COMMERCIAL & CONSUMER LAW

Success Without Tears

COMMERCIAL & CONSUMER LAW

GRAHAM STEPHENSON, LLM, Solicitor
Principal Lecturer in Law, Lancashire Polytechnic
PETER CLARK, LLB
Principal Lecturer in Law, Lancashire Polytechnic

Series Editor C.J. CARR, MA, BCL

BLACKSTONE
PRESS LIMITED
Aldine Place, London W12 8AA
Telephone 01-740 1173/01-740 1111
Facsimile 01-740 1184

First published in Great Britain 1987 by Financial Training Publications Limited, Holland House, 140-144 Freston Road, London W10 6TR

ISBN: 1 85185 043 0

Typeset by LKM Typesetting Ltd, London EC1
Printed by Livesey Ltd, Shrewsbury, Shropshire

CONTENTS

PREFACE

We were delighted to be asked to write this, our second book in the SWOT series. We have been particularly pleased with the response to our earlier work SWOT Law of Torts. The real satisfaction has come, not from the vast royalties accumulated, but rather from the kind and substantial support for the idea which these books represent, received from academics in colleges, polytechnics and universities throughout the country.

Writing this book was no easier than the first. We faced the same dilemma of choosing topics which were representative of wide ranging and varying syllabuses. We came to accept the absence of topics such as insurance and agency only by reminding ourselves that the essential purpose of this book is the promotion of study and examination technique. Constraints of a different kind caused a delay of some significance in the completion of the book. We are indebted to the staff at Financial Training and especially to Heather Saward whose patience and understanding at times quite surpassed belief. Finally, our thanks to Lesley Maunder and Madeleine Walsh for their efforts in transforming the most indescribable handwriting into manuscript.

Graham Stephenson
Peter Clark
Lancashire Polytechnic

INTRODUCTION

Commercial and Consumer law are normally second or third year subjects in most law degrees. Generally, the reason why this is so is because some knowledge of basic principles of contract and tort is thought to be an essential prerequisite to the study of consumer and commercial law. We assume that most, if not all students, will have already passed law degree examinations in contract and tort by this stage. For those students not familiar with our previous title in this series, *Law of Torts,* we feel the need to explain precisely what is the purpose of this book. For those who have read the previous title and have, coincidentally perhaps, passed their torts examination, the advice contained in chapters 1 and 2 of this book, though essentially the same as that given in the earlier book, is, we believe, worthy of a second reading.

As a second or third year law undergraduate you will no doubt realise that your examination performance will count towards the class of honours which you will achieve. We assume that your objectives will be to obtain the best possible class of honours degree, the immediacy of which now seems more pressing. You may well have realised (whether or not you have read our previous work) that to obtain a good honours degree knowledge as to legal rules is not of itself sufficient. You may well have experienced in the context of tutorial discussion a sense of inadequacy when the tutor's questions have probed beyond the mere descriptive answer as to what the law is. Alternatively, your essay may have been returned with comments such as 'too descriptive' or 'insufficient analysis'. The purpose of this book, as is indeed that of others in the series, is to help improve your analytical and reasoning abilities particularly in relation to legal concepts.

Commercial and Consumer law is a mixture of common and statute law, civil and criminal, and in that sense requires the development of a full range of lawyer's skills. For those students whose first and/or second year diet of subjects has not included a significant amount of statute law the study of this subject, which includes grappling with the complexity of the likes of the Consumer Credit Act 1974 and the Trade Descriptions Act 1968, may come as something of a shock. Additionally, the subject matter transcends the traditional criminal/civil law divide, which, whilst adding interest to the subject, also makes it more demanding on the student.

The attainment of the necessary qualities of reasoning and analysis by the student is regarded as the sole objective of the learning programme. Students by their second or third year will have recognised that lectures and tutorials are almost exclusively devoted to that end. They may also have realised just how little institutional effort is directed towards the acquisition of study skills, which are an extremely important means to that end. If they have not already done so in the first year or years of their law degree studies, students have to learn how to study law more efficiently, so as to gain maximum benefit from the three different learning situations — lectures, seminars and private study — which are common features of undergraduate courses.

Furthermore, a student needs to develop some fairly sophisticated communicative skills. In order to achieve his goal of a good honours degree he has to communicate his knowledge and understanding and demonstrate his analytical powers through the somewhat peculiar medium of law examinations — examinations in which very often those qualities are tested by means of legal problems.

As indicated above it is our experience that many students, even those in the second and third years of their studies, consistently underperform because they fail to develop sufficiently their study and communicative skills and we believe this results largely from the fact that in many institutions very little, if anything, is done in the way of providing students with effective guidance as to how to study law efficiently, present papers in seminars, and develop a reasonable examination technique. This book seeks, in a modest way, to provide that guidance and to help students to achieve examination results which do not understate their abilities. It is important that students should appreciate that underperformance through poor examination technique may affect not only the student clinging to the pass mark by his finger-nails, but also those who obtain better results. A student who obtains a third-class mark may have been afflicted far less in this respect than a student who underachieves, albeit with a higher mark.

How can this book help students?

First, a word of warning, reading the book of itself will do little to enhance a student's performance. That will only be achieved by the student giving diligent thought to, and being dedicated in the application of, the advice given.

In chapter 1, we have set out some basic guidance on study methods and the organisation of work. Chapter 2 contains a fairly detailed analysis of examination technique including some advice on revision. These chapters deal with quite a number of points which may be regarded as so obvious as not to require stating. This is not our experience: students quite commonly make some extremely elementary errors.

The rest of the book is devoted entirely to illustrating the application of examination techniques by way of a series of questions on various topics within the area of consumer and commercial law. In this respect it has been necessary to be selective. The title and content of syllabuses does vary between institutions. We have therefore tried to select those topics which are likely to be common to most if not all syllabuses. For each of these topics we have drawn attention to those aspects of the law which, for one reason or another, are likely to be found in examination questions and with which students experience some degree of difficulty. Our treatment of the substantive law is therefore selective. This book is not intended as a textbook nor will it satisfactorily serve as such.

In seeking to provide both guidance and explanation on points of technique as well as the substantive issues involved in the illustrative questions, we have deliberately avoided giving what might be termed as a 'model answer' or 'crib'. Indeed, such a format would have been impracticable for these purposes. Further, we recognise that there exists a variation in individual style and approach which is perfectly acceptable and we would not wish to create any contrary impression.

What we have attempted to do is to indicate with regard to each topic what are the difficult issues and to embody those issues, or at least some of them, in the questions. We have sought to do this in a fashion which will give students an insight into the examiner's technique — hopefully this book will reveal as much about that as it does about the technique of the student's response.

Our objectives have largely dictated the content of each chapter which is as follows:

(a)   An outline of the substantive issues with which the student may find difficulty.
(b)   Sample examination questions.
(c)   Notes explaining points of technique and the substantive issues raised in the questions.

Each of the sample questions has been constructed so as to raise numerous substantive issues, consequently the explanatory notes may occasionally be quite lengthy. We have not felt the need to restrict the construction of the questions according to the constraints of examination conditions. The questions are rather exercises to be undertaken as you progress through the course when the amount of time taken is a far less pressing consideration.

This book is primarily aimed at improving a student's examination technique, but this cannot be done in and around examination time. As we stress at various places in the first chapters, preparation for examinations starts from the moment your course starts. You should read chapters 1 and 2 right at the outset as we believe they contain useful information on study techniques and so on. Subsequent chapters can be looked at as and when your tutors consider the relevant topic in class. This will give you more experience of coping with examination-type questions.

ONE

STUDY TECHNIQUES

As a second or third year student, you will have become familiar with the teaching methods employed in your particular institution. This will in most institutions comprise a series of lectures and seminars or tutorials in each subject, leaving the individual with considerable responsibility to advance his knowledge and understanding through private study. However, familiarity with the system does not necessarily mean that students have become particularly competent at obtaining the optimum benefit from it. Time and again we have seen the effect of bad study habits acquired in the first year carried through second and even third year studies. Old habits die hard, but die they must in order to enhance your chances of success in the examinations. An additional burden in some second and third year subjects, and consumer and commercial law are no exceptions, is that the student may be faced with having to grapple for the first time with a subject which is essentially statute-based by nature.

The advice offered in the following pages is designed to enable the student to overcome this additional difficulty. We feel compelled to repeat our caution in the introduction to the effect that merely reading the chapters and recognising your shortcomings is not of itself sufficient: your performance is only likely to improve by positive action throughout the year to deal with those shortcomings.

Lectures

We believe students will find it useful if we begin by restating the basic objectives of a lecture programme. Once a student understands these objectives, he or she will be better able to appreciate his or her own role in the lectures and thus derive greater benefit from them.

The second or third year student should by now recognise that one of the major objectives of lectures, namely, the conveying of basic knowledge and understanding of the law, is not always a straightforward operation. In seeking to achieve this objective a lecturer may indulge in a close and detailed examination of case law and/or statutory provisions. In a subject such as consumer and commercial law, the lecturer may focus on the very detailed wording of legislation. This may involve a comparative analysis both of sections within one statute and similar provisions in other legislation. This exercise demands, amongst other things, the total concentration of the student. The student sitting on the back row of the lecture theatre reading a popular tabloid is hardly likely to achieve this.

Perhaps the student will by now have begun to appreciate that lectures also provide important guidance to students so as to enable them to reinforce their understanding through an informed and selective approach to legal materials.

But lectures are much more even than this. They represent a most important opportunity to stimulate the interest of students and to cultivate in them the spirit and practice of critical analysis. The continuing development of the critical faculty assumes greater significance for the second and third year students. The extent to which you can demonstrate such development is likely to be a decisive influence on the class of degree awarded.

It is our experience that second and third year students do not benefit as much as they might from their lecture programme. The reason for this may be that they have not given thought as to what their role is in lectures. Many students continue to adopt a passive role, 'silent, unthinking scribes' to use our words in *Law of Torts*.

Whilst lectures are not normally a forum for discussion students should nonetheless be able to participate more actively in the sense of devoting more effort attempting to understand the content and being far more selective in their note-taking. Given this a student will be better able to ask a more meaningful question at the end of a lecture than, 'What was the word after . . .?' Second and third year students will recognise by now, as we do, the need for a good set of notes from which to revise later in the year.

The sensible way to approach this is to realise that those notes should be built up in stages through lectures and private study and notes made in preparation for, or during, seminars. Notes taken in lectures should only be regarded as the foundation upon which to build. Viewed in this way a more useful perspective will be gained as to what and how much should be noted in lectures themselves.

We believe that the practice of recording succinctly what the lecturer has to say, as far as possible in the student's own words, is enormously important. It is not simply that the amount written down is reduced, but it helps to order the student's involvement in the lecture to one of listening, thinking, and then writing selectively and briefly.

In many institutions lecturers have sought to alleviate student difficulty in this respect by the use of lecture handouts which contain a summary of the essential points of a lecture, case references and the text of statutory provisions. Often such a simple and basic innovation remains unemployed. The following advice is offered on the assumption that there is little use made of handouts and that students are expected to make notes whilst the lecturer is in full flow. In general terms the purpose of our advice is to try to ensure that only the most relevant information is recorded in lectures in a manner which will enable greater concentration upon the content, thus providing a more informed approach to private study and facilitating additional note-taking at that stage. In view of the fact that the subject of this book is a mixture of statute and common law, with the emphasis on the former, we begin with some advice on how to cope with and note often complex statutory provisions.

How to note statutory provisions

It is not our objective to give instruction in the matter of statutory interpretation as such. The relevant knowledge and skill should have been acquired to some degree by this stage of your studies. We would, however, emphasise the importance of the need to apply some of that knowledge and further develop those skills in relation to the subject matter covered in this book. We believe this to be important for two reasons. First, it will enable a student to understand better why a court has reached a particular decision. Secondly, a student may well be called upon, in the context of problem questions in examinations, to interpret statutory provisions, sometimes without the assistance of any decided cases.

It is not necessary to attempt to record verbatim any particular provision to which the lecturer may refer. He will be concerned to discuss those cases in which certain phrases have fallen to be interpreted by the courts. It is sufficient *at this stage* that the particular phrase in question is accurately noted. You should concentrate your efforts towards understanding and explanation or interpretation, rather than worrying about the fact that you have not written down the precise wording of the section. It might be useful to leave a space in your notes for insertion of the relevant more precise detail later. For example, s. 14(6) of the Sale of Goods Act 1979 contains a definition of the phrase 'merchantable quality' as follows:

> Goods of any kind are of merchantable quality if they are as fit for the purpose or purposes for which goods of that kind are commonly bought as it is reasonable to expect having regard to any description applied to them, the price (if relevant) and all the other relevant circumstances.

The lecturer may not dictate in full the detail of this subsection, but simply select for discussion the more important issues. For example, from s. 14(6), he might choose to discuss what is meant by fitness for a usual purpose and the relevance of price and description, looking at the various decided cases. These three key phrases could form subheadings in your notes.

What are the important points to note about cases?

First, students need to assess the individual lecturer. Lecturers vary in their approach, from the exceedingly detailed and technical treatment of cases on the one hand, to the overview style on the other. Where the latter approach is adopted, a lecture may take the form of a commentary upon development in the law in general or doctrinal terms with no mention whatever of the details of any particular decision. Where this line is taken the lecturer may well expect that a basic knowledge and understanding of the subject-matter have been acquired through prior reading of the textbooks, cases, etc.

Most lecturers fall between these extremes but nevertheless demonstrate a degree of variation in approach which needs to be recognised and may result in a different method of taking notes for different lecturers. Generally, the more unselective the lecturer the more selective the notes of the student should be and vice versa. Below are the essential points upon which a student should make clear and concise notes. We have assumed that the student has a good grasp of the doctrine of precedent.

(a)   The stated common law principle or statutory provision in relation to which the case is to be considered.

(b)   The *ratio* of any case as indicated by the lecturer, i.e., the material facts together with the decision thereon. If the lecturer confines himself to stating only the material facts a precis of those facts should be made and usually this need only occupy a couple of lines. In the event that a lecturer overindulges in factual detail (most of us are guilty of this at some time), the student should be guided by his common sense and the experience he acquires. When reading cases later notes on facts may be embellished. Try to ensure at that stage that the facts noted are both necessary and sufficient to the proposition of law said to be stated in the case.

(c)   Any *obiter* statements to which the lecturer may refer should be noted. Though such statements are said to be only of persuasive authority, their impact upon the subsequent development of the law may well be far greater than the ratio of the case in question, especially in decisions of the House of Lords or even the Court of Appeal. An obvious example of this would be Lord Atkin's statement of the so-called 'neighbour principle' in *Donoghue* v *Stevenson* [1932] AC 562 at p. 580. Yet that statement has been of fundamental importance in the subsequent development of the tort of negligence. Other less prestigious *obiter* statements may well be referred to by your lecturer. Clearly he or she regards them as being of some importance and so should you by noting them, albeit as *obiter* statements.

(d) As to the lecturer's evaluation of cases under review, especially noteworthy are observations on:

(i) How the decision in any particular case relates to a stated common law principle or statutory provision and to decisions in other cases. Did the decision in *Smith* v *Smith* appear to widen or narrow the principle? Was some previous case distinguished, overruled or followed? How does a particular decision fall within the mischief at which a statutory provision is aimed?

(ii) The considerations underlying the formulation of the statement of law in any particular case. The decision in *Millar's of Falkirk* v *Turpie* 1976 SLT 66 affords a good illustration and one to which we shall return in due course. Was the remedy claimed by the buyer, namely, rejection of the motor car, the reason why the court decided that the vehicle, despite minor defects, was merchantable?

(e) Where full references to cases are given in lectures, e.g., *Christopher Hill Ltd* v *Ashington Piggeries Ltd* [1972] AC 441, you will no doubt wish to record them in full. However, you should not allow yourself to be distracted if you fail to catch every detail of the case reference. The case name is important and, in the context of the lecture itself, the court in which it was decided: House of Lords, Court of Appeal, etc. Do make a point of checking and correcting case names as necessary at a later stage. The incorrect spelling of a case name may give the examiner the impression that you have not read the case in question. Other information in the reference, i.e., the title, year, volume and page reference in the reports is useful but not vital at this stage, as are page references to particular points in the judgments. Noting this information accurately can save valuable time later.

There are certain other matters concerning the content of lecture notes to which a student should give particular consideration. Below we advise you to use headings and subheadings when taking notes. On balance we regard this as a helpful and sensible way of recording information. Any such system of compartmentalising information does not, however, promote the ability to perceive how the constituent parts of an issue interrelate or indeed, enable you to gain an overall perspective on a subject as a whole. This is, perhaps, illustrated in the context of consumer and commercial law by the teaching in separate component parts of the criminal and civil law. Any observations by the lecturer, however, on the interrelationship are worth noting.

Not every point made by the lecturer will be fully understood at the time. Quite often you will be aware yourself that you have not fully understood and it is a sensible practice to physically emphasise any such points in your notes. You should make every attempt to resolve any such misunderstandings either through questions to your lecturer or tutor if the opportunity arises, or through your own efforts. Your lecturer will usually be the person who sets your examination paper. He knows through experience the issues with which students have difficulty. You will appreciate therefore that it is no accident that many of those issues which students find difficult are to be found in examination questions.

Note form

Students would also be well advised to give some thought to the following points as to the form in which they make notes:

(a)   Bearing in mind the advice given above, use and physically emphasise headings and subheadings as appropriate and in general be generous in terms of the spacing of notes. These twin practices are in our view beneficial for a number of reasons. The generous spacing allows for complementary detail to be added at a later stage without having to rewrite the whole of one's notes. The headings and subheadings provide structure and create an obvious skeletal framework of the topic covered. This promotes clarity and enables the material to be more easily ingested. Students will find this of considerable assistance when revising, for revision inevitably involves a process of distillation.

(b)   We would advise students to maintain a reasonable standard of neatness and legibility. We suspect that many students take the view that it is sufficient if they themselves can read and follow their notes as and when required. The danger which lies in the habit of writing in this subjective fashion is the likely production under pressure in the examination of an illegible script. It is probably true to say that nothing exasperates an examiner more than this. Do not on any account fall into the trap of taking 'mayfly' notes, i.e., notes scribbled in such a fashion that they have to be rewritten afterwards in relative leisure. The remedial effort must be made in lectures if legibility is to be maintained under pressure in the examination.

(c)   Whilst the maintenance of legibility in note taking may well prove valuable in examinations, the same cannot be said of any system of abbreviation which a student might adopt. Abbreviation is a time-saving device to be employed essentially in lectures. Some limited abbreviation is acceptable in examination, e.g., P = plaintiff, D = defendant, or the names of parties involved may be signified by the appropriate initial. In examinations a student should not go beyond this general boundary except where absolutely necessary where perhaps he has allowed himself insufficient time to write a full answer to his final question. So far as lecture notes are concerned a system of abbreviation can be carried much further so long as the student understands his own system. In the course of a single lecture various words and phrases are used with almost monotonous frequency. In a lecture on the sale of goods the term 'merchantable quality' may be reduced to m.q. We would think it not beyond the wit of students to abbreviate this and many other such terms.

(d) We see the use of precis as being quite separate from that of abbreviation outlined above. Simply put, it is the art of capturing in fewer words the essential point of a larger statement. Many students make absolutely no attempt to summarise the lecturer's statements, as each word falls from the lecturer's lips it appears at the end of their pens producing page after page of undistinguished, unselective notes. We believe that the practice of succinctly recording what the lecturer has to say, as far as possible in the student's own words, is enormously important. It is not simply that the amount that is written is reduced, but it orders the student's involvement in the lecture to listening, thinking, then writing selectively and briefly and that is how we believe it should be.

Seminars and tutorials

Seminars and tutorials perform an important function in any degree programme and should be given considerable attention both with regard to preparation beforehand and contribution during class. Class contact is at a premium in most institutions of higher education and far too many students do not put what little they have to good use. We propose to say something about both aspects of seminar work, but a lot of what we say in the following chapter on private study has a bearing on the way you should prepare for seminars.

Seminars should ideally be a dialogue between *all* those involved. It is your opportunity to show your understanding of the subject under discussion, to clarify any misconceptions and, most importantly, to air your views and have them tested by your tutor and your fellow students. This is an opportunity which unfortunately many students spurn.

Preparation

Preparation for seminars or tutorials is essential if you are to play your part in the discussion in class. Some students, however, for one reason or another do not prepare at all but nonetheless attend. Our view is that they may as well be in the library catching up on the work they have omitted to do. Other students' perceptions of what is involved in preparation vary somewhat, from those who merely bring their lecture notes along and try to answer questions while leafing through them, to those who do virtually all the reading but fail to spend any time considering the questions set for group discussion. These variants and all in between are unsatisfactory and the student is failing to use the opportunities given by class contact hours.

You must attempt to read as much of the material listed as possible. How much of it you do will depend upon your capacity for absorbing material, and we shall make some further comments shortly in the section on private study on how to cope with cases, textbooks, articles and other reading matter.

In our experience we have found that the majority of students have done enough preparation in the sense of having read a substantial amount of material. However, the major shortcoming in seminar preparation is the failure to apply the knowledge gathered in the reading to the problems or essays set for discussion. Time and again students come to seminars or tutorials with little idea how to tackle the problem under discussion. Our experience shows that ability to answer such questions, rather than lack of knowledge is a persistent factor in student failure to achieve their potential. If students were to think more about the problems set for seminar work, there is every chance that their technique would improve and consequently their examination performance. It must be stressed that we are not suggesting a full written answer to seminar problems (unless this has been specified by the tutor) but that you should try to answer the problem in note form for easy use during class discussion. An additional bonus may well be that it is common practice for tutors to use past examination questions as a basis for class discussion. The benefit of adequate preparation before the seminar should be obvious and will no doubt result in an improved technique when examination time comes round.

Seminar contribution

There are many different ways to conduct a seminar but what should be produced, as we have said before, is a dialogue between all concerned. It is all very well doing a large amount of preparation for a seminar merely to turn up and remain mute throughout the proceedings. Unfortunately, too many students, for whatever reason, are prepared to allow the burden of discussion to fall on the few, usually the tutor and one other. There is a tendency to treat a seminar as just another note-taking session. Notes can be taken but only sparingly when, perhaps, a point you had not thought about crops up. The tutor may emphasise a particular issue, then it may be justifiable to note it. Otherwise, the emphasis in seminars should be on discussion. You should be prepared to contribute not just factual information but also to make points of an evaluative nature. Your views may be fairly uninformed at an early stage in your study of the subject, but nonetheless you should attempt to take up a tenable position.

Whatever career you eventually choose following your degree studies, oral as well as written skills will generally be essential. Seminars are the appropriate forum in which to develop such skills.

One final point on this topic is to remind you to collect together your lecture notes, as amplified and clarified, and the notes made for and during the seminar into a coherent whole. This will be of immense value when you come to examination revision. You can ill afford time spent just before the examination in compiling and rationalising various sets of notes on individual topics.

Private study

Very few people are capable of passing an examination by merely attending lectures and seminars without in addition doing a substantial amount of private study. This aspect of your degree studies is probably the most crucial. One or two students may succeed by doing very little during the academic year and then doing a revision crash course, but inevitably their

'a revision crash course'

marks will be a lot lower than they otherwise would have been. Indeed, such students are often on the borderline between pass and fail completely. Degree-level studies should be regarded as a learning rather than a teaching exercise and great emphasis is placed in this book on the need for a large measure of private study on your part. We shall make some comments on the amount of time which should or might be spent on this aspect of your studies and also make some suggestions as to how that time might usefully be employed. Naturally, how much time you are prepared to devote may depend on other interests and/or the capacity of any particular individual to assimilate and absorb materials and what we say can only be by way of general guidance.

How much time

No hard and fast rule can be given for the reason expressed in the previous comment but you may find some of the following points useful:

(a)   It is essential that you establish some sort of routine; whether you stick to it rigidly or not does not matter, as long as it can be maintained more or less.

(b)   Get into the good habit of trying to work between classes, even if there is only an hour available. You could perhaps read a couple of cases or a short chapter in your textbook in that time.

(c)   You should be prepared to work for at least three evenings per week until the library closes. This may result in your having your weekends completely free for relaxation, sport or other leisure interests. These are also important aspects of studies. You *must* take some time off — how much is a matter for each individual.

(d)   If your library opens on Saturdays, then you should try to use this time for finding those cases, articles or other materials which you could not find during the week. Pressure on available resources is increasing and you are much more likely to obtain popular materials on a Saturday.

(e)   Try not to work too late in the evening. You should rarely work after 9 p.m. as your mind is less receptive the later you work. It is better to go to bed early and get up early in order to work. You can probably achieve more in an hour before breakfast than you can in a late evening session. Also shorter spells of work are generally more productive in terms of assimilation of material, as concentration lapses the longer you are studying in any one spell.

What to do in the time

From what has already been said in the parts on lectures and seminars you should have gathered to some extent what you should be doing during private study. For the sake of emphasis we consider you should be doing the following:

(a)   Amplifying and clarifying lectures on a topic, including reading of cases, textbooks and recommended articles.

(b)   Seminar preparation, some or all of which may overlap with (a) but *remember* to attempt answers to seminar problems as already mentioned.

(c)   Course work, whether assessed or not, is worth doing well. Effort put into essays is usually repaid with a bonus at revision and examination time, particularly where the topic of the essay reappears in some form in the examination, a common occurrence in our experience.

Technique

We propose to take a closer look at the reading materials you have been recommended and we have a few suggestions to make as to how you go about your task of reading and noting them. Your reading list will no doubt contain references to what seems to be an abundance of cases, textbooks, articles of one kind or another and reports by Government departments or bodies such as the Law Commission. Even to a second or third year student this may be offputting, particularly since tutors in other subjects will be giving you comparable lists on the apparent assumption that their course is the only one you are doing and you have unlimited time to pursue the finer points.

The best advice we can give you is not to be put off, do not despair and become frustrated. If you have established a routine of working and follow some of our suggestions below, the reading lists should become manageable. You may still not be able to read everything on every reading list. Few students can achieve this, but you should aim to do a substantial amount, so that you can say something useful in tutorials.

Cases   The aim in reading case reports is to extract exactly what you need with a minimum of effort. Good casebooks will do this for you, although it must be remembered that any such book will reflect in the extracts selected the choice made by the persons who compiled it. In addition, it may be slightly out of date and you will still need to read the latest case reports. The student who does not have ready access to a law library or those who prefer to work at home may well find casebooks useful and convenient. Part-time students, particularly, are recommended to obtain good casebooks.

For those who cannot or do not use casebooks, there is obviously more work involved until one develops with experience a technique for getting to the crux of any case. Below are a few practical points which in our experience should prove useful and time-saving.

(a)   Read the headnote which will normally be an accurate reproduction of the facts and the decision.

(b)   The reporter himself may well refer you to the important parts of any particular judge's speech. This will enable you to go immediately to the relevant part of the judgment. In some instances this should suffice and it will not be necessary to read the whole or all of the judgements. Certainly, however, in leading cases you should read the judgments and see the way each judge approaches the legal issue involved. Reading judgments in full may be no bad thing in itself, although time is a factor. You should be guided, where appropriate, by your tutor's or lecturer's comments. The reading of judgments may also provide a spin-off in the sense that the exercise may well help you to acquire a style to be adopted in your own legal arguments.

(c)   As far as note taking of cases is concerned, if you adopt a card-index system then this will ensure you do not take too many notes and that those you do take are concise. What you need is a brief statement of facts, the decision preferably in your own words and any important statements by a judge. In leading cases, you may wish to have a note of any differing approaches.

(d)   In those series of reports where the arguments of counsel are set out, it will normally not be necessary to read them. Nonetheless, it is occasionally good practice to read counsel's arguments, particularly if you are interested in mooting, as it may well give you some hints on how to prepare and submit a legal argument.

(e)   Dissenting judgments should also be considered, as they may provide useful ammunition in future cases for arguing that a decision was wrong or is capable of being distinguished or that the position is not really settled beyond doubt.

Textbooks   Textbooks in the main should be read with a view to clarifying ambiguities and difficulties in lecture notes and for purposes of amplification on points referred to in lectures. This may, however, depend on the lecturer's technique — if he or she is taking the overview approach you may have to make substantial notes from your recommended text. Again, it is worth emphasising that too many notes can cause problems at revision and examination time. It should not normally be necessary for you to follow up references in footnotes or elsewhere in your textbook, unless either this course of action is suggested by the lecturer on a particular point, or you are researching a point for course work or tutorials. Material in footnotes is likely to be less important, the main material being included in the text. Also a further word of warning needs to be given. Textbook writers tend to allude to every possible case or other reference, even where the case does not take the principle of law any further, but is merely an example of its application. It is important to remember that cases are examples of principles or propositions of law, and normally one or two cases only are required to show how the principle works. The excessive citation of cases in indiscriminate fashion is to be discouraged.

Articles and reports   Nowadays, there is a wide range of materials available to which students are referred. We are not talking just about learned articles in a whole variety of journals published world-wide, but reports by the Law Commission, Royal Commissions, Government departments and so on. There is a wealth of material, some of which is of great value to students. It can be off-putting and again we must emphasise that too many notes on items in these various sources is not desirable.

Articles   The scope of articles in legal journals varies. Some are fairly descriptive of case law or recent statutes, others will be an attempt to be critical and say something original or enlightening on a particular topic. All have their uses. There is little point in making detailed notes on an article at the outset. You should read it through to gather a general impression of the writer's argument. It may well be that the article has been given to you not with a view to its detailed argument on any point, but with regard to the general point (if any) being made by the writer. It may well be merely this aspect which you need to note and nothing more. The writer may be critical of the approach taken in a series of cases or in recent legislation. It may well be that your lecturer, in citing an article, wishes you to grasp one main, essential point, although reading the article in full will inevitably improve your understanding of the cases and the points discussed. It may be unnecessary to take detailed notes on such an article, and in most cases the taking of such notes is to be avoided.

Reports   Law Commission working papers and reports are an extremely useful source both of existing legal rules and proposals for reform. A student may obtain an excellent critique of existing law in such a document and also from the reform proposals develop a critical attitude towards the material. However, note taking should be kept to a minimum: you should attempt to precis the proposals and any conclusions drawn by the authors in such materials. Quite often, reports, and for that matter articles, will contain useful material for course work, in particular apposite quotations or statements which can be used to support your argument. You should, therefore, be on the look-out for useful phrases and make a note of them or where they can be found. This applies generally.

We have indicated earlier in this chapter that consumer and commercial law is now predominantly a statutory subject. The advice given above is particularly relevant in the context of almost the whole of this subject area. For example, the amendments to the Sale of Goods legislation, the Supply of Goods and Services Act 1982 and the Unfair Contract Terms Act 1977 are all substantially based upon Law Commission Reports. When you are looking at a statutory provision, you are likely to find it extremely useful to consult the relevant report.

Conclusion

Private study, it needs repeating, is probably the most crucial aspect of your studies. The amount of study and the way you go about studying on your own will in nearly every case have an impact on whether you pass or fail, or obtain a third or a lower second and so on. Ultimately, however, overall success depends on how well, during the year at least, you combine private study with your class contact in the form of lectures and seminars or tutorials.

TWO

REVISION AND EXAMINATION TECHNIQUES

Revision

You will by now have discovered that revision time can be a soul-destroying period. Through experience you may well have identified for yourself some of the points of advice given below. Despite the fact that you may have promised yourself that you would take steps to remedy any defects recognised in your revision programme, our experience is that often such promises are not kept. In the light of this, we make no apologies for giving the advice to second and third year students in the hope that at least some of the points made will strike home.

It is worth repeating that how you go about your revision will vary from individual to individual. Some prefer to mix with their fellow-sufferers, to others this is something to be avoided at all costs. Wherever and however you revise, you should try to ensure that you take sufficient time for relaxation and that you do not work too late in the evening or for long spells.

(a)   The first point is a reminder that good preparation during the academic year will save a lot of heartache when it comes to revision. During the last few weeks running up to the examination period, the last thing you want is to be preparing notes on a topic for the first time. This work should have been done steadily over the previous months.

(b)   Routine is once again an important factor. You should plan your weeks and days, so that revision work becomes a habit, but not an unthinking habit.

(c)   Assuming that you have done your preparation during the year, you should have a series of separate and identifiable topics within the subject area. As has already been mentioned, it is dangerous to compartmentalise materials in this way without remaining aware of the interconnection between the various topics. Nonetheless, it is still a useful and probably essential way to proceed. It may be that at this stage you can clearly identify some 10 to 12 topics which might justify a full examination question. Factors which will be a good indication of whether a topic may be examined will include whether a seminar was devoted to the topic and the types of questions set in past examination papers. This later source is probably the most fruitful in terms of enabling you to assess the likelihood of questions on particular topics. Attempting answers to past examination papers at this stage is a useful way of assessing the effectiveness of your revision.

(d)   If you are not fortunate to be in that small minority of people who have the ability to revise every topic and, consequently, be in a position to answer every question on an examination paper, then it is better to be realistic and be selective in the number of topics you revise. If the examination allows you a choice of four or five out of nine or ten questions set, then it may for many people be a wasted effort to find yourself embarrassed for choice in your examination, and as a result not spend enough time on your other subjects. It makes sense to select, say, at least six topics and possibly seven which you consider likely to appear in some shape or form on the examination paper. You need some margin of error, just in case a favourite examiner's topic is omitted from the paper. In addition, even if your forecast is right and questions on your five main topics appear as expected, it is possible that a question set may be particularly difficult. If you have revised one or two reserve topics, you may be able to avoid a difficult question.

(e)   The material you should be revising from should ideally be that compiled on your own together with lecture and tutorial handouts, lecture notes, notes on articles, reports and cases collected during the year. It is unwise to attempt revision from textbooks, articles and reports themselves. You will find it much easier to recall information that you have written yourself. Reading from textbooks and so on may well be unproductive and far too time-consuming at this stage of the academic year when time is of the essence.

(f)   We do not propose to give very specific advice on how to organise your entire revision programme but some points are worth emphasis. You should not concentrate on any one subject to the detriment of others. There may be a temptation to do this if you feel particularly weak in one of your subjects. If you have four subjects and eight weeks before your examinatin, it is probably not a good idea to divide your time into four two-week blocks. The subject studied first will suffer considerably if you have no time to refresh your memory on it. A more suitable way of approaching this problem might be to spend initially one week on each subject and then as the material becomes more familiar, progressively less time as the examination period approaches. The more often you read through material the better will be your understanding of it and your ability to recall information. We would not recommend rote learning as a rule but some students feel happier with this technique and that is entirely up to them. We would, however, advise students to learn off by heart, for example, the definition of 'merchantable quality' in s. 14(6) of the Sale of Goods Act 1979. Of course, your choice of definitions to be learnt in this way will depend upon which statutes, if any, are provided in the examination room itself. The practice varies from institution to institution; get to know what the practice is in yours at an early stage. We need to give a further word of warning; if you are provided with say, the Consumer Credit Act 1974, there is a need to be familiar with the provisions and layout of such an Act in advance to avoid wasting valuable time in the examination room. In addition, you must avoid at all costs the mere copying out of the text of a section in your answer. No marks will be given for this.

You may, if you wish, construct your own accurate precis of the more important statutory provisions, rather than learning them verbatim. This can easily be done by using key phrases from your lecture notes, in the way we mentioned earlier.

When a student is confronted with a problem question his first task is to identify a significant number of specific issues involved. When the facts of the problem are searched against a definition or precis of a statutory provision he is likely to recognise more of those issues than would otherwise be the case. In a sense the definition tells the student to some extent what he ought to be looking for in the facts of the problem.

In advocating the use of this technique in this limited way it should not be thought that we are encouraging parrot-like regurgitation, or simplistic thinking. The use of definitions as a 'teaching aid' should be 'temporary'. Whilst they enable the student to see the 'wood for the trees', they should be given with the caveat that, in the light of the knowledge the student subsequently acquires, he should recognise definitions as the oversimplifications which they often are. We have already warned of the compartmentalising effect of using headings and subheadings. Students should not allow definitions to bridle or blinker their understanding of the subject. There is no reason why their use as an *aide-mémoire* should have that effect.

Students often delude themselves about their lack of ability to recall material. Most have little confidence in their mental powers at some stage and their fears are often unfounded.

(g) As the examinations approach you should only attempt to read the material through in a relaxed manner. By this time you should be as familiar with it as you could possibly be and you should slacken off the intensity of concentration a little. The last day or two before the examinations should be fairly relaxed. There is little use cramming and working all hours possible. This approach is as likely to be counter-productive as anything else. Some advise that you should do no work at all the day before an examination, but if you feel the need to do something a quick glance through your notes on one or two of the more difficult topics you have chosen will probably be all that is necessary.

(h)   Any time between examinations can be used productively, but unless the gap is at least a fortnight between two exams, it is extremely unwise to leave your entire revision of a whole subject to that period. You should be merely consolidating and refreshing your memory during such gaps.

(i)   Revision should ideally be a process of distillation. It should be the time when your year's work comes to fruition — not when it starts.

Examination technique

The moment towards which all the year's work has been geared arrives all too quickly for most people, not least examiners who have the unenviable task of marking a vast number of papers. Before making some specific points about what you should or should not do once you are sitting at your desk, a couple of general comforting points. First, the examiner wants you to pass — he is not trying to catch you out. You are being provided with the opportunity to show you can assimilate and understand material and apply it to given situations. Secondly, if you have followed most of the advice given earlier in this book, then you should be able to approach your examination with a lot less dread and you may even enjoy it. Whether you enjoy it or not your year's hard work should stand you in good stead. What you must not do is throw all that away by doing something stupid once in the examination room. Time and again we have seen students throw away the chance of a good examination mark because they fail to observe one or more of the points below. This may say something about the all-or-nothing nature of the examination system and its pressures. It also often says something about the student. Preparation for your examination starts at the begining of the year as we have said, but it continues right up to the moment you sit down at that desk in the examination hall. Make sure you are there on time at the right place and on the right date and that you have all the items necessary to do an examination.

Apart from these general and apparently obvious points we feel it necessary to emphasise the following matters:

(a)   Do not just read the examination paper rubric, but also read carefully what any question asks you, for example, does it say 'Discuss' or 'Advise X'. For example, does the question require a discussion of both criminal and civil provisions? Read the whole of the paper and identify which questions you can and/or wish to answer. Assuming you have not drawn a complete blank, you should seek to identify the legal issues in the problem questions. In essay-type questions you need to devise quickly and briefly a structure for your answer.

(b)   Allocate your time evenly between questions. Some students find it useful to write down finishing and starting times for questions. This problem of making sure you answer or attempt to answer the required number of questions is so often the downfall of many students. It surely is obvious that it is easier to collect more marks on a fresh question than it is to continue writing on a previous topic. The law of diminishing returns has something to do with it. A student who writes too much on a question at the expense of others clearly has not mastered the technique of the examination game.

(c)   Concise, accurate answers are preferable. You should only elaborate on facts of cases where the question demands it, i.e., where the facts of a problem may differ from the facts of a case and you are being asked to decide whether the distinction is material. Regurgitation of all you know on a topic is a common phenomenon and one to be avoided. It shows a lack of discrimination on your part.

(d)   This follows on from (c). You should try to answer the question set, not the one you would have liked the examiner to set. You must adapt the material you have revised to suit the demands and requirements of the question being asked. Too often students ignore this advice — they see examinations as being merely a question of showing knowledge to an examiner rather than showing how to use that knowledge to best effect.

(e)   Students are often reluctant to evaluate and put forward their own viewpoint on a particular issue. Provided you have arguments to justify your position, you should state your view if the question calls for it. Examiners are looking for signs that students have given some thought to the material and are attempting evaluation. Often questions dictate that a student attempts a critical analysis. For example, the question may say 'S. 13 of the Sale of Goods Act 1979 is of little value to the disgruntled consumer'. A student who merely plunges into the appropriate case law on the section without attempting to assess the accuracy of the statement is not really answering the question. The material relating to this question must be geared towards answering it. This may well involve a process of selecting appropriate cases to either agree or disagree with the proposition.

In conclusion, we would remind you that the examiner is looking for a legible, well-balanced script which reflects a good assimilation of knowledge combined with an attempt to apply that knowledge in an effort to answer the question set. In the following chapters we will be exploring difficulties with particular substantive topics in consumer and commercial law but the general points we have discussed so far should not be forgotten.

Examination technique and legal problems

Whilst the points made above should be sufficient to enable students to cope with essay questions, legal problems and the technique necessary to deal effectively with them deserve more detailed attention. Legal problems are extremely popular with examiners as a means of testing the student's knowledge and understanding. Often by virtue of the number of such questions in an examination paper a student will be compelled to deal with at least one and probably more. In our experience this type of question does appear to cause students more difficulty than essay-type questions. We are of the opinion that a good deal of student underperformance in this connection is due to a lack of the required technique which is, of necessity, more sophisticated than that which is required to respond to essay questions.

We have taken the view that students would probably find it helpful if, in addition to giving guidance as to the technique which they need to acquire, we also gave some insight into the techniques employed by the examiner when constructing problem questions. First, a few words of reassurance. We have already pointed out that examiners are not in the business of trying to fail students. When creating problem questions the examiner will try to ensure that they are balanced and fair and allow a student capable of achieving a pass to do so. By the same token problems must not be pedestrian, so as to prevent the better student from doing justice to himself. There is no golden rule that problem questions suit the better student. Good technique is essential to all students and all are capable of mastering the requisite technique

The examiner's approach

When constructing problem questions the examiner has first to decide which legal issues he wishes to raise for discussion, and secondly how he will do so. Such questions will usually raise a number of issues and the facts chosen should be such as to enable the student to identify those issues at least in general terms.

Questions may be restricted to raising issues which arise from one particular statutory provision, e.g., the implied obligation as to merchantability of goods in s. 14 of the Sale of Goods Act 1979. Alternatively, questions may raise issues which range across numerous provisions either in the same or different statutes. Problem questions on consumer credit, e.g., will often require the student to determine whether the agreement is regulated; how it is classified under the Act of 1974, before dealing with the specific points at issue. This approach will necessitate the examination of a significant number of provisions in that Act.

This matter of limitation and identification of issues may also be covered to some extent in the rubric to a question. An obvious example of this would be an instruction to 'Discuss the civil liability of D'. Time and again we have seen such an instruction ignored.

But beware, the guidance to students will almost never be solely confined to the rubric. It is important that you are able to appreciate the legal significance of facts and the examiner will use the facts of questions both to provide guidance and to test that ability. For the same reasons, the examiner may deliberately omit a legally material fact. Examiners find this a useful ploy for other reasons. Assuming that a student spots the omission, he is then forced to speculate, to argue an issue in different ways. Suppose, for example, you are concerned with the problem of whether a purchaser of a motor vehicle which is the subject of a hire-purchase agreement has acquired a good title to it from the hire-purchaser. The examiner may deliberately omit any facts which might indicate one way or the other whether the purchaser was a 'private purchaser' as opposed to 'a trade or finance purchaser'. This is crucial to the issue (see Hire-Purchase Act 1964, Part III; Consumer Credit Act 1974, Schedule 4, Part 4).

An examiner will frequently build in 'prompts' and clues drawing students towards specific issues and even particular cases. Whilst doing so he will avoid using facts which are identical to those in any decided case, for he will be seeking to ensure that students argue through the use of principle and analogy. Gauging the appropriate strength of the 'prompt' can be a difficult exercise, some may be more subtle than others to allow for the varying abilities of students.

Constructing 'good' problems is something of an art. Examiners differ substantially in style and approach. We believe it is enormously helpful for students to become familiar with the varieties in style. In this connection students should obtain and study carefully copies of past examination papers. The problem questions found on seminar sheets are often past examination questions. Where this is so it affords an invaluable opportunity to develop a satisfactory technique long before the dreaded examinations time. We cannot overemphasise the importance of application and practice not only at revision time but throughout the year. Merely reading the advice which follows will assist you very little, the techniques have to be applied.

The student's technique

The approach to problem questions has two quite distinct aspects. First, a student must identify as many of the detailed issues as possible and secondly, he has to deal with those issues in a manner which will impress the examiner.

Identification of issues   As we have indicated above guidance as to the identification and limitation of the issues involved may well be contained both in the rubric and the facts of the problem. Read the rubric carefully and note precisely what it requires of you. Now for the facts. Think of the problem question as a carefully constructed crossword puzzle. This is in many respects an accurate analogy. Clues are provided, but you need to think in a particular way. Above all you need concentration, a receptive state of mind and experience gained through practice. There are, we believe, certain techniques which can assist significantly not only in identifying issues but also in promoting a more structured answer.

First, we would draw attention to the usefulness of definitions. Earlier in this chapter in the part on revision we gave warning of that usefulness in this context. When the facts of a problem are searched against such a definition, it is far more likely that the right interconnections will be made and the legal issues identified. An important and integral part of this whole process is the making of a rough plan in note form. The plan should begin with the definition itself. As you search through a problem identifying issues, the detailed points and relevant case and statute law which spring to mind should be briefly noted. This plan should then be used as the basis for your answer. No doubt as you consider and write the final version of your answer further relevant material will be recalled which you will wish to incorporate therein.

These rough plans are not only helpful in terms of the content of your answers but may also assist enormously in achieving a sensible structure and balance. Difficulties in structuring an answer may well be exacerbated, for example, by the presence in the problem of two or more potential plaintiffs and/or defendants. Preparatory work along the lines indicated will, in so far as it reveals the number of relevant issues involved, allow the student to balance the depth of treatment given to individual issues with the need to say something meaningful about all of them.

Anxiety experienced in examinations often leads students to neglect this preparatory work. The failure to identify important issues, lack of structure, unbalanced treatment of the recognised issues, are the hallmarks of an ill-prepared answer. The message is loud and clear. Time spent in preparing answers using the above-mentioned techniques, whether or not under examination conditions, is an invaluable investment.

Dealing with the issues   In order to avoid underperformance students must develop the skills which are necessary to communicate effectively via the medium of the legal problem: a medium which requires the application of knowledge to hypothetical situations. Effective communication involves considerations of both content and style. Students must ensure at all times that the material deployed in their answer is relevant. The sheer bulk of relevant material and the severe constraints upon time in examinations pose problems of selection and treatment. Students often leave examination rooms expressing their disappointment that they 'knew all the stuff' but 'didn't have time to get it all down'. This may well reflect inadequate examination technique. The advice which follows is given to enable students to avoid such disappointment which all too frequently results from poor examination technique. We repeat an earlier observation that a number of points made below appear to be so obvious as not to require stating. That unfortunately has not been our experience.

(a)   A basic error which in our experience is still made to some extent by second and third year students is that they suggest solutions to problems in common-sense terms rather than by way of legal principles and decided cases. Often such answers have very little of the law in them and will gain very few marks indeed.

(b)   When answering examination questions, whether essays or problems, the unselective regurgitation of notes, even if verbatim, is hardly a satisfactory approach. Students must demonstrate their understanding through the selective application of principles and cases to move towards a solution to a problem.

(c)   Be prepared to adopt a standpoint and argue. An examiner not only hopes for argument but expects it. Often he will have chosen to raise an issue on which the authorities support the possibility of tenable alternative views. The absence of authority supporting a particular viewpoint should not of itself be regarded as a bar to argument. It is not of any great significance that the examiner and yourself reach different conclusions, unless that demonstrates misunderstanding on your part.

Relevance   On the general point of ensuring that the material deployed is relevant the following should be borne in mind:

(a)   When dealing with a problem question do not write a long-winded, general and/or historical introduction to the relevant area of law. You may state briefly how you intend approaching the problem and then embark immediately upon providing answers on the specific points which you have identified.

(b)   One matter with which many students experience difficulty is how much of the facts of cases they should incorporate into their answers. Evidence of that difficulty is to be found in the extreme positions adopted in numerous examination scripts. Some students appear to be totally averse to ever stating facts, whilst others insist upon devoting half a page to the facts of a simple case. In the former situation the student's level of knowledge may not be effectively communicated to the examiner, whilst a student indulging in the latter practice may to some extent be wasting valuable time.

As a working rule you should state only those facts which are necessary in support of the particular point of law which you assert. With regard to 'landmark' cases such as *Donoghue* v *Stevenson*, you may safely assume that the examiner is aware of the facts. Do not insist upon informing him in graphic detail of the alleged presence of the decomposed snail in a bottle of ginger-ale. On the other hand it may be appropriate to refer specifically to the facts of cases, even to those of the 'landmark' decisions. The following illustration will hopefully demonstrate that it is quite within the grasp of most if not all students to incorporate authorities into an answer in a way which clearly conveys the relevance of a decision to the point of law in question whilst at the same time avoiding the need to state the detailed facts of that decision.

Suppose you were dealing with a problem concerning the extent to which pure economic loss was recoverable in the tort of negligence from a manufacturer.

Whilst the possibility of such liability appears small (see *Junior Bookshops* v *Veitchi Co. Ltd* [1983] 1 AC 520 and more recently *Muirhead* v *Industrial Tank Specialties Ltd* [1986] QB 507), you would no doubt wish to point out that the duty of care in this context is not confined to situations in which the actual identity of the plantiff is known to the defendant, but could extend to other situations where the plaintiff is readily identifiable. This could be supported in the following terms:

> Such a position was clearly anticipated by the House of Lords on the facts, in the seminal decision in *Hedley Byrne* v *Heller*.

As examiners we would accept that statement as an adequate demonstration that a student understood the material facts of *Hedley Byrne* without him having spelled them out in a more detailed statement occupying a further three or four lines.

A good answer to a question will obviously demonstrate a thorough knowledge of case law and statutory provisions on a particular topic. Such an answer will not only explain the relevance of certain decisions, but will also explain why other decisions are not regarded as relevant. We have already warned that the facts of the problem may well have been carefully chosen in order to provoke and facilitate this kind of discussion. In giving such an answer a student may well be involved in handling a significant number of authorities. Many students simply lack the necessary technique to do so. We suspect that some students appreciate that certain cases which appear to be relevant on the facts of the problem may be properly distinguished. But they refuse to become involved in saying so simply through pressure of time. We know that other students try to deal with this matter by stating, for example, 'The decision in *Smith* v *Jones* is distinguishable', but fail to give any explanation as to why this may be so. At the other extreme, in distinguishing a single case, some students allow themselves to be drawn into making a far more detailed statement of facts than is necessary and find they have insufficient time to deal adequately with other issues they have identified. These difficulties may be avoided by adopting a style similar to that above which should enable you to say a good deal in relatively few words. Furthermore, your script is likely to be far more readable, a point which may count substantially in your favour in the tired eyes of the examiner.

We would describe such a style as 'functional'. It should help you cope more adequately with the demands of examinations. However, this impressionism should not be carried too far. Try to ensure that your style overtly demonstrates your understanding of the authorities. On the other hand you should make every effort to avoid writing an answer the text of which is interspersed with, indeed interrupted by, 'block' statements of detailed factual information. The names of cases can and should be memorised. They facilitate the employment of the style advocated above. Valuable time might otherwise be wasted by having to identify cases by stating their facts. However, as a final resort you may do so and you should recognise that the level of the decision and its date is of greater significance than the name of the case. From a presentational point of view it is customary wisdom to advise students to physically underline the names of cases incorporated in their answers so as to emphasise their presence and thus impress the examiner.

(c)   We believe it is important that students should have a clear understanding of when and to what degree it may be appropriate to speculate on facts other than those set out in a problem, especially in view of the possibility that an examiner may have deliberately omitted legally material facts. To this end the following advice should not only be borne in mind but put into practice:

(i)   Do not speculate on facts contrary to those actually stated in a problem unless the examiner specifically asks you to do so.

(ii)   Be prepared to recognise that legally relevant facts may be *implicitly* stated in a problem and deal with them accordingly.

(iii)   Approach problem questions on the assumption that certain legally relevant facts may well have been omitted. Obviously your ability to identify as relevant, facts which are omitted, comes from your detailed knowledge of case law. If you feel you have identified a legally relevant fact which is not stated in the problem you should hypothesise as to what the legal solution may be alternatively taking into account the presence of the fact and its absence.

In the following problem we have sought to illustrate these three basic points:

> P, a self-employed courier went to D Garages Ltd and informed a salesman that he was interested in buying a small secondhand van but insisted that it should be especially reliable. The salesman recommended a one year old Ford Escort van standing in the showroom and assured P that it was an 'extremely reliable model'.
>
> P bought the vehicle for cash and signed an agreement which contained the following clause 'All second hand commercial vehicles are sold subject to our three months free parts and labour warranty. All other conditions or warranties express or implied by statute or common law are hereby excluded'.
>
> During the three month period after purchase the vehicle broke down on five occasions due to minor electrical and mechanical faults. Although these were remedied free of charge by D Garages Ltd, P incurred expenses through having to hire another van. D Garages Ltd refused to accept responsibility for those expenses.
>
> Four months after purchase the van has broken down again and P seeks your advice.
>
> Advise P.

(a)   First, the problem clearly states that the exemption clause is incorporated in the agreement by virtue of its signing by P. There would, therefore, be no point in speculating as to the legal position had the agreement not been so signed.

(b)   On the other hand, however, the question does not state whether P examined the vehicle at the time of sale, or whether any specific defects were brought to his attention. Speculation as to such matters would indeed be expected by the examiner in the light of the provisions of s. 14(2) of the Sale of Goods Act 1979.

(c)   Finally, the fact that the problem states that P is 'a self-employed courier' and the fact that the vehicle is a van, imply that it has been purchased for business use, rather than for private use. This raises the legal issue as to whether he has 'dealt as a consumer' (see s. 12 of the Unfair Contract Terms Act 1977).

Summary

In chapters 1 and 2 we have drawn attention to, and advised how to avoid, what we perceive as the major failures in study methods and examination technique. We have sought to illustrate that advice at various points. In doing so we inevitably became involved with the substance of consumer and commercial law. These illustrations should become more meaningful as you progress through the course and acquire knowledge of relevant areas of law. In subsequent chapters we take this illustrative approach much further. Our purpose is to enable students to gain progressively the experience and practice which are important to the development of a satisfactory examination technique.

THREE

IMPLIED TERMS AS TO THE QUALITY
OF GOODS AND SERVICES

Introduction

In this chapter we shall consider a number of obligations which are implied as a matter of law into a wide range of contracts by virtue of the Sale of Goods Act 1979, the Supply of Goods and Services Act 1982 and Schedule 4 of the Consumer Credit Act 1974. Whilst there are numerous implied obligations in such contracts, we are here confining ourselves to those which are concerned with the description or quality in contracts for the supply of goods and services. Important obligations, such as those relating to price, and other aspects of performance, e.g., delivery of goods, will be dealt with in chapter 4. We thought it preferable to deal with the implied obligations as to title of goods in a separate chapter concerned with the property aspect of the supply of goods, namely, chapter 6.

These obligations as to description and quality are of central importance in both consumer and commercial contracts which will normally be reflected in syllabuses and examinations. Their importance in the context of consumer contracts is emphasised by the fact that liability for breach of these obligations cannot be excluded (see ss. 6 and 7 Unfair Contract Terms Act 1977, chapter 5).

Before moving on to consider the particular substantive issues, we feel that it is necessary to recognise that students experience considerable difficulty in gaining an overall perspective of this area. This is the result not only of the variety of contracts involved but also of the piecemeal nature of the statutory framework as it has evolved over the past decade, including the legislation which deals with the related issue of exclusion clauses. The following explanation will we trust serve to alleviate any such difficulty.

The present position is that obligations as to correspondence with description, merchantable quality, fitness for purpose and compliance with sample, are implied into any type of contract under which goods are supplied. One matter which confuses students is that the *statutory source of the above mentioned obligations* differs according to the type of contract concerned.

The statutory control of the effect in civil law of clauses purporting to exclude liability for breach of those implied obligations are to be found in the Unfair Contract Terms Act. Although the relevant controls are contained in different sections (ss. 6 and 7) of that Act (according to the type of contract in question), *there is in this respect* no meaningful difference between the two sections. There is however an important distinction in the *criminal law controls* over the use of exclusion clauses. The Consumer (Transaction Restrictions on Statements) Order 1976 (as amended) creates offences only with regard to the use of clauses which are 'void by virtue of s. 6' of the Unfair Contract Terms Act and does not appy to those clauses which may be rendered ineffective by s. 7 (or other provision of that Act).

The other important implied obligation concerning quality relates to work which is done or the services which are provided under contract. An obligation requiring the supplier to exercise reasonable skill and care is now implied by s. 13 of the Supply of Goods and Services Act 1982. That obligation affects not only those persons who, in the course of a business, supply services such as dry cleaning but it also attaches to the 'work element' in a contract for work and materials such as the repair of a motor car. Attempts to exclude civil liability for the breach of this implied obligation are also controlled by the Unfair Contract Terms Act, s. 2 being the relevant section. The nature and extent of the controls implied by this section differ significantly from those imposed by ss. 6 and 7. This, and other differences in the overall scheme of the 1977 Act totally baffle some students — the subject of exclusion clauses is dealt with in chapter 5. In the meanwhile we trust the following table in which we have set out the present statutory framework will be of assistance.

Type of contract	(1) Sale of goods cash/credit	(2) Hire-purchase	(3) Barter	(4) Work and materials	(5) Hire, leasing	(6) Contracts for services
Implied obligations	(a) correspondence with description (b) merchantable quality (c) fitness for particular purpose (d) compliance with sample	As per column (1) (a) to (d) inclusive	As per column (1) (a) to (d) inclusive	As per column (1) (a) to (d) inclusive *and* carry out work with reasonable skill and care	As per column (1) (a) to (d) inclusive	— Carry out service with reasonable skill and care
Source of obligations	Sale of Goods Act 1979, ss. 13 to 15 inclusive	Consumer Credit Act 1974, Schedule 4, para 35	Supply of Goods and Services Act 1982, ss. 3 to 5 (inclusive)	Supply of Goods and Services Act 1982, ss. 3-5, 13	Supply of Goods and Services Act, ss. 8 to 10	Supply of Goods and Services Act 1982, s. 13
Exclusion clause control	Unfair Contract Terms Act 1978, s. 6. Consumer Transactions (Restriction on Statements) Order 1976 (as amended)	As per column (1)	Unfair Contract Terms Act 1977, s. 7	Unfair Contract Terms Act 1977, ss. 7 *and* 2.	As per column (3)	Unfair Contract Terms Act 1977, s. 2.

Substantive difficulties

Perhaps the first issue upon which some advice might be offered is that of the relationship between the statutory implied obligations as to description, quality and fitness for purpose on the one hand and other possible heads of liability under the common law or the Misrepresentation Act 1967. Students, not surprisingly, do experience difficulty because of the number and complexity of the possible actions which may arise, under the common law or statute, from the facts of a problem question on sale of goods. We shall, as appropriate, seek to shed light on some of the more difficult points raised by this relationship.

There is however a second aspect to this issue. Lecturers and tutors may or may not have emphasised the common law framework of this subject. If they have not, there exists the real danger that students will erroneously believe that the whole of the law pertinent to a sale of goods is to be found in the 1979 Act. Any such belief will we trust be effectively dispelled by the following illustration.

A pre-contractual statement made by a vendor in respect of goods sold, which amounts to more than mere commendatory expression may, in appropriate circumstances, give rise to liability under one or more of the following heads:

(a) Where the statement does not amount to a term of the contract of sale an action may lie for:

(i) fraudulent misrepresentation under the common law;
(ii) negligent or even innocent misrepresentation under the Misrepresentation Act 1967;
(iii) breach of duty of care established under either *Donoghue* v *Stevenson* [1932] AC 562 or *Hedley Byrne & Co. Ltd* v *Heller & Partners Ltd* [1964] AC 465 depending upon whether the damage sustained is of a physical or purely financial nature;
(iv) breach of the condition implied by s. 14(2) Sale of Goods Act, on the basis that the statement was a part of the description applied to the goods and the goods were unmerchantable under that description.

(b) Where the statement does amount to an express term of the contract an action may lie for:

(i) breach of that express term, the remedy varying according to whether the term is regarded as a condition, a warranty or an innominate term;

(ii)   breach of the condition implied by s. 13, of the Sale of Goods Act 1979, on the grounds that the statement was a 'description' of the goods with which the goods did not comply;

(iii)   breach of the condition implied by s. 14(3) of the Sale of Goods Act 1979 that the goods be fit for the buyer's particular purpose. The relevance of the statement being that the vendor encouraged reliance upon his skill and judgment in this respect.

Goods are not generally sold without some oral or written statement being made about them. The range of possible actions outlined above may arise quite frequently and is not, we submit, the result of fevered imagination on our part. To what extent should students concern themselves with the possible liabilities outside the Sale of Goods Act? The obvious advice is to read the rubric to any question carefully 'Consider the possible liability under the Sale of Goods Act', essentially disposes of the matter. However your examiner may well wish to encourage a wider view of the kind of possibilities illustrated above and may simply instruct you to 'discuss' the legal issues which arise from the facts of the problem. To give what is in the view of the examiner a balanced answer to such a question is more problematic. We would suggest that it is perfectly proper for students to seek guidance from tutors on issues such as these and we would advise you to do so before examination time. Where past examination questions are used in seminars this provides an ideal opportunity to raise the matter.

A similar problem arises in those courses which include some aspects of the criminal law, in particular, the Trade Descriptions Acts. The facts of a question concerning the possible misdescription of goods will almost inevitably raise the possibility of both civil and criminal liabilities. The examiner, if it is his wish to do so, will (hopefully) limit discussion clearly by means of the rubric to the question, e.g., 'Discuss the possible *civil* liability'. The examiner may however wish to leave it open to students to explore the issues at both civil and criminal law, the rubric merely inviting students to 'discuss'. In respect of this matter we repeat the advice given immediately above. In this chapter we have primarily confined ourselves to a consideration of the civil law, but the relevance of certain aspects of the criminal law, e.g., Trade Descriptions Act, Consumer Transactions (Restriction on Statements) Order 1976 (as amended) must be and are acknowledged.

Correspondence with description

Section 13(1) of the Sale of Goods Act 1979 which embodies the requirement that goods must correspond with their description is, in a conceptual sense, perhaps the most difficult of all the implied obligations. There exists a number of interrelated issues which produce this situation, all of which may be raised by a problem question of deceptive simplicity.

The first of these matters is raised by the opening words of s. 13(1) itself. The obligation as to correspondence with description is only implied — 'where there is a sale by description' — and the obvious question arises as to what amounts to a sale by description?

It is now reasonably well established that this *will* embrace all sales of future or unascertained goods (see *Varley* v *Whipp* [1900] 1 QB 513 per Channell J at p. 516) and *may* also include the sale of specific goods over the counter where the buyer has seen and even perhaps examined them, 'so long as [the goods are] sold not merely as the specific thing, but as a thing corresponding to a description, e.g., woollen undergarments, a hot water bottle . . .' (*Grant* v *Australian Knitting Mills Ltd* [1936] AC 85, per Lord Wright at p. 100). With the addition of what is now s. 13(3) dealing with self-service sales, one is tempted at first sight to agree with the view expressed by the Law Commission (Exemption Clauses in Contracts: First Report: Amendments to the Sale of Goods Act 1893, a para. 25) that the section is, 'to all intents and purposes comprehensive'.

Unfortunately that view tends to obscure the fact that s. 13 still allows a good deal of freedom of contract. It is clearly implicit in the opening words of s. 13(1) that it is open to a person to sell specific goods over the counter, other than by description. In seeking to do so the vendor may include in a contractual document a term to the effect that the goods are 'bought as seen'.

Such a clause may however be viewed as an exclusion clause under s. 13 of the Unfair Contract Terms Act 1977 in that it attempts to exclude a 'relevant obligation' namely that of supplying goods which correspond with a description. If the clause is so regarded then in the context of a 'consumer transaction' such a clause is without effect in the civil law (s. 6 Unfair Contract Terms Act) and its inclusion in the document amounts to a criminal offence under Article 3(d) Consumer transaction (Restriction on Statements) Order 1976 (as amended).

The employment of such terms is almost customary in certain trades, e.g., second hand car sales. Given the propensity which businessman have for exploiting contractual freedom it would be more than useful to know exactly how one is to decide whether the employment of a phrase such as 'bought as seen', is a legitimate exercise of the contractual freedom preserved by s. 13 or whether it is, in the context of a consumer transaction, a criminal offence under the 1976 Order.

Proceeding upon the assumption that a sale is one by description a second question arises — precisely what amounts to the description with which the goods must comply? In seeking an answer to this question it is of crucial importance to be aware that the effect of s. 13 is to treat any such statements as a condition, breach of which will entitle the buyer who acts promptly to reject the goods.

Although s. 13(1) sheds no light on the relationship between the statutory requirement and the common law, it seems reasonably clear that the descriptive words used must have been intended as a term of the contract (rather than a mere representation) if they are to be treated as part of the description of the goods under s. 13(1) (see *Harrison* v *Knowles & Foster* [1918] 1 KB 608; *Taylor* v *Combined Buyers Ltd* [1924] NZLR 627). The need for students to refresh their memories on the common law distinction betweeen representation and terms is fairly obvious. No doubt they will be reminded of the difficulty of applying the 'intention of the parties' test: a difficulty well illustrated in this context by the decision in *Beale* v *Taylor* [1967] 1 WLR 1193.

This leaves us with the proposition that s. 13 elevates, to the status of a condition a descriptive statement which under the common law might only be regarded as a warranty giving rise to an action only for damages. Certain earlier cases took that view and indeed required strict compliance with the descriptive words in question with the result that the buyer was entitled to reject goods notwithstanding the fact that the deviation from the contractual description had caused him little if any loss (see *Arcos Ltd* v *E. A. Ronaasen & Son* [1933] AC 470; *Re Moore & Co. Ltd and Landauer & Co.* [1921] 2 KB 519).

The results in such cases bear remarkable contrast with the present common law under which the likelihood of a term being regarded as a condition (allowing automatic repudiation in the event of breach) has been dramatically reduced notwithstanding that the term may be so defined in the contract (see, e.g., *Bunge Corpn., New York* v *Tradax Export SA, Panama* [1981] 1 WLR 711 per Lord Wilberforce at p. 715; see also *Wickman Machine Tool Sales Ltd* v *L. Schuler AG* [1974] AC 235). Furthermore, through the notion of the innominate term what may be described as a doctrine of 'substantial damage' has been developed since the seminal decision in *Hongkong Fir Shipping Co. Ltd* v *Kawasaki Kisen Kaisha Ltd* [1962] 2 QB 26. Under this doctrine the innocent party is only entitled to repudiate the contract if he has been substantially deprived of the whole of the benefit of the contract.

The Law Commission has recognised this inconsistency between the statutory regime and the common law and envisaged the possibility of substantial changes to the remedies available under the Act (see Law Commission Working Paper No. 85, Sale and Supply of Goods (1983) para. 2.30. However in their subsequent report (Law Commission Report,

Sale and Supply of Goods, CM 137, 1987) the changes actually proposed are relatively minor ones. Meanwhile students face the somewhat daunting task of trying to understand how the courts have themselves sought to address the problem by a restrictive interpretation of s. 13 and in particular what amounts to 'the description' with which the goods must comply. Two decisions of the House of Lords are relevant in this respect: *Christopher Hill Ltd* v *Ashington Piggeries Ltd* [1972] AC 441 and *Reardon Smith Line Ltd* v *Hansen-Tangen (trading as H. E. Hansen-Tangen)* [1976] 1 WLR 989. The upshot of these decisions would appear to be that the strict approach illustrated by the decision in *Arcos* v *Ronaasen* (above) is likely to be confined to sales of future unascertained goods. In all other cases a much more restrictive approach is to be adopted, by treating only those words which go to the identity of the goods as part of the description with which the goods are required to comply. As we shall see below a similarly restrictive approach has been taken with regard to the meaning of 'merchantable quality' in s. 14(6) of the 1979 Act as a solution to the problem of the rigidity of remedies which also affects the other obligations implied by the 1979 Act. Though it is not entirely free from doubt it seems that the same problem exists with regard to the remedies available for breach of similar obligations implied in other contracts by the Supply of Goods and Service Act 1982.

A further issue which appears not to be well understood by students or at least not very well emphasised in examination answers, is the relationship between s. 13 of the 1979 Act and the other implied obligations, especially the obligation to supply goods of merchantable quality. Whilst little if any difficulty seems to be experienced in understanding the proposition that goods which may be of merchantable quality may not correspond with their description (and vice versa) students often fail to demonstrate sufficient appreciation of the enormous difference which exists between the restricted meaning of 'description' under s. 13 and the much wider view, expressed in s. 14(6) that, '*any* description applied to the goods' may be relevant to determine whether or not goods are of merchantable quality.

Finally, it is of course the case that s. 13 applies to sales by both private individuals and businessmen alike whereas the implied obligations as to merchantable quality and fitness for purpose are implied only where the sale is 'in the course of a business'. Now this is not a difficult point to grasp but how often it is overlooked in the heat of the examination room!

Merchantable quality

The obligation to supply goods of merchantable quality is, in our view, the most important of the implied obligations and is likely to be regarded as a 'core' topic in either a consumer law or commercial law syllabus. Questions on the subject are likely to appear on examination papers with predictable regularity. The questions themselves may be problem or essay questions. Where the topic is examined in a problem question the examiner may well raise a range of issues concerning not only merchantable quality but also correspondence with description, fitness for the buyer's particular purpose and the possible exclusion of liability by a supplier of goods. An essay question requiring an analysis and evaluation of the statutory definition of merchantable quality may prove to be an attractive alternative to the examiner. This is particularly so at the present time in view of considerable dissatisfaction with that definition. Despite Lord Denning's view that it is, 'the best that has yet been devised' (see *Cehave NV v Bremer Handelsgesellschaft mbH* [1976] QB 44 at p. 62), the definition of merchantable quality has subsequently been referred to the Law Commission for consideration. The Commission has now recommended certain reforms (see Law Commission Report (above), paras 3.1-3.67). Students ought not merely to be aware of the possible reform but ought to have formed their own view of it. The substantive issues involved in the implied obligation to supply goods of merchantable quality with which students experience difficulty will be dealt with under the following heads:

(a)   In what circumstances is the obligation as to merchantable quality implied?

(b)   The meaning of merchantable quality in law.

To assist we have incorporated the text of the provisions in s. 14(2) and (6) of the Sale of Goods Act 1979.

In what circumstances is the obligation to supply goods of merchantable quality implied?

Where the seller sells goods in the course of a business, there is an implied condition that the goods supplied under the contract are of merchantable quality, except there is no such condition —

(a)   as regards defects specifically drawn to the buyer's attention before the contract is made; or

(b)   if the buyer examines the goods before the contract is made, as regards defects which that examination ought to reveal.

From the text of s. 14(2) we can see there are a number of basic requirements all of which have to be satisfied before the obligation is implied.

Unlike s. 13 the obligations implied by s. 14(2) and 14(3) are confined to sales 'in the course of a business'. Students often fail to recognise the two different requirements involved here with the result that their discussion of the case law tends to be confused. The first issue is whether or not the vendor's activities amount to 'business' at all (taking account of the non exhaustive definition to be found in s. 61(1) of the 1979 Act). Assuming that to be the case a second question arises: is the sale *in the course of* a business'?

Similar phraseology is to be found in numerous civil and criminal statutes in this area, e.g., Supply of Goods and Services Act 1982; Trade Descriptions Act 1968; Business Advertisements (Disclosure) Order 1977; s. 2(1) Unsolicited Goods and Services Act 1971. There appears to be some divergence of views expressed in the decided cases. It would seem that the phraseology is subjected to a more restrictive interpretation under the criminal law than under the civil law and in our experience students generally do not show a sufficient appreciation of that distinction.

Your examiner may seek to explore your knowledge (or lack of it) as to the legal position where goods are sold by, e.g., an auctioneer on behalf of a private seller: are the obligations as to merchantability and fitness for purpose implied? He may also raise, in this context, the validity of an exclusion clause. This is in our view a classic example of a topic which many students never quite understand. The answers to the questions posed above are to be found in s. 14(5) of the Sale of Goods Act 1979 and s. 12 of the Unfair Contract Terms Act 1977. Careful study of these provisions may well pay a handsome dividend.

The two provisos, as to examination and specific defects being brought to the buyer's attention, do not appear to cause students any great difficulty, except that a number do tend not to emphasise sufficiently that the test as to what defects might have been discovered by 'that examination' is a subjective one. Similarly some fail to make the point that whilst a *general notice of defects* e.g., 'shop soiled', may not be sufficient to oust the implied obligation, such notice may be relevant as part of the 'description applied to the goods' under which they may be regarded as merchantable.

Definition of merchantable quality   The definition of merchantable quality in s. 14(6) of the 1979 Act, is of course the central issue and is as follows:

Goods of any kind are of merchantable quality . . . if they are as fit for the purpose(s) for which goods of that kind are commonly bought as is reasonable to expect having regard to any description applied to them, the price (if relevant) and all the other relevant circumstances.

The meaning of merchantable quality is a problematic issue per se, which results to a considerable degree from the less than satisfactory statutory definition set out above. Our experience is that the subject causes students even greater difficulty when raised in a problem question as opposed to an essay question. There are a number of reasons for this. First, it is intrinsically more diffcult to apply the definition to a particular factual situation and to 'Advise P' than it is for example to explain the deficiencies of the definition and suggest how those deficiencies might be rectified. The issue of merchantability is a mixed one of fact and law. At the factual level it can be a difficult (if not impossible) question of judgment to decide on the basis of a very limited statement of facts in an examination question whether or not goods are in fact as fit as is reasonable to expect. Whilst the proper interpretation of the definition of merchantable quality is a matter of law the provision is of such an open textured nature that 'it is on an empty vessel into which the courts can pour their own meaning' according to the circumstances of any particular case (Atiyah, *Sale of Goods*, 7th ed. at p. 136). Examiners are aware of the degree of artificiality and difficulty involved when asking students to 'Advise the Purchaser'. In anything except the clearest of cases it is therefore of no great consequence if the views of the student and examiner do not entirely coincide, unless that shows a substantial misunderstanding of the relevant cases on the part of the student. What is of crucial importance here is that students must be prepared to discuss issues both ways, for a failure to do so may well result in a student not dealing with important points. Suppose for example a problem question includes issues as to the merchantability of goods and consequent possible remedies of the buyer, together with the validity of an exemption clause. A student who concludes on the given facts that the goods are merchantable may then simply not bother to discuss the other issues with disastrous results.

Merchantable quality is one of those subjects on which there appears to be an almost infinite number of specific points which may be raised by an examiner. Having acquired knowledge of most if not all of these, students then tend to deploy the whole of their knowledge indiscriminately whether or not it is relevant on the given facts of a problem. Examiners tend to be rather selective, choosing the facts of problem questions to raise specific points and therefore react quite unfavourably to the kitchen sink approach. Perhaps because of the large number of points from which the examiners can and do select, students tend not to identify points raised as well as they might. In that respect we would refer students back to the advice given in chapter 2 at p. 26. In order to provide further assistance in this respect we have below identified and outlined briefly many of the issues which may be raised on the subject by an examiner. We have done so largely by posing questions concerning certain key phrases in the statutory definition.

Fitness for usual purposes Under s. 14(6) of the 1979 Act goods are required to be '*as fit for the purpose(s) for which goods of that kind are commonly bought as is reasonable to expect.* . . .' This phrase represents the nucleus of the definition of merchantable quality. Whilst the central question may also have to take account of the price and the description of goods a number of important points arise from this phrase alone:

The wording requires that goods be reasonably fit for their *usual* purpose(s). An examiner may well focus upon the purpose to which goods are put in order to provoke a discussion of the *further requirement in s. 14(3)* that goods must be fit for the buyer's particular purpose even though that be an 'unusual purpose'. But in what circumstances is this so?

The definition was intended to enshrine what was thought to be the law as developed through the cases prior to 1973. To what extent does the definition achieve this? Does the definition in some way incorporate an 'acceptability test' as well as a fitness for purpose test? If so, which words in the definition do that? If not, can a buyer successfully claim that the refrigerator he unpacks to find a large scratch across its door is unmerchantable?

Where goods are commonly bought for several different purposes for how many of those purposes must goods be reasonably fit in order to be of merchantable quality? Section 14(6) requires the goods to be fit for the 'purpose or *purposes*'. Does this now mean that goods have to be fit for all their usual purposes before they are regarded as merchantable (see *M/S Aswan Engineering Establishment Ltd* v *Lupdine Co.* [1987] 1 WLR 1? Contrast the views of Law Commission in the 1987 Report (above) at paras 3.32-3.36.

The goods are required to meet one's reasonable expectations and this has generally been taken to mean that goods need not be perfect. This 'less than perfect' standard seems to be more than the mere application of the *de minimis* rule. The standard is set by the courts. Most reported consumer cases have been concerned with motor vehicles (and so may your examination question). Is it reasonable to expect a new car to be free of minor defects? Is it reasonable to allow a new vehicle to be rejected and the purchase price reclaimed when a new vehicle has minor defects? There can be little doubt that the issue of reasonable fitness has been decided by courts with one eye on the resultant remedy (see *Millar's of Falkirk* v *Turpie* 1976 SLT 66; *Cehave NV* v *Bremer Handelsgesellschaft mbH* [1976] QB 44; *Bernstein* v *Pamsons Motors Ltd* [1987] 2 All ER 220; *Rogers* v *Parish (Scarborough) Ltd* [1987] 2 WLR 353).

The supplier, it is said, is strictly liable in the event that the goods are unmerchantable or indeed unfit for the buyer's particular purpose as required by s. 14(3). What precisely does this mean?

The description of the goods   The reasonable expectations as to the quality of goods is to be judged, *inter alia*, in the *light of 'any description applied to them. . . .'* Several points arise from this phrase.

The word 'description' here has a much wider meaning than is attributed to the same word under s. 13. But do the descriptive words in question have to have been intended as a term of the contract before they are of relevance under s. 14(6)? How widely is the word 'any' to be construed?

The supplier is clearly free to affect the level of the reasonable expectation by describing goods as 'shop-soiled' etc. Where goods prove to be defective does the description applied have to give some indication of the possibility of the particular defect manifesting itself? Would a coat described as 'shop-soiled' be merchantable under that description in the event that a sleeve came adrift due to defective sewing? This kind of question points to the need to consider carefully the meaning to be given to such descriptive words (see for example the discussion as to the meaning of 're-conditioned' in *Minster Trust Ltd* v *Traps Tractors Ltd* [1954] 3 All ER 136 at p. 144.)

In this context what is the position where goods are described as 'bought as seen'? Is this a legitimate means of reducing the reasonable expectation as to quality, or an attempt to exclude the implied obligation? If it is the latter, the clause is void in a consumer transaction by virtue of s. 6 of the Unfair Contract Terms Act 1977 and a criminal offence under Article 3(d) of the Consumer Transactions (Restriction or Statements) Order 1976 (as amended). You will recall we asked a similar question earlier in the context of correspondence with description (see *Hughes* v *Hall (Gillian)* [1981] RTR 430; *Cavendish-Woodhouse Ltd* v *Manley* (1984) 148 JP 299, 82 LGR 376).

The general view is that instructions and directions as to use placed upon containers, etc., are to be regarded as a part of the description applied to goods. But might goods be regarded as unmerchantable by reason of the absence of clear user instructions (see *Wormell* v *RHM Agriculture (East) Ltd* [1986] 1 WLR 336)? Observations in this very recent case pose some interesting questions which may well prove attractive to an examiner despite the reversal of the actual decision on appeal (see [1987] 1 WLR 1091).

The price of goods   Merchantability may have to be measured by reference to the price of the goods '(if relevant)'. When is the price paid relevant and when is it irrelevant? Since s. 14(6) is supposed to reflect the pre 1973 case law one could presumably find the answer therein. The test of merchantability involving the price consideration is to be found in the House of Lords decision of *B. S. Brown & Sons Ltd* v *Craikes Ltd* [1970] 1 All ER 823, but the decision sheds no light on the questions posed above. Is the price of goods relevant when the goods are damaged (and that is not known to the buyer)?

Goods must be fit for the buyer's particular purpose

Section 14(3) of the 1979 Act states that:

> Where the seller sells goods in the course of a business and the buyer, expressly or by implication, makes known —
>
> (a)   to the seller, or
> (b)   where the purchase price or part of it is payable by instalments and the goods were previously sold by a credit broker to the seller, to that credit broker, any particular purpose for which the goods are being bought, there is an implied condition that the goods supplied under the contract are reasonably fit for that purpose, whether or not that is a purpose for which such goods are commonly supplied, except where the circumstances show that the buyer does not rely, or that it is unreasonable for him to rely, on the skill and judgment of the seller.

Whilst the provision gives rise to fewer problems in practice than does s. 14(2), it does involve a number of issues which exercise considerably the minds of students. The above mentioned obligation is, like that as to merchantability, only implied 'where there is a sale in the course of a business. . . .' We have already identified the difficulties associated with this requirement (see above p. 41). There exists a good deal of overlap between subsections 14(2) and 14(3) in that both provisions require that goods be reasonably fit for their usual purposes, so that in many cases a breach of s. 14(2) will also automatically amount to a breach of s. 14(3). There are other cases in which, though the goods are purchased for a usual purpose, the provisions as to examination and reliance by the buyer in the respective subsections are such that in certain circumstances an action under s. 14(3) may hold a greater prospect of success.

The importance of s. 14(3) lies, however, in the requirement that the goods be reasonably fit for *any particular purpose even though this may not be a purpose for which such goods are commonly bought*. It is the student's understanding of this requirement that the examiner is most likely to explore. Many of the central issues involved in the provision are essentially questions of fact. Such matters as the reasonable fitness of the goods, whether the buyer has sufficiently communicated the purpose for which he requires the goods, and extent and reasonableness of the buyer's reliance upon the skill and judgment of the supplier or credit broker, can only be determined by reference to the detailed circumstances of a particular transaction. The absence of this kind of factual information from the typical examination problem places the student in some difficulty. As we pointed out in the context of merchantable quality the examiner will be aware of this and will make allowance accordingly. What the examiner will expect of students is that they identify the specific issues and deal with the possibilities and consequences arising therefrom.

It should not however be thought that all the matters raised in questions of this kind are exclusively matters of fact upon which one can simply suggest different possible results according to the alternative views which may be taken of the facts. The whole question as to the proper interpretation of statutory provisions is a matter of law, and the examiner may well raise a number of points concerning the interpretation of certain key words in s. 14(3). The examiner will have chosen facts which raise these points of law on which he will expect an answer which deals accurately with the relevant case law.

Thus, for example, in the context of the reasonableness or otherwise of the buyer's reliance upon the supplier's skill and judgment, it seems that a court may take into account the supplier's lack of expertise where he sells goods which he did not originally acquire with a primary intention of resale (as where a grocer sells off a freezer cabinet secondhand). Can a supplier, as a matter of law, plead an absence of expertise on his part (which may be real rather than conveniently invented) with regard to goods purchased for resale?

The following questions indicate some of the issues involved in s. 14(3) which examiners often explore and upon which students frequently flounder.

(a)   What is the meaning of the phrase 'particular purpose'?

(b)   The section requires goods to be fit for '*any* particular purpose'. Does this mean that the goods have to be fit for any purpose to which the buyer chooses to put the goods? Where goods have a variety of purposes is the seller's potential liability more onerous under s. 14(2) or 14(3) (see *Henry Kendall & Sons* v *William Lillico & Sons Ltd* [1969] 2 AC 31 and *Christopher Hill Ltd* v *Ashington Piggeries Ltd* [1972] AC 441)?

(c)   To what extent if at all does s. 14(3) require goods to be of a higher standard than that required by s. 14(2) (see *Baldry* v *Marshall* [1925] 1 KB 260, CA)? In the light of the decision in the Baldry case what do you make of the view taken in *Porter* v *General Guarantee Corpn. Ltd* [1982] RTR 384 that the facts did not disclose a breach of s. 14(2) or s. 14(3)?

(d)   Does the buyer's reliance upon the seller or credit broker need to be total? Given the enormous amount of brand advertising by manufacturers at the present time does the consumer rely on the supplier/credit broker where he requests or selects a particular brand of goods?

(e)   Since the obligation as to fitness for the purpose is a condition, the breach of which entitles the buyer to repudiate the contract, how are the courts likely to react to claims in respect of 'minor defects' (see *Millar's of Falkirk* v *Turpie* 1976 SLT (Notes) 67)?

(f)   Section 14(3) like s. 14(2) preserves a good deal of freedom of contract. It seems clearly open in theory for a supplier to refuse to warrant goods as being fit for *any* particular purpose by doing so in terms. As we indicated earlier the dividing line between what amounts to the legitimate exercise of that freedom as opposed to an exclusion of liability as defined by s. 13 of the Unfair Contract Terms Act 1977 can be a difficult one to draw.

Remedies for breach of the implied obligations

Problem questions concerning the implied obligations will almost inevitably require students to show their knowledge and understanding of the remedies available to the buyer where the supplier is in breach of any one or more of those obligations.

The law concerning remedies is sorely in need of reform and together with the question of the redefinition of merchantable quality, it was the subject of the Law Commission, Working Paper No. 85 (1983) and is now dealt with in the 1987 Report (above) see paras 4.1-6.17. We would strongly recommend students to read and carefully digest these valuable documents. There is quite a number of specific points on which one can question students in connection with remedies. Some are straightforward and do little other than test the student's memory, whilst others are in the nature of insoluble conundrums. Examiners tend to raise issues which fall between these extremes but into that category of issues which students 'never quite understand'. We would suggest that that category includes in this context the following matters:

(a)   We drew attention earlier to certain decisions which clearly demonstrate a tendency to interpret the substantive provisions of the 1979 Act with one eye on the available remedy in the belief that once a breach of the implied condition is established the buyer is automatically entitled to repudiate the contract and claim back the contract price with no reduction for user of the goods (assuming the buyer has not waived the breach or accepted the goods) (see, e.g., *Christopher Hill Ltd* v *Ashington Piggeries Ltd* [1972] AC 441 above p. 39). To what extent has that belief been challenged by, for example, the Court of Appeal in *Cehave NV* v *Bremer Handelsgesellschaft mbH* [1976] QB 44 and the Scots case of *Millar's of Falkirk* v *Turpie* 1976 SLT (Notes 66)? Does this difficulty affect the equivalent obligations in other supply contracts? If not, why (see the Law Commission Working Paper (above) at para. 2.39)?

(b)   Section 11(4) of the 1979 Act makes provision for the loss of the right to reject, the buyer then having only an action for damages. The circumstances in which this may be so are broadly spelled out in ss. 34 and 35. These include lapse of a reasonable period of time without the buyer intimating rejection. What is a reasonable period of time is essentially a question of fact but the examiner would expect an understanding on the part of the student as to the guidance which is to be derived from the decided cases. Is it possible that such period might differ according to whether the contract was one of sale or hire-purchase? Does the principle of recovery of money paid without reduction for user apply equally to both kinds of contract in the event of an established breach of the implied obligations? To what extent if at all are the above questions related? Finally, the question as to the buyer's aquiescence in attempted repair by the supplier or the possible commission by the buyer of an act 'inconsistent with the ownership of the seller' are likely to figure frequently in both consumer and non-consumer problems alike.

The quality of services

The contractual obligations of the supplier of services bear quite a remarkable contrast with those of the supplier of goods. Perhaps the first point to note is that it is fairly simple to state the legal principles applicable to services. The obligation formerly implied only under the common law has now been placed upon a statutory footing and is contained in s. 13, Supply of Goods and Services Act 1982. It states that 'in a contract for the supply of a service where the supplier is acting in the course of a business there is an implied term that the supplier will carry out the service with reasonable skill and care'. The apparent simplicity of this principle belies the difficulty of its application in practice, but this should not render the matter any more difficult to deal with in an examination. Whether or not a person has exercised reasonable skill and care is predominantly a question of fact and in that respect students should bear in mind the advice previously given of being prepared to discuss such issues 'both ways'.

There are, however, certain legal issues which arise in this context which are quite often either overlooked or poorly explained by students:

(a)   The standard of care in law is contained in the often quoted dictum of McNair J in *Bolam* v *Friern Hospital Management Committee* [1957] 1

WLR 582 at p. 586. Students fail to state the principle with sufficient accuracy and perhaps because of that their discussion of the principle is frequently flawed. The only other observation we would make in this respect is that students should spell out clearly the substantially lower standard this principle requires of suppliers of services by comparison with the standard required of the suppliers of goods.

(b) Students tend to have a very blinkered view and fail to make any observations whatever upon the possibility of any alternative action by the purchaser under the common law (see our previous advice on this matter in connection with the supply of goods, above). Given the relatively low standard required by the statutory obligation, it is important to consider the possible existence of alternative and perhaps more exacting obligations. The existence of the implied obligation in s. 13 of the 1982 Act does not, as a matter of law, preclude a court from holding that a stricter warranty has been given. In that regard your examiner may well have chosen his facts so as to imply on those facts the existence of a higher obligation (see *Greaves & Co. (Contractors) Ltd* v *Baynham Meikle & Partners* [1975] 1 WLR 1095 CA).

(c) An important recent development which we suspect will by now have found its way into most syllabuses is concerned not so much with the standard of care expected from a supplier of services but rather with the question: to whom is the duty to exercise such care owed? Recent decisions have established that a supplier may owe a duty of reasonable care in tort not only to a contracting party but also to a non-contracting party with regard to foreseeable injury whether of a physical or purely financial nature. The prospect of this wider liability is enjoyed by those who supply goods as well as those who supply services (see *Junior Books Ltd* v *Veitchi Co. Ltd* [1983] 1 AC 520; *Ross* v *Caunters* [1980] Ch 297; *Yianni* v *Edwin Evans & Sons* [1982] QB 438; *Muirhead* v *Industrial Tank Specialities Ltd* [1985] 3 WLR 993; *MS Aswan Engineering Ltd* v *Lupdine* (above)). These cases are more appropriately considered in chapter 7 which deals with tortious liability.

Quite apart from the development illustrated by the above mentioned cases one ought not to overlook the prospect of the recovery of damages by a non-contracting party following the decision of the Court of Appeal in *Jackson* v *Horizon Holidays Ltd* [1975] 1 WLR 1468.

Illustrative question

In the earlier pages of this chapter we sought, *inter alia*, to convey an appreciation of the sheer volume of issues arising out of the implied obligations which we considered. Many of them no doubt feature frequently in examination questions. It is not however our intention to try to deal with all or even most of those points in the illustrative question in this chapter. We have deliberately deferred consideration of a number of issues to later chapters. Thus, in chapter 4, the illustrative question raises a mixture of issues in relation to description and quality as well as matters concerning time of performance and the price of goods. That question is a sort of 'examiner's cocktail'. Some examiners are very fond (perhaps over fond) of

'some examiners are very fond of cocktails'

'cocktails'. The topic most noticeably deferred for later consideration is the implied obligation as to reasonable skill and care. This, together with certain other issues will be raised in chapter 5 (dealing with exemption clauses) and helps provide the basis of the illustrative question in that chapter.

The chosen question is of the essay type and is essentially concerned with the difficulties which stem from the present statutory definition of merchantable quality. Our choice in this respect is motivated not so much by the fact that in the present circumstances this topic is likely to be the subject of an examination question, but by the need to remind students that essay questions are not invitations to write all you know about any particular topic. Such questions will, as a matter of course, require thoughtful analysis and the selective deployment of material and that which follows is no exception.

'Much of the present criticism of [the obligation to supply goods of merchantable quality] comes down, at the end of the day, to being little more than a dislike of the word 'merchantable' which appears old fashioned and rather meaningless in a consumer transaction' (Atiyah, *Sale of Goods*, 7th ed. at p. 36). Discuss.

Commentary

We may begin appropriately by reasserting some fundamental points of technique. Whilst we shall not use a rough plan on which to base our commentary we would remind students of our earlier recommendation in this respect (in chapter 2, p. 26). The above quotation has been carefully chosen so as to express what might appear to be a somewhat provocative view in the hope of stimulating a positive and argumentative response. This kind of response to such questions is crucial if you are to impress your examiner. You may agree or disagree (to varying degrees) with such propositions but for goodness sake do not sit on the fence. Your answer should be a series of arguments based upon a careful selection of the most relevant issues. You will certainly not impress an examiner by an unselective, uncritical regurgitation of lecture notes at the end of which is tagged a note of agreement or disagreement with the quotation.

The particular quotation has been selected for quite a different reason: whilst it indicates, in general terms, the subject matter on which a discussion is required, it stops short of identifying detailed specific issues, the onus in this respect remains firmly with the student. In that sense the quotation strikes the kind of balance commonly sought by examiners and in the light of that we would emphasise yet again the need for careful thought as to exactly what is or is not relevant to any particular question and your proposed response thereto.

The selected quotation appears to make light of the criticisms of the provision as to merchantable quality. We therefore need first to identify and then to evaluate the relevant criticisms. In so far as those criticisms may have been repeated or commented upon in the Law Commission Report (above), an answer which did not demonstrate some awareness and understanding of the views expressed in that Report is unlikely to score particularly well.

Should one weave into the answer the views of the Law Commission point by point or, should one opt for a more basic structure (e.g., Part 1: The Criticisms, Part 2: The Law Commission's Views)? Whilst the former approach is more likely to impress an examiner it does require a greater familiarity with the material, more self confidence and it is probably more time consuming. This kind of decision on what is a common structural problem should have been made long before you get into the examination room.

We would suggest a response to the question along the following lines:

It is misleading to convey the view, as the quotation appears to do, that the only or even major criticisms of the provision as to merchantability in the Sale of Goods Act 1979 are merely terminological ones. Whilst there is dissatisfaction with the term 'merchantable quality' itself, more important substantive difficulties arise from the statutory provision. This is in fact recognised in the Report recently published by the Law Commission. Whilst the Commission recognises that it would be desirable to replace the term 'merchantable quality' with 'acceptable quality', the Commission countenances the possibility of far more important and substantive changes in the light of more serious weaknesses in the present statutory provision.

By adopting such an approach the student straightaway nails his/her flag to the mast in a way which is likely to stimulate a little greater interest on the part of the examiner. As we are now moving on to deal with the detailed criticisms, specific references to the wording of the statutory provision will become necessary. Assuming a copy of the Act is not available to you in the examination room, we would suggest that it is unnecessary (and a waste of valuable time) to write out the whole of the statutory provision even if you have total recollection of the text. In our view it is more efficient and impressive to employ an accurate precis of the provision and to select the key phrases which lie at the heart of the issues which are to be discussed (hopefully identified in your rough plan). In this way the relevant parts of the provision can be drawn into the text so as to produce a smooth, flowing and more polished answer.

Students will no doubt be aware that the legitimate criticisms of the present provision are not of equal importance, so why not show a little boldness and imagination? Make that point to the examiner, deal with those criticisms of less import in a fairly brief manner thus leaving a little more time for the most deserving issues. The criticisms which warrant some evaluation in the context of the quotation concern:

(a)   The generality of the provision which creates practical difficulty in application and in particular the failure of the statutory definition to spell out clearly many of the relevant considerations.

(b)   Certain apparently unintended differences in the law as stated in s. 14(6) and that to be found in the pre-1973 case law.

(c)   The strained interpretation placed upon the meaning of merchantable quality as a direct result of the remedies available in the event of breach, which are themselves unacceptably rigid and inconsistent with the reality of the market place.

The criticisms arising under (c) above are in our view of greater importance than those under (a) and (b) and should be given appropriate weight in an answer to the question.

The provision in s. 14(6) of the Sale of Goods Act 1979 requires in essence that goods be reasonably fit for their usual purpose(s) having regard to, *inter alia*, their price and description. It is widely accepted that the provision is so general in nature that it affords little real guidance as to when goods are or are not of merchantable quality. This is seen by some as inevitable, in that the provision has to apply to the sale of all kinds of goods in all kinds of differing circumstances. The Law Commission Report takes the view that, in so far as the subsection fails to clearly specify a number of factors which are thought to be relevant, it is perhaps unnecessarily vague. To that end the Report recommends a new definition of 'acceptable quality' comprising a statement of basic principle which is expanded by a non-exhaustive list of matters most germane, such as fitness for purpose, appearance, finish, freedom from minor defects, safety and durability. The failure of the present provision to specify all but the first of these factors is regarded by some academic writers as being relatively unimportant. Such matters as safety are in their view implicit in the notion of merchantable quality. In short unsafe goods are unmerchantable goods (unless perhaps the defects in the goods were drawn to the buyer's attention at the time of sale). Such a view is arguably dangerously complacent in the light of the decision of Judge Merrilees in the Corby County Court in *Lee* v *York Coach and Marine* [1977] RTR 35. In that case the judge by a most curious process of reasoning held that a car which was clearly and dangerously defective was of merchantable quality. Happily, the decision was overturned on appeal. Similarly with regard to durability there is authority for the view that goods must not only be merchantable at the time of sale but must remain so for a reasonable period thereafter (see Lord Diplock in *Lambert* v *Lewis* [1981] 1 All ER 1185 at p. 1191). The implication of this statement has been questioned and it seems to conflict with the 'evidentiary' view of the matter taken by Lord Denning MR in *Crowther* v *Shannon Motor Co.* [1975] 1 All ER 139, CA (see Mustill LJ in *Rogers* v *Parish (Scarborough) Ltd* [1987] 2 WLR 353. See also the Law Commission Report (above) at paras 3.47-3.61 which supports the approach advocated by Lord Denning).

It is our view that the changes proposed by the Law Commission (outlined above) are a sensible response to justifiable criticism of the present provision. Those changes are not merely cosmetic, but may help reduce avoidable uncertainty in the definition itself. We accept however that the difficult judgments which have to be reached will remain in many cases. The introduction of a new statutory definition which specifically recognises the relevance of such matters as the appearance and finish of goods, would resolve another point of uncertainty. The existing provision appears to concentrate upon the fitness of goods in a functional sense to the exclusion of aesthetic qualities. In that respect the present definition (introduced by the

Supply of Goods [Implied Terms] Act 1973) is arguably unrepresentative of the pre 1973 case law. That case law clearly recognised not only a 'fitness for purpose' test but also a 'saleability' (or acceptability) test (see *Henry Kendall & Sons* v *William Lillico & Sons Ltd* [1969] 2 AC 31, especially Lord Guest at p. 108 and Lord Reid at p. 75). This latter test is well illustrated by the decision of the Court of Appeal in *Jackson* v *Rotax Motor Cycle Co.* [1910] 2 KB 937 where it was held that scratched, dented but functional motor horns were not of merchantable quality. Academic opinion is that the language of the present provision is wide enough to cover such defects so that, e.g., a new refrigerator with a large scratch across its door would not be reasonably fit for its purpose. That opinion is however based upon a rather strained interpretation of 'fitness for purpose' (see *Rogers* v *Parish (Scarborough) Ltd* (above), where Mustill LJ in the CA took the view that a new car might be unmerchantable if its appearance was such that the buyer was unable to take 'pride in the vehicle's outward and interior appearance'. See also *Shine* v *General Guarantee Corpn., The Times,* 18 August 1987, CA.) Clarification along the lines anticipated by the Law Commission is to be welcomed, not least for the separation of this issue from that of 'minor defects' to which we should turn shortly.

Before doing so it would perhaps be appropriate to raise here one other point in respect of which the present definition appears to have departed from the pre-1973 case law. The present definition could be taken to require that multi-purpose goods be fit for *all* their normal purposes whereas, under the common law, goods were of merchantable quality if they were fit for only one of a number of usual purposes, provided that a purchaser fully acquainted with their defects would buy them without substantial abatement of the price (see *B. S. Brown & Son Ltd* v *Craiks Ltd* [1970] 1 WLR 752). In *M/S Aswan Engineering Establishment Ltd* v *Lupdine* [1987] 1 WLR 1, the Court of Appeal rejected the view that goods need to be fit for all purposes in order to satisfy the statutory requirements. Contrast the views of the Law Commission expressed in the 1987 Report (above) at para. 3.36, where it is proposed that this position be reversed so that 'if the seller knows that his goods are not fit for one or more of the purposes for which goods of that kind are commonly supplied, he may ensure that the description of the goods excludes any common purpose for which they are unfit . . . If he does not do so, and it is not clear from the other circumstances, then the seller may be in breach . . . if he sells goods which are commonly supplied for two purposes but which are fit only for one'.

Most concern and dissatisfaction with the present law arises from the rigid and inappropriate regime of remedies available for breach of the implied obligations. This is due mainly to the fact that the obligation to sell goods of merchantable quality is a *condition* of the contract, breach of which (subject to the buyer having accepted the goods) automatically entitles the buyer to reject the goods, to reclaim the price and claim any foreseeable consequential losses.

A discussion of the issue of remedies is really crucial in any attempt to refute the suggestion contained in the quotation that the criticism of the present law is merely terminological. The topic is however fairly complex and one upon which much could be written. This is especially true in that students would need to show some appreciation of the views of the Law Commission on the matter. Even if (following our earlier advice) more of the time available in an examination was to be devoted to this topic it would still be necessary to be both selective and concise. But beware: the dividing line between effective summary and unconvincing impressionism may be a fine one. A discussion of the issue of remedies sufficient to respond to the quotation might be approached in the following manner.

As indicated above the most serious criticism of the classification of the implied obligation as a condition is that under the 1979 Act any breach of this condition automatically entitles the buyer (who has not accepted the goods) to reject them and reclaim the price. To a large extent this rigidity has been eradicated from the common law through the development of the innominate term approach (see *Hongkong Fir Shipping Co. Ltd* v *Kawasaki Kisen Kaisha Ltd* [1962] 2 QB 26). The statutory regime of remedies is therefore inconsistent with those applicable under the general law of contract. Thus, whilst the failure to provide goods of a specified quality may only entitle the buyer to damages for breach of an express term, that failure might entitle the buyer to reject if pleaded as a breach of the implied obligation. The courts have reacted against such a conclusion by a restrictive interpretation of the provision of merchantability which precludes minor defects even in new goods (see *Cehave NV* v *Bremer Handelsgesellschaft mbH* [1976] QB 44, CA). Where, however, there is no express provision in the contract as regards quality (as is often the case in consumer transactions) such a restrictive interpretation of the implied condition may leave the buyer completely without (see *Millar's of Falkirk* v *Turpie* 1976 SLT (Notes) 66).

The conclusion that defective goods are nevertheless merchantable might then be reached where the defects are relatively minor and the supplier is willing to cure the defects. Such considerations strongly influenced the court in *Millar's of Falkirk* v *Turpie* (above), and this seems inconsistent with the views expressed in the Court of Appeal in *Jackson* v *Rotax* (above) and more recently in *Lee* v *York Coach and Marine* [1977] RTR 35. Is it not more than a little illogical to suggest that goods are or are not reasonably fit for their purpose according to whether a supplier is or is not willing to cure defects in them? Such a strained interpretation of the statutory provision would be unnecessary if the buyer's right of rejection were subject to a right on the part of the supplier to first attempt cure. Whether a supplier has such a right in law (as opposed to being allowed to attempt cure in practice) is a matter of considerable uncertainty (see Law Commission Working Paper No. 85, para 2.38). The better view perhaps is that whilst some such limited right may exist under the common law no such right exists under the Sale of Goods Act.

In the absence of some such mechanism the rigidity of the position remains. If goods are unmerchantable the buyer has the right to reject; if they are merchantable (despite minor defects) the private purchaser is likely to have no legal redress whatsoever. The inflexibility of this position may explain why, under the Sale of Goods Act (ss. 11(4), 34 and 35) buyers are regarded as having a shorter period of time in which to reject than is the case under the common law doctrine of affirmation which applies to other types of supply contract (see, e.g., *Farnworth Finance Facilities Ltd* v *Attryde* [1970] 1 WLR 1053). Indeed in the recent case *Bernstein* v *Pamsons Motors* [1987] 2 All ER 220, the purchaser of a new car was held to have lost his right of rejection after being in possession of the vehicle for only three weeks. Whilst 'reasonable time' under s. 35 of the 1979 Act is a question of fact it is difficult to reconcile this decision with others under the Act in which the right to reject had been lost only after the expiry of a much longer period (see, e.g., *Lee* v *York Coach and Marine Ltd* (above)).

Despite the importance of the issue of remedies in the context of this question, we recognise that under examination conditions time is unlikely to permit a detailed analysis of the views and proposals of the Law Commission. It would therefore be sensible to offer a summary of the most important of the proposed changes, perhaps along the following lines:

Firstly, it would impress an examiner if you were able to show an awareness of the substantial 'change of heart' experienced by the Law Commission between the publication of Working Paper No. 85 and their 1987 Report. In particular the most radical change envisaged in the Working Paper, namely, to give the supplier a legal right to attempt 'cure' (i.e., by replacement or repair) is no longer favoured by the Commission. The 'formidable lines of objection' (see paras 4.13-4.14) which prevent common practice being placed upon a legal footing are, we would suggest, by no means insuperable and rather less than convincing. Instead it is proposed that the implied obligations continue to be designated 'conditions' but the remedy of automatic rejection that will continue to confer is subject to certain qualifications. In doctrinal terms perhaps the most significant proposal is that consumer and non-consumer sales should in some respects be treated differently. Thus in non-consumer sales the *prima facie* right to reject for breach of the obligations embodied in ss. 13-

15 is subject to the ability of the seller to show that the nature and consequences of the breach are so slight that rejection would be unreasonable. This is a welcome provision which should enable the courts to deal more effectively with the unmeritorious commercial buyer who seeks to escape the consequences of a change in market conditions (see cases such as *Arcos* v *Ronaasen* (above), *Re Moore and Landaver* (above) or otherwise gain some commercial advantage, see *Cehave* v *Bremer* (above)).

Proposals for changes to the provisions in ss. 34 and 35 of the 1979 Act, governing the circumstances in which the buyer may lose his right to reject are also included in the 1987 Report. Here again it is proposed that further distinction should be drawn between consumer and non-consumer transactions. It is suggested that the buyer (whether commercial or not) should not lose his right to reject by reason of an intimated acceptance unless he has had a reasonable opportunity to inspect the goods to ensure conformity with the contract. However this in itself is to be subject to contrary agreement between the parties in a non-consumer transaction; any such term restricting the buyer's remedy would need to satisfy the test of reasonableness under the Unfair Contract Terms Act 1977. Such a term would presumably have no effect on civil law in a consumer transaction (by reason of s. 6 of the 1977 Act) and also amount to an offence under the Consumer Transactions (Restriction on Statements) Order 1976 (as amended).

One further proposal which is intended to clarify the law is perhaps particularly important in consumer transactions — it is to the effect that a buyer should not be deemed to have accepted goods merely because he requests or agrees to their repair. Whilst this appears to go no further than Lord Denning in *Farnworth Finance Facilities Ltd* v *Attryde* [1970] 2 All ER 774, it will perhaps do no harm to put the principle upon a statutory footing.

Examination answers which include a clear and concise conclusion are obviously more likely to impress an examiner. In this context a conclusion should suggest that the opinion expressed in the quotation is substantially refuted by the earlier discussion of the serious criticisms of the present law. Those criticisms are endorsed by the view of the Law Commission in both the Working Paper and the 1987 Report. The proposals embodied in that report will effect changes to both the definition of the standard required of goods and the remedies available should the goods supplied fall short of that standard. We would suggest that your conclusion might also express your own views as to the likely efficacy of this combination of changes. Would the outcome of cases such as *Millar's of Falkirk* v *Turpie* (above) or *Bernstein* v *Pamson* (above) be different under the Law Commission proposals? Do you think it desirable that a different result ought to obtain?

FOUR

OTHER IMPLIED TERMS IN CONTRACTS FOR GOODS AND SERVICES

Introduction

In the previous chapter we dealt at some length with the implied contractual obligations in respect of the quality of goods and services. Such detailed and lengthy treatment of quality matters is justified on the basis that there is a vast quantity of consumer complaints relating to the quality of goods and services reported annually to the Office of Fair Trading. For those who wish to check the accuracy of this observation, reference may be made to the Annual Reports of the Director General of Fair Trading.

Those reports will also reveal that there are many other recorded complaints about matters falling outside the scope of the implied terms on quality. Many of those other complaints focus upon problems relating to the price of goods and services and issues concerning the delivery of goods and performance of services, particularly late delivery or performance. These figures, of course, relate to *recorded* individual consumer complaints and may only be the tip of the iceberg. Additionally, the figures will not encompass problems experienced by *commercial* consumers on such matters as late delivery or performance by one of the parties to a commercial contract. It may well be that such matters as price, delivery and performance will as a matter of routine be catered for specifically in a commercial contract for the supply of goods and services. Consequently, the parties will merely refer in most cases to the relevant terms and conditions and no difficulty will normally ensue. However, experience may show that the commercial as well as the individual consumer often leaves these kinds of issue to chance and to the supplier, thus generating a large quantity of difficulties and complaints. So it may well be that for the commercial or individual consumer, the issues discussed below are often as important as issues of quality discussed in the previous chapter.

Given the pragmatic importance of such matters in both the consumer and commercial spheres, we think it important to devote a complete chapter to them. Your examiner will no doubt be aware that these are of some importance and seek to include a question or questions on such issues in your consumer or commercial law paper.

The topics discussed below may of themselves not present any great conceptual difficulty for you. However, there are a few areas where the law itself is uncertain (see, for example, the discussion on 'estimates' and 'quotations'), or where the law is the characteristic hotchpotch of common law principle overlaid with statutory rules. It may be precisely these areas for that very reason, that your examiner will include the subject matter in his examination paper. This is a point we have made before, but once again it bears emphasis. This interrelationship between common law principle and statutory rule is ripe for exploitation in the topics discussed in this chapter. You will be expected to show that you have the necessary perspective leading to an understanding of these topics.

Our question in this chapter has been deliberately chosen with our foregoing comments in mind. We have selected a 'cocktail' type question: one which contains a mixture of issues. Some of these build upon the information which should have been absorbed in the previous chapter. Others contain points which mix together the common law and statutory rules. The question is of a kind which we believe might appear frequently in commercial law examination papers.

We now propose to consider the difficulties students commonly face in this area.

Substantive difficulties

The Sale of Goods Act 1979 imposes a number of different but often related duties upon the seller and buyer of goods with regard to issues such as price, delivery, time of delivery and delivery of the right quantity. In the main, these duties are cast upon the seller. It should be remembered, of course, that the Sale of Goods Act 1979 does not apply to contracts of work and materials, exchange, hire and services. You are referred to our chart in chapter 3 for the differences between these types of contract. Such implied terms as are set out in statute are to be found in the Supply of Goods and Services Act 1982, reference to which was made in the previous chapter. It is easy to overlook the fact that, whereas the 1979 Act does contain detailed provisions regulating the issues discussed below, the 1982 Act contains few provisions which regulate these issues. There is, therefore, something of a void here, which may only be resolved by appealing to common law rules, if any, governing such matters. There is a strong argument for suggesting that at common law similar rules as to time, delivery, etc., apply to those contracts which are outside the Sale of Goods Act 1979. After all this was the apparent justification behind the Supply of Goods and Services Act 1982 which was regarded by many as merely setting the appropriate common law rules into a statutory form. The first batch of duties are really concerned with the seller's, or supplier's duty of delivery in sale of goods contracts and other contracts involving the transfer of goods, e.g., work and materials contracts, etc.

The duty of delivery

Section 27 of the Sale of Goods Act 1979 imposes upon a seller of goods a duty to deliver the goods in accordance with the terms of the contract. The first point to note about this rather simple and obvious statement is that 'delivery' should not be given its popular meaning. 'Delivery' here is merely meant to cover 'a voluntary transfer of possession', according to s. 61 of the 1979 Act. There is no general rule which compels the seller to send the goods to the purchaser. However, the terms of the contract may provide for this, but in the absence of any such terms, s. 29(2) provides that the place of delivery is the seller's place of business, if he has one, and if not, his residence. In certain instances the place where the goods are located may be the place of delivery. It will be a rare commercial contract which does not contain specific detail as to the place of delivery. In consumer contracts, by way of contrast, delivery will in most instances be contemporaneous with payment, namely, at the retailer's premises. However, in those situations where delivery is to be delayed for some reason, it will be a matter of negotiation between the retailer and the consumer as to when and how it is to be effected.

One final general point on delivery under sale of goods contracts is that the delivery of documents of title, if accompanied by an intention to transfer possession and ownership of goods, will amount to such a transfer. This will normally only apply in commercial contracts and usually to goods shipped by sea or air.

As far as other types of contract are concerned, for example, a work and materials contract, it would seem, there being no equivalent of s. 29 of the 1979 Act in the Supply of Goods and Services Act 1982, that the place of delivery will depend on the terms of the contract and/or the surrounding circumstances. It would seem that in most instances of a work and materials contract, it will be the supplier's responsibility to deliver the goods to the place where the work is to be carried out using those goods.

Time of delivery or performance

So far we have considered upon whom the duty to deliver is placed and what that entails in broad terms. It is now necessary to consider the important topic concerning the time of delivery, or performance. This is an extremely thorny and often vexed question which arises frequently in practice. The difficulty in this area arises, perhaps, for two reasons. First the law is to be found partly in statute, and partly in the case law, a state of affairs causing considerable confusion. Secondly, the law seems to adopt separate approaches to the time issue, depending on whether the contract is a commercial or consumer agreement. Much of the consequential confusion surrounds the meaning of the phrase 'time is of the essence' and in what circumstances it applies and the consequences which follow from that. There are three possible situations:

(a)   A time for delivery or performance is stipulated and time is regarded of the essence.

(b)   A time is stipulated as in (a), but time is not of the essence.

(c)   The parties do not provide in their contract for delivery or performance on any specific date.

Let us look at each of these in turn.

A time for delivery or performance is stipulated and time is regarded of the essence   The parties have agreed a delivery date for goods, or a time for the carrying out of some service. Where time is of the essence, and the supplier fails to deliver the goods, or carry out the service on the due date, the innocent party is entitled to repudiate the transaction and/or claim damages for loss on the usual contractual basis. 'Time is of the essence' means no more and no less than that time is regarded as a major term of the contract and failure to comply gives rise to a serious breach entitling the innocent party to repudiate the agreement. The question remains as to when time is of the essence. Your tutors will no doubt emphasise that 'in ordinary commercial contracts for the sale of goods the rule clearly is that time is *prima facie* of the essence with respect to delivery' (per McCardie J, *Hartley* v *Hymans* [1920] 3 KB 475 at p. 484). Section 10 of the Sale of Goods Act 1979 makes a specific statement to the effect that the time of payment is not *prima facie* of the essence, but goes on to provide that whether any other stipulation as to time is of the essence of the contract or not depends on the terms of the contract. The 1982 Act contains no equivalent provision. It would seem that McCardie J's statement above will apply to all commercial contracts involving the supply of goods and services, and is not restricted merely to sale of goods contracts. So in the commercial sphere, at least, the position is reasonably well settled: there is a *prima facie* presumption that time is of the essence.

That leads us on to the position of those contracts made by a supplier with an individual private consumer. Assuming that a time is specified, is it of the essence? It would appear that time is not of the essence, but there is little or no authority on this point. We shall, therefore, assume, as probably is the case, that there is no *prima facie* presumption that time is of the essence in a consumer contract. However, provided the evidence is clear, a consumer may well be able to argue that time was regarded as important right from the outset. If time can be shown to be of the essence then the consumer will be entitled, subject to the discussion on waiver below, to treat the contract as at an end in the event that the supplier fails to deliver by the agreed date. This may be an important right in practice, for example, where completion of a job by a builder is taking longer than agreed. If time is of the essence the builder in breach of this term can be told to leave the site, leaving the consumer free to choose another builder as he pleases.

It should not be overlooked, however, that it is possible to waive a breach of the condition as to time (see s. 11(2), Sale of Goods Act 1979). In commercial contracts, as Atiyah points out (*The Sale of Goods*, 7th ed., p. 90) some of the most difficult questions that frequently arise relate to the issue of waiver. Where there is the prospect of a breach, the buyer will rarely resort immediately to his legal rights, but will, as a matter of expediency, attempt to resolve the difficulty in some other way. This may give rise to difficult issues of fact as to whether a waiver of the breach has occurred. In any event, even if waiver is found to have taken place, it is clear that a buyer can, by giving reasonable notice, make time of the essence once again. Students should make themselves familiar with the case of *Charles Rickards Ltd* v *Oppenheim* [1950] 1 KB 616. The contract concerned the delivery of a chassis by a particular date. As this was a commercial contract, time was of the essence. However after the due date the buyer continued to press for delivery, thus waiving the breach of condition. Delivery was not made and the buyer wrote giving a date some four weeks ahead as the last date for delivery. The chassis was not ready for some three months after this final date. The letter by the buyer, it was held, made time of the essence once again and the buyer was entitled to refuse delivery. The case illustrates neatly the point that time can be made of the essence by giving reasonable notice. This applies as we shall see, irrespective of whether time was originally of the essence. This is a point which an examiner may wish to explore.

A time for delivery or performance is specified but time is not of the essence
The position is that the innocent party may still have an action in contract, but this will be for damages only, should there be any foreseeable loss. What the innocent party is not lawfuly entitled to do is to treat the contract as at an end. Time can, of course, be made of the essence by adopting the procedure outlined above in *Rickards* v *Oppenheim*.

Where time is said not to be of the essence there is a tendency to forget that, nonetheless, a failure to meet a specified deadline is a breach of contract giving rise to an action for damages. What may be recovered in such a situation will depend on the normal contractual principles on remoteness and measure of damages.

Where a time for delivery or performance has not been fixed in any way by the parties   Section 29(3) provides that in such circumstances, under a sale of goods contract, the seller is bound to send them within a reasonable time. Section 29(5) provides that demand or tender of delivery may be treated as ineffectual unless made at a reasonable hour, and this is a question of fact. Section 14 of the Supply of Goods and Services Act 1982 provides a similar reasonable time rule in respect of the performance of a service. Presumably, s. 14 would apply to a contract of work and materials, involving the supply of goods and services, even though on its wording it would seem only to apply to contracts for services (see s. 12(3) of the 1982 Act).

In a commercial contract it is unlikely in practice that the issue of time of delivery will be left to chance. This is more likely to arise in a consumer contract and in reality is a source of much difficulty for consumers. As it is largely a question of fact very little can be said by way of general guidance to students. It will always depend upon the nature of the contract, and evidence from those in the trade as to how long delivery or performance should take, and so on. It is important to remember, however, that the innocent party can make time of the essence by giving reasonable notice to the other side that time is now regarded as an important term and by specifying a fixed date for delivery or performance.

The duty to deliver the right quantity

Another problematic area concerns the seller's duty to deliver the correct quantity under the contract and the buyer's remedies if this does not happen. The seller may deliver too much, too little or mixed goods. What happens if one or more of the batches is defective in some way? Does this entitle the buyer to repudiate the whole contract? There is also a complicating factor arising from the interrelationship of ss. 13 and 30 of the Sale of Goods Act 1979. These kinds of issues may be of less importance in a consumer contract, but are of fundamental importance in commercial law and you can expect examination questions on such topics. As already indicated above there is an overlap between the rules on quality and quantity. It may give the

'the seller may deliver too much'

examiner the opportunity to explore this relationship and set a question which goes across the boundaries between individual topics. This may well be seen to be a legitimate exercise for second or third year students. Indeed, our specimen question below does precisely this.

We are principally concerned here with contracts for the sale of goods and we must therefore turn to ss. 30 and 31 of the 1979 Act to discover the relevant rules. In the first instance we shall look at contracts where it is clear that delivery will be in one instalment. Where it is agreed or can be inferred that delivery is to be by a number of instalments, different considerations apply and there will be a separate discussion of such contracts.

Delivery in one instalment Here regard must be had to s. 30(1) which provides that where the seller delivers a smaller quantity than agreed, the buyer may reject the goods. If the buyer, as he may and can, accepts the goods, he must pay for them at the contract rate. Section 31(1) provides that, unless otherwise agreed, it is not open to the seller to deliver by instalments. So, for example, if the contract is for delivery of 200 tons of wheat and the seller delivers only 150 tons on the appointed day with a promise of a further

50 the next day, the buyer can refuse to accept the delivery. Of course, whether the buyer would adopt such a course would be a matter of expediency for him.

If the converse situation arises and the seller delivers too much, it would seem harsh to allow the buyer to reject the whole amount. But this is precisely what s. 30(2) allows him to do. Alternatively, the subsection permits him to accept the correct amount and reject the rest. Section 30(3) provides that if the buyer accepts the full amount delivered, he must pay at the contract rate for the excess goods. What if the seller delivers too much or too little and the buyer decides to pick and choose as to what he might take and reject the rest? Oddly, it seems that there is nothing to prevent the buyer from doing this. So, for example, if the contract figure is 200 tons, but the seller only delivers 150 tons, the buyer may, if he so wishes, take, say, 100 tons and reject the other 50.

The third situation under this heading is that where goods complying with the contract description are mixed with other goods, s. 30(4) provides that the buyer may accept those in accordance with the contract and reject the rest, or reject the whole. There will often be an overlap in this type of situation with a possible breach of s. 13 of the Sale of Goods Act, discussed in the previous chapter. If goods which conform to the contract description are supplied with goods which do not, the seller may be in breach of both the duty under s. 30(4) and that under s. 13. As Atiyah (7th ed.) points out (p. 98) the whole of s. 30 is merely an application of the duty to deliver goods conforming to description imposed by s. 13 (see *Re Moore & Co.* v *Landauer & Co.* [1921] 2 KB 519). Subject to the *de minimis* rule, it would seem that a seller's failure to comply with his obligation to deliver the correct quantity will, by virtue of the provisions in s. 30, amount to a breach of condition, although the language of s. 30 does not focus upon the condition/warranty dichotomy. (Note the Law Commission proposal that the right of commercial buyers to reject should be restricted where the breach is slight and it is unreasonable to allow rejection (see p. 57).)

Delivery by instalments   The rules as to delivery by instalments give rise to a few problems, not the least important of which is the issue of what amounts to a contract where delivery is by instalments, i.e., is the contract severable or not? In the first instance, let us deal with the more straightforward position where there is no doubt that the contract is severable. The question which requires resolving here is whether a breach in respect of delivery of one instalment gives the buyer the right to repudiate the whole contract, or merely the goods forming the basis of the single delivery.

The Sale of Goods Act s. 31(2) is supposed to answer this question, but you will be disappointed if you were to expect a complete answer. The subsection merely states that where there is a defective delivery of one or more instalments by the seller, or the buyer neglects or refuses to take delivery of or pay for one or more instalments, it is a question in each case depending on the terms of the contract and the circumstances of the case, whether a right to repudiate the whole contract arises, or whether the breach can be regarded as severable only. As is often the case the contract itself will be silent on this issue. We must then resort to the case law to see whether there are any guidelines as to how we are to resolve this essentially factual issue. The main test was established in *Maple Flock Co. Ltd* v *Universal Furniture Products (Wembley) Ltd* [1934] 1 KB 148, where it was stated by Lord Hewart CJ (at p. 157):

> The main tests to be considered in applying the subsection . . . are, first, the ratio quantitatively which the breach bears to the contract as a whole and secondly, the degree of probability or improbability that such a breach will be repeated.

This is an extremely useful and important quotation and is well worth remembering. It is also worth showing how it operates by reference to the facts of the case itself. The contract related to 100 tons of rag flock, to be delivered at the rate of one and a half tons every three weeks. The first 15 loads were satisfactory, but the sixteenth was below the specified quality. The four loads which followed were satisfactory. Applying the tests above, it was held that the breach did not entitle the buyer to repudiate the contract (c.f., *Robert A Munro Co. Ltd* v *Meyer* [1930] 2 KB 312).

Section 31(2) and its case law provides an answer where there is no difficulty in deciding whether a contract is severable, e.g., because delivery and payment are based on periodic instalments and each instalment is to be separately paid for. There are, however, other situations in which a court may regard a contract as severable. This is essentially a factual question and regard must be had to the wording of the contract and other relevant circumstances. In *Jackson* v *Rotax Motor & Cycle Co.* [1910] 2 KB 937 it was held that a contract for the sale of motor accessories 'deliveries as required' was a severable contract. This is a difficult test to apply and there is very little judicial guidance to show the way. The practical importance in the commercial sphere of the rules discussed above may persuade the examiner that it is an area upon which to test your ability.

Duty to perform in general

So far we have been looking at the duty to perform in respect of fairly specific matters such as place, time and quantity of delivery of goods. It goes without saying that there is a general duty to perform one's contractual obligations. However, as you have no doubt been told time and again, performance must be precise and exact, subject to the *de minimis* rule. This general rule is also subject to what was said in the previous section on instalment contracts.The 'precise and exact' rule may cause hardship in other respects and over the years the courts have developed the principle of 'substantial performance'. The importance of this doctrine is particularly acute where contracts to carry out building works are concerned and a large number of the cases have been in connection with such contracts. Can the consumer, in particular, lawfully refuse to pay a builder who has not finished his or her kitchen extension? If the 'precise and exact' rule were to be applied in its full severity, a builder who had all but completed the extension would find his action for the agreed price defeated and, what is more, not be able to claim a fair proportion for the work actually done. The doctrine of 'substantial performance' to some extent mitigates this harshness in certain instances but, as the case of *Bolton* v *Mahadeva* [1972] 2 All ER 1322 shows, the balance is still tilted heavily towards the consumer. In that case Cairns LJ (at pp. 1325-6) stated:

> In considering whether there was substantial performance I am of the opinion that it is relevant to take into account both the nature of the defect and the proportion between the cost of rectifying them and the contract price. It would be wrong to say that the contractor is only entitled to payment if the defects are so trifling as to be covered by the *de minimis* rule.

Thus, one must consider the defects in relation to the overall contract figure. This test did not aid the builder in the above case, as it was held that, where the cost of repairing defects was between one third and one quarter of the contract price, the builder had not substantially performed his obligation and could recover *nothing* (c.f. *Hoenig* v *Isaacs* [1952] 2 All ER 176; see also questions posed immediately following the case extract in Miller and Harvey, *Consumer and Trading Law, Cases and Materials*, at p. 105, and their implicit criticism).

The duty to pay the price

We now come to one of the most obviously fundamental issues in any contract and that is the question of payment and the buyer's duty in that respect. There seem to be three major difficulties that arise in practice here. One is the presumed difference between 'estimates' and 'quotations', and the other concerns the so-called 'Battle of forms' issue which arose in *Butler*

Machine Tool Co. Ltd v *Ex-Cell-O Corpn. (England) Ltd* [1979] 1 WLR 401. This latter issue will normally only arise in the commercial context, where both parties like to trade on their own standard terms. The battle is for the supremacy of one's own terms, including price variation clauses (if any). For more discussion on this you are referred to pp. 50-51 of our colleague Richard Taylor's *Law of Contract* (2nd edition) in this series.

As to the first issue this can be of immense practical importance for the consumer. One view is that in law an 'estimate' is a guide to the price that may be charged and is not binding on the parties. Conversely, it is said that a 'quotation' is a firm price and, therefore, binding. But the answer surely cannot depend on the word used by one or both parties. As to whether a price given at the outset is a firm one, the other words used at the time and any other relevant factors must be considered. For example, if a precise figure for the carrying out of work is given, e.g., £175.75, one can infer that this is a firm price, otherwise why specify the pence figure? The test to apply, of course, is what did the parties intend, regardless of what particular name they may have given to the price statement? Even if the figure given is regarded as an approximate figure, it is suggested that any increase must be reasonable and supported by evidence, e.g., that the cost of materials had increased, thus necessitating an increase on the 'estimated' figure.

The final issue concerns the position where no price is agreed, unlikely in a commercial contract, but frequently occurring in a consumer contract. Section 8 of the Sale of Goods Act 1979 provides for the payment of a reasonable price in respect of goods and s. 15 of the 1982 Act provides for payment of a reasonable charge in respect of a contract for services. These rather unhelpful sections are the only guidance available and the answer is one of gathering suitable evidence of prices charged by other suppliers in the same line as the supplier in question.

That concludes the discussion of the noteworthy points concerning the various implied obligations covered in this chapter. Below is the problem question to test your understanding of the relevant obligations, followed by our commentary.

Illustrative question

Bodgit Ltd agree to supply Fixit Ltd with 500 tons of raw material, X, at £400 per ton 'delivery as and when required'. Delivery of 40 tons is carried out in four monthly instalments of 10 tons each and these are paid for separately by Fixit Ltd. Fixit Ltd ask for a further instalment of 10 tons to be delivered on 31 July. The delivery is not made, and the following day Fixit Ltd telephone Bodgit Ltd, enquiring as to why the delivery was not made. Bodgit Ltd explain that the delay is due to problems with their own suppliers.

On 16 August Fixit Ltd ask for a further delivery of 10 tons for 31 August, which is duly made with no problem. A sixth instalment of 10 tons is requested and delivered on 30 September. Shortly after delivery it is discovered that this delivery is a mixture of 8 tons of raw material X and 3 tons of another material, Y. On 3 October an invoice relating to the delivery on 31 August is received by Fixit Ltd. The price indicated is £5,000. A covering letter with the invoice from Bodgit Ltd refers to the price variation clause in Bodgit Ltd's standard order form.

Discuss.

Commentary

As was mentioned earlier this is a typical commercial law problem which has a number of strands, some interrelated, others not, running throughout. It also attempts to build upon, in particular, some of the ideas discussed in the previous chapter. Some of the issues are relatively straightforward and can be dealt with accordingly. Others may require some speculation, as all the facts may not be readily available from the problem itself.

We suggest that it would make good sense to identify the main issues at the outset and then deal with the detail thereafter. It is good practice to spell these main issues out in your introductory paragraph in your answer. This should impress the examiner in that you have been able to see the wood for the trees. It should also give your answer the necessary organisation and direction rather than its being a long rambling and uncoordinated discussion of the various points. Briefly, then, the major issues would seem to be:

(a)   Is the contract severable?
(b)   What is the effect of the failure to deliver on 31 July?
(c)   What are Fixit Ltd's options in respect of the delivery of mixed goods on 30 September?
(d)   Finally, what are the effects of the invoice for £5,000 and the reference to the price variation clause?

Is the contract severable?   This particular issue should not present any undue difficulty. As we remarked in the earlier part of this chapter, even where the agreement does not specifically state that delivery is to be by instalments, a court may infer that to be the case when the words of the contract and other circumstances are considered. We would have thought that it would be safe for you to say quite simply that this is a severable contract when the words 'delivery as and when required' are considered (see *Jackson* v *Rotax* (above)). In addition this view is supported by the way in which the parties themselves have acted from the outset of the agreement.

What is the effect of the failure to deliver on 31 July?   The failure to deliver on 31 July as requested is a little more difficult and requires much fuller discussion and explanation. Perhaps the place to start here is to make the point that in a commercial contract time of delivery is *prima facie* of the essence (see *Hartley* v *Hymans* [1920] 3 KB 475, per McCardie J at p. 484). Consequently, the failure to deliver on 31 July would amount to a breach of condition entitling Fixit Ltd to treat itself as discharged from the obligation to accept delivery of and pay for that particular instalment, claiming in addition any consequential losses on the usual contractual damage basis. However, whether such a breach would entitle them to repudiate the whole contract is extremely doubtful in the light of Lord Hewart CJ's dictum in the *Maple Flock* case, mentioned earlier. As the previous four deliveries had been satisfactory at the time in question of the breach, it is unlikely that a court would have held that Fixit were lawfully entitled to repudiate.

In any event, there is a further argument which would probably prevent Fixit from taking such a course of action. By merely enquiring the day after as to the reasons for the delay and then, apparently, doing nothing further about it, this would be interpreted as a waiver by them of the breach of condition, relegating their claim at the most to one of damages (see *Charles Rickards* v *Oppenheim* (above). Nor does it appear that they have made time of the essence by giving a fresh date for the delivery of that instalment. However, it must not be forgotten that Bodgit are in breach. What could Fixit Ltd claim by way of damages? We are not told what steps (if any) Fixit may have taken early in August. They may have, of course, lost profits, as a result of the failure by Bodgit Ltd to supply the raw materials. You should, however, point out that Fixit Ltd have a duty to mitigate their loss, for example, by trying to obtain the materials from an alternative source. Naturally, if this step is taken and Fixit Ltd have to pay more than the contract price, they will be entitled to damages representing the difference. We think that it is important that you should try to deal with issues of damages in this type of problem, although it may be that damages are a remedy not specifically covered in your present course. There seems little point in advising or discussing problem questions unless this task is undertaken. There is a tendency amongst students to state that there may be a breach of contract and go no further. Your examiner, as well as the parties, is interested in your views on remedies.

What are Fixit Ltd's options in respect of the delivery of mixed goods on 30 September?   The question of the delivery of the mixed goods on 30 September raises some difficult questions. First, we have to consider Fixit Ltd's rights in respect of the individual instalment, and secondly, if this is a further breach of contract, does it affect Fixit Ltd's rights in respect of the whole contract?

As regards the individual instalment, Fixit's options would seem quite clear. Section 30(4) provides that, in these circumstances, a buyer may accept the goods which conform to the contract, i.e., the 8 tons of X and reject the other materials, i.e., the 3 tons of Y. Alternatively, they may reject the whole delivery. There is also a breach of s. 13 of the Sale of Goods Act 1979, because the buyer has received something different in kind from that for which he contracted. In practice, it does not seem to matter under which head a claim is pursued, as a breach of s. 30(4) amounts in effect to a breach of condition, as does a breach of s. 13 (see *Re Moore & Co.* v *Landauer & Co.* [1921] 2 KB 519). A comment along these lines would certainly impress an examiner.

The more difficult issue to consider is whether this second breach of contract in conjunction with the earlier failure to deliver on time may give rise to the right on the part of Fixit Ltd to treat the whole contract as repudiated (see s. 31(2) (above))? Consideration must here be given to the influential quotation in the *Maple Flock* case referred to earlier in this chapter. We must look at the ratio which the breaches bear in a quantitative sense to the contract as a whole. So far there have been two breaches out of seven instalments which, on the face of it, would appear to be a significantly high proportion, compared with the facts in the *Maple Flock* case (one load in 16 unsatisfactory). On the other hand in *Robert A Munro & Co. Ltd* v *Meyer* [1930] 2 KB 312 where nearly half of the total quantity had been delivered and was found to be seriously defective, the court had little difficulty in accepting that the buyer was entitled to repudiate. Our facts fall between these two situations. In these circumstances it may be necessary to have regard to the other test, namely the likelihood of a further breach of contract. The whole contract is less than one fifth completed and already there are two breaches. Is it possible to say that there is only a small degree of probability that another breach might occur? In the absence of any assurance by Bodgit Ltd that there will be no further breaches, it is likely that a court might accept the argument by Fixit Ltd that the right to repudiate the whole contract had arisen. If we assume that Fixit Ltd is entitled to treat itself as discharged from further obligations under the contract, it may be necessary to consider the position with regard to the instalments accepted and paid for already. As Atiyah points out (at p. 387) s. 31(2) looks to the future and not to the past, but concludes that it would seem that the buyer, in such circumstances as these, might be able to reject earlier instalments. This, of course, assumes that he is in a position to return them, i.e., they have not been consumed or used up in some way. This point has not arisen for consideration so far by the courts and it may therefore be the case that it just does not arise in practice.

What are the effects of the invoice for £5,000 and the reference to the price variation clause?   The final issue to be considered in this problem is that relating to the price increase. The examiner has deliberately not given any indication as to whether the buyer, Fixit Ltd, made the order on its own standard order form, thus leaving open to speculation the issue of 'battle of forms' referred to earlier. This issue seems to be resolved by looking to see who 'fired the last shot' and accepting that his or her terms will have supremacy should there be any conflict. All that you can do here is to refer to the possibilities. If Fixit Ltd were to win the so-called 'battle', then Bodgit's invoice claiming £5,000 is incorrect and can be successfully challenged by Fixit Ltd. On the other hand if Bodgit Ltd's price variation clause is a term of the contract, then Fixit Ltd will be bound by it to some extent. It is probable that a price variation clause which allows for a large increase, or has no limits as to any increase, would be subject to intervention on the part of the courts. Any increase would have to be reasonable in the circumstances. Bodgit Ltd should produce evidence to show that their costs had increased, for example, and that they were merely passing this increase on. One further point which a student might raise is whether there is a breach of s. 11 of the Trade Description Act 1968 by Bodgit Ltd in attempting to charge the higher price for the instalment. As we shall see the divisional court in *Miller* v *F. A. Sadd & Son Ltd* [1981] 3 All ER 265, has effectively said that there is no offence in these circumstances. However if you were to make such a comment, this might persuade an examiner to raise the mark on this question.

In conclusion, the question above can be seen to be easier to manage provided you separate out the various issues and deal with them in a concise and efficient manner. An examiner will be impressed with the clarity with which the answer is presented. One of the things most dreaded by an examiner is the long, rambling answer which covers the issues, but slips from one to another at random. This kind of answer is extremely difficult to assess. You should try to avoid putting your examiner in such a position.

FIVE

EXCLUSION CLAUSES

Introduction

The law concerning the use of exclusion clauses will have been studied by most degree students at a very early stage of their course, normally within the confines of a general principles of contract syllabus. The Unfair Contract Terms Act 1977 is therefore no stranger to students when they subsequently embark upon the study of commercial and consumer law. Yet when the subject is raised in this context the look of panic which crosses the faces of some students defies belief. This obvious discomfort stems from the less than happy previous experience of the topic. There seems little doubt that first year students do find this a difficult subject to master for a number of reasons. The 1977 Act may well be one of the first statutes with which they have had to grapple at a time when their understanding of statutory interpretation was at an early stage of development. Students are required to appreciate the meaning and effect of a number of individual provisions within an act which appears to lack a rational plan. The variation in the patterns and criteria of control within the Act is, in our view, probably the major cause of much confusion.

The Act does not of course abolish the common law, indeed the common law principles governing the incorporation of terms are expressly saved by s. 11(2). Equally the common law rules of construction continue to be relevant, though their importance is seen (perhaps wrongly) to be diminished. The need for students to refresh their memories as to the common law is patently obvious. The common law principles are not in themselves particularly problematic and we thought it unnecessary to rehearse them here. Those students who wish guidance with regard to the common law may usefully consult another title in the SWOT series: *Law of Contract* by Richard Taylor, chapter 6 of which contains an excellent résumé of the common law position. Since tension clearly exists between the common law rules and the statutory provisions, a number of interesting and difficult questions do arise from that relationship, the more important of which are addressed below. It is not our intention, in this chapter, to construct a narrative of the statutory provisions. In particular we have consciously omitted any consideration of s. 8 of the Act (dealing with exclusion of liability for misrepresentation); s. 4 (dealing with unreasonable indemnities) and s. 9 (which amends the common law on the issue of fundamental breach). We shall only consider here the provisions of s. 2 in so far as this section deals with the exclusion of liability in contract. Section 2 will however be dealt with in chapter 7 to the extent that the provision affects the ability of manufacturers to exclude liability in tort, along with s. 5 of the Act which creates additional controls in that particular respect.

We have deliberately adopted this strategy in order to enable students to see the 'wood for the trees'; it will we hope allow the student to perceive more readily the three different patterns of control the Act creates with regard to the exclusion of a wide range of contractual liabilities, which we have represented in diagrammatic form below. An appreciation of those different patterns may also be gained from a careful perusal of the Law Commission's Second Report on Exclusion Clauses, Law Commission No. 69 (1975) on which the Act is substantially based. Special caution is necessary here, for the Act differs significantly in certain respects from the recommendations contained in the body of the report and the draft Bill appended thereto. Perhaps most significant amongst those differences is that in relation to the control of exclusion clauses in respect of death or personal injury resulting from negligence. In that regard the broad sweep of s. 2(1) of the Act bears little relation to the far more selective controls which were advocated by the Law Commission (see paras. 70-74). We have in the following pages attempted to draw attention to what we regard as the more difficult substantive issues and subsequently to advise how those issues might be dealt with in an examination question.

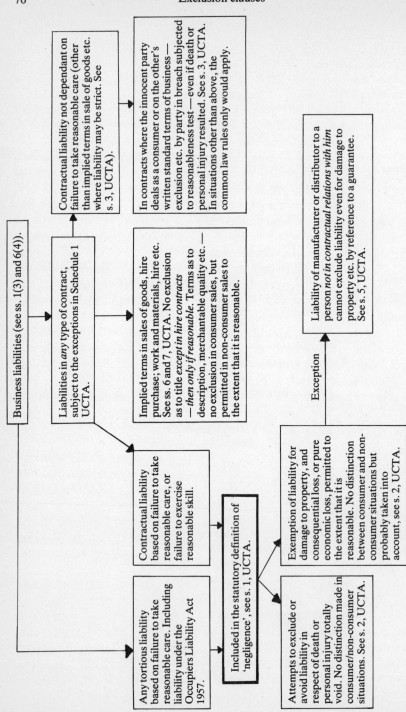

Effects of the Unfair Contract Terms Act 1977

Substantive difficulties

Exclusion of contractual liability: The three different patterns of control

As we indicate above the Act appears to lack any overall scheme to which one can relate the interpretation of any particular provision. The Act is in effect a combination of three different patterns of control which are represented by ss. 2, 3 together with ss. 6, 7 (combined). Individually each of these provisions represents a comprehensible and arguably rational policy, whilst collectively they appear as something of a 'dog's dinner'. As between these three regimes there is no common theme, other than a general policy aim to control the use of exclusion clauses. The criteria used to justify intervention and the extent of control are to some extent different in each case.

Before turning to the relevant provisions we need to recognise that in the context of the exclusion of contractual liability the Act has nothing to bite upon until a breach of contract is alleged and the person allegedly in breach seeks to rely upon a clause which negates or in some way limits his responsibility for the resultant injury, loss or damage. In deciding whether or not any particular clause is governed by the Act two preliminary points need to be made. First, we shall assume, for our purposes, that the contract in question is not exempt from control by Part III or Schedule 1 of the Act. We shall further assume that the person seeking to rely upon an exclusion clause contracted 'in the course of a business' (see s. 1(1), 1(3)), or is a private individual seeking to exclude liability for supplying goods which do not correspond with their description (see s. 6(4)).

Given those assumptions there is a substantial probability that at least one of the provisions in ss. 2, 3 or 6, 7 will apply to the exclusion clause in question — but which? Students will find it somewhat easier to identify and apply the appropriate provision if they accept the existence of the three different patterns of control, two of which create fairly specific controls, the third being of a much more general nature. The algorithm on p. 76 should assist in identifying the section of the Act applicable to any exclusion clause.

Exclusion of liability for negligence — s. 2 UCTA It is notable that clauses subject to s. 2, which seek to exclude liability for negligence, are either rendered totally ineffective in respect of death or personal injury and subjected to a test of reasonableness as regards 'other loss or damage'. This is so, irrespective of the status of the person who sustains the injury, loss or damage. These rules apply even as between business parties despite the absence of any inequality of knowledge or bargaining power. Whether the rules are based upon some strong moral conviction, or a policy intent upon the promotion of liability insurance as opposed to loss insurance, is unclear. If it is the latter, it is difficult to see how it will succeed in the absence of a compulsory insurance requirement. The rationale behind the more selective intervention proposed by the Law Commission in the Second Report on Exclusion Clauses (above) at paras. 85-94 is noteworthy by way of comparison.

Exclusion of implied obligations as to title, description, merchantability, fitness, or sample in contracts for supply of goods — ss. 6 and 7 UCTA
Section 6 of the 1977 Act controls clauses which purport to exclude liability in sale of goods or hire-purchase contracts arising from the breach of the obligations implied as to title, description, merchantability, fitness for purpose and sample (see ss. 12-15 Sale of Goods Act 1979, Schedule 4, Consumer Credit Act 1974). The clauses covered by this section are again rendered either totally ineffective or subjected to a test of reasonableness. Under s. 6, however, the criteria by which this is decided has nothing whatever to do with the nature of any damage which may result from the breach. Instead, the matter is determined by reference to the status of the buyer: if he deals as a consumer (see s. 12) any such clause is ineffective but otherwise the clause is subject only to a reasonableness test. The justification for the intervention in 'consumer transactions' is the frequent inequality of bargaining power and lack of real choice as to the terms on which consumers contract. It should be noted that clauses in consumer sale or consumer hire-purchase contracts which seek to exclude liability for breach of *some other express or implied obligation are not affected by s. 6.* These may be subject to a reasonableness test by virtue of s. 3 (see below). Greater importance seems therefore to be attached to the obligations as to title, description, quality, etc., than to other strict liability obligations such as that to deliver goods at the promised time or within a reasonable time.

Section 6 replaces, with certain important amendments, s. 55(7) of the Sale of Goods Act 1979 (as amended). That provision was itself introduced by the Supply of Goods [Implied Terms] Act 1973. The Law Commission in the Second Report merely adopted, without any detailed explanation, an amended provision. The more informative exposition of the rationale underlying the present provisions is therefore to be found in the Law Commission Exemption Clauses in Contracts First Report: Amendments to the Sale of Goods Act 1893 (Law Commission No. 24 (1971), paras. 64-119). The intervention by way of the reasonableness test in non-consumer transactions was substantially influenced by arguments that retailers would otherwise be placed in a difficult position given the restrictions placed upon their use of exclusion clauses vis-à-vis consumers.

Section 7 of the 1977 Act applies similar controls to clauses which seek to exclude liability for breach of the obligations as to description, merchantability, fitness for purpose and sample, which are implied into other types of supply contracts by Part I of the Supply of Goods and Services Act 1982. With the exception of clauses relating to title, there is no meaningful difference between the provisions of s. 6 and 7. There is however, one very important point of distinction in the criminal law. The Consumer Transactions [Restriction on Statements] Order 1976 (as amended) applies to the publication, etc., of clauses which are ineffective by virtue of s. 6 of the 1977 Act and does not apply to clauses which are rendered ineffective by, e.g., ss. 2 or 7 of that Act.

Section 3 — A Residual Provision   The controls so far considered can be seen to be fairly specific at least in the sense that they apply to clauses seeking to exclude or limit liability arising from the breach of particular contractual obligations. The scope of ss. 2, 6 and 7 is not difficult to grasp since, subject to our earlier assumptions, s. 2 applies to all contracts in which there is an express/implied obligation to exercise skill and care and s. 6 or s. 7 apply to all contracts for the supply of goods.

Section 3 is something of a residual provision, which will catch many, but not all, clauses which are outside the scope of ss. 2, 6 and 7. The precise ambit of s. 3 is a matter which not surprisingly causes a great deal of difficulty and, we suspect, not only to students. The reason for this is that to ascertain the scope of the section, three questions need to be answered.

(a)   Assuming that the person seeking to rely on an exemption clause contracted in the course of a business does s. 3 apply to *all such contracts*?

(b)   Within the contracts covered, does s. 3 apply to the exclusion of *any kind of contractual obligation*?

(c)   Does the section apply only to 'conventional' exclusion clauses?

We shall here address only questions (a) and (b). Question (c) will be dealt with below in the context of our analysis of s. 13 which seeks to define the varieties of exemption clauses covered by the 1977 Act.

To which contracts does s. 3 apply?

Section 3 applies to any contract where one person deals as a consumer (see s. 12) or 'on the other's written standard terms of business'. Thus many contracts between 'business' parties are quite clearly caught by s. 3. The justification for intervention in this type of case is the perceived need to control the excess of those businesses with superior bargaining power. Put another way, s. 3 applies to all contracts except those between business parties which are 'freely negotiated'. In the light of the proliferation of written standard conditions of contract, s. 3 assumes immense importance. No doubt the mere mention of standard terms will conjure up memories of the 'Battle of Forms' and more particularly the decision of the Court of Appeal in *Butler Machine Tool Co. Ltd* v *Ex-Cell-O Corpn. (England) Ltd* [1979] 1 WLR 401. Whether s. 3 applies to any exclusion clause will depend on whose written standard conditions the parties have contracted upon. It is unclear whether a person can be regarded as contracting 'on the other's written standard terms of business' where the parties contract on the basis of standard terms created by another body or agreed as between the trade associations representing the respective parties (see for example *R. W. Green Ltd* v *Cade Bros. Farms* [1978] 1 Lloyd's Rep 602, actually decided under s. 55 Sale of Goods Act 1893, the clause in question relating to merchantable quality). Given the fact that s. 3 merely subjects clauses to a reasonableness test, one would imagine the courts will take a pretty broad view as to the meaning of the above mentioned phrase.

To which contractual obligations do the s. 3 controls relate?

We may safely presume against duplication by the various provisions of the Act and therefore that the s. 3 controls relate to contractual obligations not already 'protected' by the controls embodied in ss. 2, 6 and 7.

Since s. 2 deals with clauses which attempt to exclude or limit liability for contractual negligence then s. 3 must be assumed to relate to obligations the breach of which is not dependant upon proof of fault. Thus s. 3 would appear to apply to clauses which seek to exclude or limit responsibility for breach of *any express or implied strict liability obligation other than those implied strict liability obligations as to title, description, quality, etc., which are the subject of ss. 6 and 7*. Despite these eliminations the range of obligations embraced by s. 3 is considerable indeed since the majority of express undertakings are strict in their nature.

The kind of clauses caught by s. 3 would include, for example, those which seek to relieve a supplier of goods from liability for late or non-delivery. The obligation to deliver goods within a certain time may be express or implied by virtue of s. 29(3) Sale of Goods Act 1979. In either case liability is strict, i.e., not dependent upon proof of fault. Given the narrow, almost non-existent doctrine of frustration in English Law one can readily appreciate the presence in contracts of clauses seeking to exclude liability for late or non-delivery whether or not the cause is within the control of the supplier. Such clauses including (it is thought) the ubiquitous 'force majeure' clause, are now subject to a reasonableness test by virtue of s. 3.

We believe it important to remind students that although s. 3 is extremely far reaching in effect it is not of universal application in particular, as we pointed out above, it does not apply to contracts between business parties the terms of which are freely negotiated. Clauses excluding liability for breach in this type of contract (other than those caught by ss. 2, 6, 7) are subject only to the common law rules.

One other significant difference as between the three patterns of control represented by ss. 2, 3 and 6, 7 is worth highlighting. Each of the ss. 2, 6 and 7 render a limited number of clauses wholly ineffective. The isolation within those sections of the clauses which attract such severe sanctions enables a greater degree of flexibility in the far reaching residual provision of s. 3. Thus all clauses falling within s. 3 are subject only to a reasonableness test.

A student can only be reasonably certain of applying the correct provision of the Act to any particular exclusion clause if he appreciates and learns the different requirements of each of the above mentioned sections. We hope the algorithm assists in this respect. May we suggest in addition a complementary exercise. Consider carefully some of the cases concerning exclusion clauses which were decided under the common law. Try to ensure that your selection embraces a mixture of both consumer and commercial cases. Using the algorithm, try to identify which section(s) of the 1977 Act (if any) would now apply to the clauses in question. In the event that the Act would now apply, would the clauses be ineffective *ab initio* or subject to the test of reasonableness?

Assume the contract is not exempt by Part III or Schedule 1 and that the person seeking to rely on the exclusion clause contracted in the course of a business (or is a private seller covered by s. 6(4)).

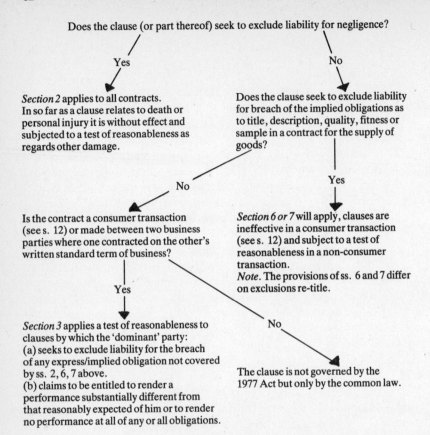

Does the clause (or part thereof) seek to exclude liability for negligence?

Yes

Section 2 applies to all contracts. In so far as a clause relates to death or personal injury it is without effect and subjected to a test of reasonableness as regards other damage.

No

Does the clause seek to exclude liability for breach of the implied obligations as to title, description, quality, fitness or sample in a contract for the supply of goods?

No

Yes

Is the contract a consumer transaction (see s. 12) or made between two business parties where one contracted on the other's written standard term of business?

Section 6 or 7 will apply, clauses are ineffective in a consumer transaction (see s. 12) and subject to a test of reasonableness in a non-consumer transaction.
Note. The provisions of ss. 6 and 7 differ on exclusions re-title.

Yes

Section 3 applies a test of reasonableness to clauses by which the 'dominant' party:
(a) seeks to exclude liability for the breach of any express/implied obligation not covered by ss. 2, 6, 7 above.
(b) claims to be entitled to render a performance substantially different from that reasonably expected of him or to render no performance at all of any or all obligations.

No

The clause is not governed by the 1977 Act but only by the common law.

What kind of terms does the Act control?

We have deliberately delayed consideration of this matter in order to concentrate our efforts in the earlier pages towards an understanding of the threefold pattern of the controls affecting contractual exclusion clauses. Thus in our earlier observations upon s. 3 we specifically deferred consideration of the question as to whether or not the section governed only 'contractual' exemption clauses (see p. 79).

The Act is somewhat misleading in regard to which terms fall within its scope. The title of the Act might at first glance suggest that the purpose of the legislation is to control the use of *contractual terms only* which may be regarded as unfair according to the underlying policy and the criteria established within the Act itself. We need only note here that the Act regulates not only contractual terms but also non-contractual notices affecting certain liabilities in tort. In the context of contractual relationships, which terms does the Act control? Could one reasonably infer from the title of the Act that this legislation controls *any contractual term* which is capable of being regarded as unfair, with the exception only of those terms specifically saved by the Act such as arbitration clauses (as to which see s. 13(2))? The predictable and to some extent understandable response to this question one gets from students is a confident, 'NO! the Act only controls exemption clauses'. That answer demonstrates a degree of misunderstanding of what is perhaps the most controversial aspect of the whole Act. Much of the problem stems from the manner in which the Act seeks to define the contract terms within its embrace. At the heart of the definitional difficulty with which the draftsman had to cope, is the argument concerning the distinction to be drawn between terms which purport to exclude liabilities for breaches of established obligations and those which a party may employ to define the obligations which he is prepared to undertake. The Act seeks to deal with this and other issues through two distinctly different provisions, namely, s. 13 and s. 3(2)(b). The reasons behind the inclusion of two different provisions will emerge in the course of the observations which follow.

Section 13, Unfair Contract Terms Act A careful examination of the wording of s. 13 reveals a definition of 'exemption clauses' which is non-exhaustive and so broad that it is capable of embracing an extremely wide variety of terms. In particular the section provides that to the extent that ss. 2, 6 and 7 prevent the exclusion or restriction of liability they 'also prevent excluding or restricting liability by reference to terms and notices which exclude or restrict the relevant obligation or duty'. No distinction is drawn between clauses which exclude liabilities and those which define obligations. In effect a term such as 'the seller does not warrant the goods fit for any purpose' is as much caught by s. 13 as a clause which states 'all conditions and warranties express or implied by common law or statute are hereby excluded'. This aspect of s. 13 has been strongly criticised on the grounds that the effect is:

> . . . to insist that a party has undertaken a particular liability in contract when he has expressly negated such intention [and that is] if not merely perverse, to treat the law of contract as if it were an arm of the public law (Coote (1978) 41 MLR 312 at p. 314).

The provision is similarly condemned by Palmer and Yates ((1981) CLJ 108 at p. 127) who claim that, 'if taken literally [s. 13] deprives the parties of virtually all capacity to agree and define the content of the obligations undertaken'.

Whilst some difficulties will inevitably arise from the wording of s. 13, little purpose would have been served by an Act, the provisions of which could be circumvented by a simple change in drafting technique. As the earlier example showed, a term purporting to define a supplier's obligations may be equally repugnant to the underlying policy as one which proclaims to exclude liability for breach. We believe it is improtant that students obtain a balanced view of the extent to which this Act interferes with contractual freedom and in so doing they will more readily appreciate the areas of significant difficulty and avoid at least some of the obscurantist arguments.

In assessing the impact of s. 13 upon contractual freedom we should first note that this controversial aspect applies only to ss. 2, 5 to 7, the provisions of which, by comparison with s. 3, serve to protect a relatively narrow range of obligations (mostly implied by law) which secure *minimum standards* of performance. They are largely of a kind which social policy requires that a party should enjoy.

Secondly, the mere fact that a particular term is caught by s. 13 does not mean that it is, *ipso facto*, ineffective. Those contractual terms which are rendered ineffective *ab initio*, are confined within narrow limits (i.e., s. 2: clauses relating to death or personal injury arising out of negligence; s. 5 affects any exclusions of negligence liability contained in a 'guarantee document'; ss. 6 and 7 relate to terms affecting the obligations as to title, description, quality, etc., *mainly* in consumer transactions). In a vast number of cases to which s. 13 applies the term concerned will be subject only to a test of reasonableness.

Given the flexibility of that test we could fairly predict the expansive approach to the interpretation of s. 13 which was taken by the Court of Appeal in *Phillips Products* v *T. Hyland and Hamstead Plant Hire Co.* [1987] 1 WLR 659. Whilst that decision is technically concerned with a claim in tort (in which respect s. 13 is perhaps even more controversial: see the above mentioned articles), it is not unreasonable to expect a similar approach in a contractual context. The clause in that case purported to place the responsibility for any negligence on the part of the driver of an excavator upon the plaintiff hirers. The argument that the clause in question prevented any obligation on the part of the defendants from arising and was thus outside the scope of the Unfair Contract Terms Act, was rejected. In the view of the Court of Appeal the concluding words of s. 13 of the Act brought this type of clause within the Act (for a brief but interesting analysis of the decision see Palmer (1986) BLR 57).

Such clauses can however only be said to 'exclude liability' where person seeks to rely upon the clause as against, e.g., the victim of his negligence (or negligence for which he is vicariously liable). The Court of Appeal has in *Thompson* v *Lohan (Plant Hire) Ltd and J. W. Hurdiss Ltd* [1987] 1 WLR

649 insisted upon and explained the fundamental distinction that is drawn between exemption clauses and indemnity clauses. That distinction is recognised in the 1977 Act. Thus where the term of contract between A and B requires B to indemnify A for liability which he (A) may incur to C, such a term is not subject to control under the 1977 Act unless B happened to deal as a consumer (in which case such a term will be subject to a test of reasonableness under s. 4).

In other circumstances, the dividing line between terms which reflect the legitimate exercise by the parties of their contractual freedom and those which in some way represent an abuse of that freedom by one party alone, may be exceedingly fine and difficult to draw. A study of the contrasting decisions of the Divisional Court in *Hughes* v *Hall (Gillian)* [1981] RTR 430 and *Cavendish-Woodhouse Ltd* v *Manley* (1984) 148 JP 299, 82 LGR 376, should enable students to gain an appreciation of this difficulty. Similarly it will continue to be necessary to distinguish between exclusion clauses covered by the 1977 Act and other clauses which warn of dangers and by which a duty of reasonable care (in tort or contract) may be discharged. A careful reading of the decision in *Hurley* v *Dyke* [1979] RTR 265 (the facts of which arose before the 1977 Act came into force) should serve to warn students of the dangers of taking too simplistic a view as to the kind of clauses covered by s. 13 of the 1977 Act. Lord Denning's view in that case that a clause 'sold as seen with all faults and without warranty' would amount to an exclusion clause under the 1977 Act (see [1979] RTR 265 at pp. 281-282) has to be treated with a certain degree of caution.

'sold as seen with all faults'

Section 3, Unfair Contract Terms Act   We pointed out above (at p. 83) that the wider definition of exclusion clauses in s. 13 applies only to ss. 2 and 5 to 7 of the Act. In so far as this represents a significant interference with contractual freedom, it may be justified on the grounds that parties (often in a weaker bargaining position) would otherwise be 'deprived of rights of a kind which social policy requires that they should enjoy' (Law Commission, Exemption Clauses, Second Report (above) paras. 143-146).

Section 3 on the other hand is almost a catch all provision protecting an enormous variety of contractual obligations both express and implied, in a wide range of contracts, in respect of which the priority was given to flexibility rather than specific prohibitions. In the context of s. 3 it is open to a person to argue that the clause on which he seeks to rely prevented any obligation to the other arising. Thus to take the Law Commission's own example (*ibid.*):

> if a decorator agrees to paint the outside woodwork of a house except the garage doors, no-one can seriously regard the words of exception as anything but a convenient way of defining the obligation.

Whilst s. 3 intrudes less upon contractual freedom than does s. 13, s. 3(2)(b) represents some attempt to ensure that contractual freedom is not abused by controlling the manner in which contractual obligations are defined.

Section 3(2)(b)(i) and (ii) provide that the 'dominant' party cannot claim to be entitled to render a contractual performance substantially different from that which was reasonably expected of him, or, claim to be entitled in respect of the whole or any part of his contractual obligations to render no performance at all — except in so far as the 'dominant' party can show that the term satisfies the requirement of reasonableness.

Section 3(2)(b) is aimed at the practice of 'defining' obligations in general terms and then substantially reducing those obligations by 'further definition' in clauses often in small print, strategically placed so as to minimise the likelihood of close scrutiny by the other party.

The reasonableness test

The relevant provisions of the 1977 Act are to be found in s. 11 and Schedule 2. Those provisions are not in themselves particularly difficult to comprehend. We shall examine here only a limited number of substantive points some of which conern the interrelationship between the statutory reasonableness test and the common law rules. The real dififculty arises in connection with the application of the reasonableness test. This issue is more appropriately dealt with in the context of our commentary upon the illustrative question.

Whether any particular clause can be shown to be reasonable is largely, but by no means exclusively, a question of fact. There is a number of important substantive points of which students need a thorough understanding, some of which will be applicable to all clauses. One such point is raised by s. 11(1) which requires that the reasonableness (or otherwise) of a clause is to be judged at the time the contract is made, rather than the time at which a party seeks to rely upon the clause (which is the test under s. 55 of the Sale of Goods Act 1979). Section 11(1) reflects the views of the Scottish Law Commission, such an approach being preferred on grounds of certainty and consistency with general principles of contract law (see Law Commission, Exemption Clauses, Second Report (above), paras 170-183). The English Law Commission on the other hand favoured a 'reasonable to rely on test' mainly on the grounds that to hold a clause to be unreasonable simply on the basis that it could theoretically operate unreasonably was unacceptable. The English Law Commission would therefore have preferred that clauses be judged in circumstances wider than those which appertained at the time of contract including the nature and the extent of a breach, its effect upon the contract and the surrounding circumstances (see Law Commission, Exemption Clauses, Second Report (*ibid.*)).

Section 11(1) however renders irrelevant events subsequent to the making of the contract except to the extent that they are 'circumstances which were or ought to have been, known to or in the contemplation of the parties when the contract was made'. The judicial interpretation of this phraseology could be most interesting in a situation where a clause, drawn in extremely wide terms (and arguably unreasonable to include in the contract) is relied upon in circumstances which are such as to evoke a more lenient response. It is not beyond the imagination of your examiner to devise such situations.

Section 11(1) does not however prevent a court from applying the normal rules of construction to determine whether or not the parties intended the clause to cover the particular breach which has occurred. If the wording of the clause (construed *contra proferentem*) does not clearly cover the particular breach the clause will be totally ineffective. In seeking to satisfy the rules of construction and ensure that a clause would be effective in a wide variety of circumstances, draftsmen have resorted to wide language. The use of such phrases as 'howsoever caused' or 'howsoever arising' is now almost traditional. In as much as this broad language is clearly capable of excluding liability which might arise in circumstances which could not be contemplated by the parties at the time of contract, such clauses may well be unreasonable to include in the contract. Similarly, a clause which purported to exclude liability for any 'injury, loss or damage' arising through negligence might well be ineffective either:

(a)   on grounds that part of the clause offends s. 2(1) of the Act rendering the whole clause void, *or*

(b)   that such a clause was not a reasonable one to include in the contract.

Conclusion (a) or (b) could be reached despite the fact that the clause was being set up only against a claim for financial *loss*.

The combination of the rules of construction together with the reasonableness test created something of a dilemma for those who draft conditions of contract. A narrowly drawn clause may be entirely reasonable but fail to cover the breach in question, whilst the broadly worded clause may achieve the reverse result. It should come as no surprise to students that examiners will seek to test the student's knowledge and understanding of this kind of issue.

Section 11(4) provides for differential treatment as between those clauses which represent partial limitation on the amount of damages recoverable as opposed to those which seek to exclude liability for any damages. The provision came into existence as a result of a late amendment to the Bill during its passage through Parliament. This may explain this rather odd provision. Why are such considerations as the defendant's resources and the availablity to him of insurance cover only to be taken into account where the particular clause limits liability to a specific sum? It seems more than a little illogical to so restrict these considerations. A literal interpretation of s. 11(4) would even preclude consideration of such matters where the liability was limited by reference to the type of damage rather than to some specific sum. By contrast the more lenient application of the rules of construction to limitation clauses so clearly signalled in *Ailsa Craig Fishing Co. Ltd* v *Malvern Fishing Co. Ltd* [1983] 1 WLR 964 HL are not so confined. Perhaps the likely interpretation of s. 11(4) is that whilst the consideration of the factors here mentioned is *mandatory* where the clause limits to a specific sum, this does not by implication exclude consideration of those factors in other cases.

Illustrative question

P, the sole proprietor of a restaurant, signed a written agreement under which S Ltd would supply and install an underfloor electrical heating system at P's premises. The particular make/type of system was specified by P. It was agreed that the work would be completed in the second two weeks of July when P and his staff took their annual holiday.

The work was delayed and the restaurant had to remain closed for a further two weeks resulting in a loss of earnings to P of £2,000. Two months after installation the system overheated causing a fire which resulted in damage to P's premises and other losses estimated at £100,000. P was injured whilst trying to ensure the safety of his customers. The whole of the reverse side of the agreement signed by P contains, in small print, the terms of business of the Association of Heating Installation Engineers and includes, *inter alia*, clauses which provide that:

(a)   S Ltd accepts no responsibility for latent defects (or losses consequential thereon) arising in equipment supplied to the customer's specification.

(b)   Any dates given for delivery or completion are estimates only.

(c)   Without prejudice to any other term, the liability of S Ltd howsoever arising, whether by reason of negligence or otherwise, shall not exceed £10,000.

Discuss any liability which S Ltd may have incurred to P.

Commentary

We should like to preface the analysis of the question by repeating advice given in earlier chapters, namely, to plan at least the structure of your answer before you begin casting your pearls of wisdom upon the script. The labyrinthine path which we trace in part of our analysis will we hope convince any doubters as to the real value of investing a few minutes sorting out identified issues into some sort of logical sequence.

The discussion of this question should include a reasoned explanation as to whether or not any or all of the three different 'losses' sustained by P are likely to be recoverable. We have chosen to approach them in the following order. First we shall deal with the loss of £2,000 earnings due to the delay in the completion of the work. How to order the other issues is perhaps not so easily decided. The contract in question is one for the supply of work and materials. Under such contracts suppliers have obligations as to the quality of both the materials and the work. There are significant differences between these obligations and also in the provisions of the Unfair Contract Terms Act regarding the exclusion of liability arising from their breach. In that respect the cause of the system overheating would be of considerable legal significance. We have deliberately omitted to state this cause so as to elicit a discussion of the alternative positions if the fire resulted from: (a) defective materials, or (b) defective workmanship. We propose to consider the issues of the injury to P and the damage to his property (and consequential losses thereon) in relation to each of these possible alternative causes.

Loss of earnings due to delay

The question tells us that 'it was agreed that' the work would be completed within the first two weeks of July. Can we assume therefore that S Ltd are under a contractual obligation in that regard and that the delay beyond the second week in July is automatically a breach of that obligation, entitling P to recover the foreseeable loss of income. The difficulty in the way of any such assumption is the clause in the agreement signed by P, which states that the completion date given is only to be regarded as an estimate. Your answer on this issue would need to focus sharply upon the likely legal effect of such a clause. Though the contract is arguably not a consumer transaction (see below), P appears to contract upon the standard written terms of business of S Ltd. Assuming that to be so we may safely conclude that s. 3 of the Unfair Contract Terms Act would apply to clauses affecting a wide range of strict liability obligations which might be contained in the contract. This would include clauses affecting any express or implied obligation as to time of performance (you may reach this conclusion by means of the algorithm on p. 76).

On the brief facts of the illustrative question a court might take any one of these possible views:

(a)   An express obligation existed to complete the work within the first two weeks of July of which S Ltd are in breach. The clause in question is regarded as an attempt to exclude the consequent liability and is subjected to a test of reasonableness by virtue of s. 3(2)(a) of the Act.

(b)   An alternative view, which might well be taken by S Ltd, is that the clause prevented the creation of any express obligation to complete within the first two weeks of July. Even if this construction was to be accepted the effectiveness of the clause may be called into question employing two different lines of argument:

(i)   If the clause has the effect suggested in (b) above, then the parties have in effect not agreed any time for the performance of the contract, in which case s. 14 of the Supply of Goods and Services Act 1982 would be relevant, and an obligation to complete within a reasonable time would be implied into the contract. What amounts to reasonable time is a question of fact in every case. The question is likely to be determined to some extent, by reference to the conduct of the parties. If S Ltd were aware of P's reason for having the work done at that time, it is by no means inconceivable that a court might hold that a failure to complete by the end of the second week of July (or at least before the date of actual completion) amounted to a breach of that implied obligation. In the event that such a breach could be established (with *prima facie* liability for some if not all P's loss of £2,000), it might be argued that the clause affected this liability. Two points are worth making. Since the clause appears to refer only to express statements as to dates of completion then, as a matter of construction (*contra proferentem*) the clause has no application to liability arising by reason of breach of an *implied* obligation and is therefore totally ineffective. Alternatively on the assumption that the clause could be construed to affect this liability it would be subjected to the test of reasonableness by reason of 3(2)(a) of the Act.

(ii)   The second line of argument which may be employed in the event that the clause is regarded as one defining the obligations of S Ltd, arises under s. 3(2)(b)(i) of the Act. This provision subjects to the test of reasonableness, a clause by which the 'dominant' party claims to be entitled 'to render a contractual peformance substantially different from that which was reasonably expected of him'. One should emphasise that, in order for the clause in question to be subjected to a test of reasonableness, it would be necessary to establish that performance by the end of the second week of July was reasonably expected of S Ltd *and* that the late performance was a 'substantially different' performance. Assuming that these points could be established the clause in question would be subject to the test of reasonableness under the 1977 Act, to which we now turn.

Whilst considering the substantive law and its application to the facts of our problem it is also appropriate to re-emphasise certain points relating to technique. The reasonableness test is one of those issues which, in our experience, students do not handle particularly well and their failure to do so is often due to a failure to observe certain basic points of technique which we identified in chapter 2. The difficulty in arriving at a conclusion as to the reasonableness or otherwise of an exclusion clause appears to disconcert students. Some are afraid that they might arrive at the 'wrong' conclusion and will be penalised for that. These students react to the issue in different but equally unsatisfactory ways. Some will refuse to indulge in any analysis or evaluation, merely stating, e.g., 'the clause would be subject to the reasonableness test under the 1977 Act, see s. 11, Schedule 2'. Others will regurgitate without analysis or evaluation all the provisions of s. 11 and Schedule 2 of the Act, whether or not they are relevant on the facts of the problem questions. Apart from the obvious waste of time and effort involved, such an approach is also likely to give an examiner the impression that the student lacks the capacity to distinguish between the relevant and the irrelevant.

Whether on the facts of any particular case a clause would be regarded as reasonable or not may well be an extremely difficult question of judgment. Furthermore the brevity of facts in examination questions renders the exercise somewhat artificial. Examiners are well aware of these difficulties. Students should 'grasp the nettle' and should offer a reasoned conclusion on such issues with the assurance that it is of no great significance in itself that the student's conclusion might differ from that of the examiner. In dealing with the clause concerning delivery dates in our question, the following points would need to be made.

Certain provisions of the Act will be relevant to all clauses. This would include s. 11(5) which places the onus of proof, in this case upon S Ltd, to show that the clause satisfies the test of reasonableness. The burden which S Ltd bear is to show that the clause was a fair and reasonable one to include in the contract 'having regard to the circumstances which were, or ought to have been, known to or in the contemplation of the parties when the contract was made' (see s. 11(1)).

In the light of this, as a rule of thumb, the wider the language and effect of the clause the less is the likelihood that the clause can be shown to be reasonable. Whilst the clause in question is fairly narrow in the sense that it relates only to delivery dates, it purports to be comprehensive in that regard. The clause seeks to exclude liability (or avoid any responsibility) irrespective of whether the relevant circumstances were 'known or ought to have been in the contemplation' of the parties at the time of the contract. On the face of it the clause attempts to exclude liability for delay even though the cause of the delay was within the control and due to the negligence of S Ltd. The clause is therefore in certain respects much wider than the traditional *force majeure* clause. In the context of s. 3(2)(b)(i) of the Act, it is not easy to see how it can be reasonable to include a clause which would allow a dominant party to offer a performance substantially different from that which was reasonably expected of him. Given that the above mentioned provision anticipates this to be a possibility we should not disregard that possibility. We would doubt whether any difference in result would occur according to whether a clause is subject to a test of reasonableness by virtue of s. 3(2)(a) rather than s. 3(2)(b)(i).

Section 11(4) of the Act (which provides for differential treatment of limiting clauses) is worth mentioning here, although we give fuller consideration to the clause limiting the liability of S Ltd to £10,000 below. Though the clause is expressed to be without prejudice to any other term, it would not be inappropriate to consider whether its presence is likely to render more difficult the task of showing that other more restrictive clauses (such as that affecting delivery) to be reasonable to include in the contract.

The discussion of the guidelines in Schedule 2 of the Act should perhaps be prefaced first by drawing to the examiner's attention that, whilst strictly speaking the guidelines contained in the Schedule apply only to clauses which are subject to the reasonableness test under ss. 6 and 7, the likelihood is that they will be applied in other cases. Such cases may arise under s. 2(2) or indeed under s. 3 (see *Stagline Ltd* v *Tyne Ship Repair Group Ltd* (1985) 4 Trading Law Reports 33). Assuming that the guidelines were to be considered relevant to the question in hand, an understanding of the difficulty inherent in applying the relevant guidelines and reaching a conclusion might usefully be demonstrated by, e.g., quoting Lord Bridge in *Mitchell* v *Finney* (above): 'The court must entertain a whole range of considerations, put them in the scales on one side or the other and decide at the end of the day on which side the balance comes down.'

The guidelines to which our chosen facts point (a little obviously perhaps?) are those listed (a), (b) and (c) in Schedule 2. Guideline (a) requires the court to take account of the relative strength of bargaining position of the parties. The fact that P contracted upon the written standard terms of business of S Ltd would indicate that S Ltd enjoys a superior bargaining position. Furthermore, the terms of contract employed are those of a trade association of which S Ltd is presumably a member. This should indicate the probability that P's freedom of choice as to the terms on which he is able to contract may be significantly reduced. Freedom of choice appears to be a relevant cnsideration under two guidelines (a) and (b) though guideline (b) would appear to be most clearly relevant, i.e., whether in accepting the clause P has an opportunity of entering into a contract with other persons without having to accept a similar term.

Students would be expected to show an awareness and understanding of any relevant case law on this issue. Two cases, *Mitchell* v *Finney* (above) and *R. W. Green Ltd* v *Cade Bros. Farms* [1978] 1 Lloyd's Rep 602 are particularly relevant. This is perhaps an appropriate opportunity to demonstrate and re-emphasise certain points of technique. When dealing with cases the amount of factual detail must be kept to a necessary minimum. Explanations and observations have to be concise yet sufficient to convince the examiner of a good level of knowledge and understanding. As we indicated in chapter 2 this is to a considerable extent a matter of style. In dealing with the two cases mentioned above we would suggest something along the following lines:

Whilst both cases were decided under s. 55 of the Sale of Goods Act 1979 they are thought to be authoritative with regard to the UCT Act. Recognising the danger of examining issues in isolation from other relevant factors in particular cases, the upshot of those decisions would appear to be as follows. Where, as in Green's case, the terms of the contract are the product of negotiations between trade associations representing both buyer and seller the more likely a clause would be upheld as reasonable. Conversely, where trade association conditions are 'forced upon' the purchaser as is perhaps the case here, the less likely it is that any exclusion clause will be reasonable, see *Mitchell* v *Finney*. The clause in question is concerned with delay in delivery (as opposed to the quality of goods in the above mentioned cases). In the absence of decided cases precisely in point it is not possible to state affirmatively that the difference is immaterial.

The fact that the whole of the reverse side of the document which P signed contained conditions in small print raises the need to discuss guideline (c) which requires the court to consider:

whether the customer knew or ought to have known of the existence and extent of the term (having regard, amongst other things, to any custom of the trade and any previous course of dealings between the parties).

Let us assume for the sake of argument no trade custom exists, and there has been no previous course of dealings between P and S Ltd. It is important to convey to the examiner the understanding that the statutory reasonableness test makes important inroads into the common law as reflected in such cases as *L'Estrange* v *F. Graucob Ltd* [1934] 2 KB 394. Despite the fact that the party affected by the clause has signed an agreement in which the clause is incorporated, it is clearly open to a court to hold a clause to be unreasonable on the grounds that the clause has not been given sufficient prominence relative to its importance; the language in which the clause is expressed renders the meaning of the clause difficult to comprehend by those affected (see *Stagline Ltd* v *Tyne Ship Repair Group* (1985) 4 Trading Law Reports 33); or that the party affected had insufficient time to study the detail of the conditions (see *Phillips Products* v *T. Hyland and Hamstead Plant Hire Co.* (above).

So far the decided cases seem to suggest that these are makeweight factors rather than being in any way decisive factors in themselves. Perhaps this is a sign that the weight to be attributed to such matters will be balanced in the judicial mind against the danger of being seen to encourage the feckless. By way of conclusion on the issue of the loss caused through the delay, we would venture to suggest that S Ltd would in all probability be liable for some if not all of that loss. We would doubt very much the ability of S Ltd to persuade a court that the relevant clause was a fair and reasonable one to include in the contract.

Injury, loss, damage resulting from defective materials

Assuming that defective materials were the cause of the malfunctioning of the heating system and subsequent fire, the following points would need to be discussed. Arguably this is a work and materials contract which S Ltd appears to have made in the course of a business with the result that the obligations as to merchantable quality and fitness for purpose would be implied by virtue of s. 4 of the Supply of Goods and Services Act 1982. On the facts of the question there seems to be no reason to supppose that the obligation as to merchantable quality may not be implied by reason of examination, or defects having been brought to P's attention at the time of contract. The fact that P himself has specified a particular make/type of system would be unlikely to negate reliance on the skill and judgment of S Ltd with regard to fitness for purpose under s. 4(4) of the 1982 Act (see for example *Young & Marten Ltd* v *McManus Childs Ltd* [1969] 1 AC 454).

The supplier's liability with regard to the materials supplied is strict, i.e., the fact that the defect which renders goods unmerchantable is not discoverable by reasonable skill and care on the part of the supplier is immaterial. Whilst numerous cases make this point there would seem to be little purpose in making reference to more than one or two of them (see, e.g., *G. H. Myers & Co.* v *Brent Cross Service Co.* [1934] 1 KB 46.

Assuming the materials supplied are not of merchantable quality and/or not fit for the buyer's particular purpose, we should now recognise that the clause relating to latent defects is an exemption clause within the meaning of s. 13 of the Unfair Contract Terms Act 1977, as the clause purports to restrict liability that would otherwise arise by virtue of the obligations implied by s. 4 of the Supply of Goods and Services Act 1982. The clause will therefore be subject to the controls embodied in s. 7 of the 1977 Act which vary according to whether or not P dealt as a consumer. Where the buyer deals as a consumer any such clause would be void, but otherwise subject to a test of reasonableness.

Section 12 of the 1977 Act contains three criteria all of which must be satisfied in order to establish that P dealt as a consumer. The first, that S Ltd supplied the goods in the course of a business, is clearly satisfied. Secondly, the requirement that the goods supplied must be 'of a type ordinarily supplied for private use and consumption' may also be fulfilled. Some brief speculation as to whether the type of heating system supplied to P was normally only installed in commercial/industrial premises would not however be misplaced. The third requirement, that P does not 'buy or hold himself out as buying in the course of a business' will, on the facts, warrant greater discussion especially in the light of the decision in *Peter Symmonds & Co.* v *Cook* (Lexis Transcript 131 (1981) NLJ 758). In that case Mr R. Rougier QC held that a firm of architects who purchased a secondhand Rolls Royce motor car 'dealt as consumers' under the 1977 Act and that an exclusion clause which sought to exclude liability for unmerchantable goods was void by virtue of s. 6 of the Unfair Contract Terms Act. He took the view that for such a sale to fall outside s. 12, the purchase of the particular goods would need 'to form at least an integral part of the buyer's business or a necessary incidental thereto. Only in those circumstances could the buyer be said to be on an equal footing with the trade/seller'.

If we were to apply that decision to the facts of our problem then both the clause relating to latent defects and the clause limiting liability to £10,000 would be void by virtue of s. 7 of the Unfair Contract Term Act. On an issue such as this an examiner would expect students to contemplate the alternative view namely, that it was a 'non-consumer transaction', (on the grounds that P was buying in the course of a business) and to discuss the reasonableness test in relation to both the clauses mentioned above. An examiner would no doubt award marks to students offering some critical analysis of the decision in *Symmonds* v *Cook*. Does the decision introduce an unnecessarily wide interpretation of the Act? What difficulties does the decision raise in connection with offences which might be committed under the Consumer Transactions (Restriction on Statements) Order 1976 (as amended)? Would it be preferable to reach the same result via the 'alternative route' (i.e., that the transaction is a 'non-consumer transaction' but the clause is unreasonable; see, e.g., the *obiter dicta* of Lawson J in *Rasbora Ltd* v *JCL Marine Ltd* [1977] 1 Lloyd's Rep 645)?

Assuming for argument's sake that P is not regarded as dealing as a consumer then we need to offer some view as to the likely success of clauses (a) and (c) under the reasonableness test. It would not be necessary in an examination to repeat in detail points which, though relevant, have already been discussed earlier. It would be perfectly acceptable to refer the examiner to the earlier discussion of matters such as the burden of proof and inequality in bargaining power, thus concentrating one's efforts upon a discussion of those factors peculiar to clauses (a) and (c) in the question.

We would suggest that the matters most deserving of discussion arise in relation to clause (c). The clause is a limitation clause rather than a total exclusion clause and the provision in s. 11(4) of the 1977 Act is therefore relevant. The decision in *George Mitchell (Chesterhall) Ltd* v *Finney Lock Seeds Ltd* [1983] 2 AC 803 though pre-dating the Act is also relevant and suggests that as a matter of policy, the suppliers of goods and services are expected to carry liability insurance, at least in regard to the quality of goods and services they provide. Unless S Ltd can show that there exists some difficulty in obtaining insurance cover, which is sufficient to justify the limitation, then arguably the clause will be regarded as unreasonable, especially in the light of the inequality of bargaining power and limited choice indicated above. Furthermore, it should be pointed out that the clause, albeit a limitation clause, is so widely drawn that it purports to limit the liability of S Ltd for death or personal injury resulting from negligence.

Although in the context of a claim based upon defective materials, the clause is not relied on to exclude liability for negligence, that is strictly irrelevant. The point in issue is that the clause is only effective 'in so far as it' can be shown to be a fair and reasonable one to include in the contract. It may well be argued that it can never be reasonable to include a clause which is, at least in one respect, void by virtue of s. 2(1) of the Act. The counter argument is to the effect that the use of the phrase 'in so far as' in s. 7(3) (and in other sections) enables a court to uphold a part of a clause as reasonable, striking out or disregarding other parts which are objectionable. The difficulty with this line of argument is that the wording of s. 11(1) seems to suggest that it is the whole term which has to be reasonable to be included in the contract. The point has yet to be decided and an examiner would be happy that the student had identified the issue and indicated an understanding of the present difficulties. It would certainly be worth drawing attention to the decision in *George Mitchell (Chesterhall) Ltd* v *Finney Lock Seeds Ltd* [1983] 2 AC 803 in which the House of Lords rejected the argument that the phrase 'to the extent that' in s. 55(4) Sale of Goods Act 1979 could be interpreted to permit a partial reliance on a limitation clause, so as to allow the purchaser to recover a percentage of his losses (see [1983] 2 AC 803 per Lord Bridge at p. 816).

To conclude on this point, we would suggest that S Ltd would be liable for the damage to P's property and for the injury to P himself in the event that the fire resulted from materials rendered unmerchantable by reason of a latent defect. The injury to P would probably not present any difficulties in terms of remoteness of damage. A lengthy discussion of the relevant principles would not therefore in our opinion be justified, though a brief reference to both the relevant principles and decided case would be commendable. On the brief facts of the problem even if the contract were regarded as a 'non-consumer' transaction, the balance would seem to be against either of the clauses being upheld as reasonable.

Injury, loss, damage resulting from defective installation

Under this head it is important to emphasise the legal implications of the assumption that P's injury and losses resulted from 'defective' work rather than defective materials. The issues to which particular attention should be paid concern differences in the nature of the potential liability which S Ltd may incur, together with the different provisions of the 1977 Act governing the validity of exclusion clauses which would apply.

With regard to quality of the installation in such contracts there will often be no express obligation undertaken. Most frequently the supplier's only obligation in this regard will be that which is implied by s. 13 of the Supply of

Goods and Services Act 1982, namely, to exercise reasonable skill and care. A stricter duty may in certain cases be implied from particular facts (see *Greaves & Co. (Contractors) Ltd* v *Baynham Meikle & Partners* [1975] 1 WLR 1095 CA). The most significant point which needs to be highlighted is that the statutory obligation (which is likely to apply) is discharged provided S Ltd exercised the 'ordinary skill of an ordinary competent man exercising that particular art' (see McNair J in *Bolam* v *Friern Hospital Management Committee* [1957] 1 WLR 582 at p. 586). Though there is nothing in the facts of our problem to suggest that it is the case, it should be pointed out that P may find it more difficult to establish liability under this head than he would if the injury, etc., were caused by a breach of the strict liability obligation to supply merchantable goods.

Assuming P can show that there has been negligence, the only clause which needs to be considered is the limitation clause. So far as P's injuries are concerned the clause would have no effect whatever, by virtue of s. 2(1) of the Unfair Contract Terms Act. It should be pointed out that this would be so despite the fact that the clause is a limitation clause rather than an exclusion clause. In regard to the damage to P's property and losses consequential thereon, the points made previously would be relevant here, i.e., does the fact that the clause is partially ineffective mean that the whole clause must fail? If not, then the clause would be subject to the test of reasonableness by virtue of s. 2(2) of the 1977 Act. Is the clause a reasonable one to include in this particular contract? We do not propose to repeat our earlier discussion of these issues nor would it be necessary to do so in an examination script. We would only add, by way of conclusion, one brief observation. Where negligence is established against a defendant (rather than him being in breach of a strict obligation by reason of matters beyond his control) the burden of persuading a court that any exclusion or limitation is reasonable is likely to be a heavy one.

We hope that the commentary in this chapter has impressed upon readers the value and tangible benefit to be gained from attempting to draft answers to questions of this kind both during term time and revision. Do not be put off by the length of our commentary. We have included a fair amount of comment upon points of examination technique and we would remind readers that our commentaries are in no way intended as model answers.

SIX

TITLE, PROPERTY AND RISK

Introduction

In this chapter we propose to consider a number of interrelated topics concerned essentially with ownership of goods under a contract for the sale or supply of goods. The very fact of the interrelationship between the topics is itself a source of much confusion. The kind of questions that we are looking at here are:

'if a seller sells goods which he does not own'

(a) If a seller or supplier sells or supplies goods which he does not own, what are the buyer's rights against him?

(b) Are there any circumstances in which an innocent purchaser may obtain a good title to goods, despite the fact that the supplier himself does not have good title to them?

(c) If, after a contract for sale of goods is made the seller retains possession of them pending delivery, and the goods are damaged, who must bear the risk of the loss?

(d)   Where a supplier delivers goods in pursuance of a contract, but payment has not been made by the buyer, who then goes into liquidation, can the supplier recover the goods from the buyer's liquidator?

The answers to these and other ancillary questions may often be crucial in determining the rights of the parties, including third parties, in relation to the goods. They are issues which may easily find their way into a consumer or commercial law examination in appropriate circumstances.

There has been mounting criticism over the years on the state of the law in these particular areas. Cranston comments that 'the law contains some highly technical and in some cases unjust rules.' He continues by saying that the origin of these rules 'in some cases derives from historical considerations quite out of touch with modern conditions' (*Consumers and the Law*, 2nd ed. at p. 161). The Crowther Committee (1971, Cmnd. 4596), in its important report on Consumer Credit, remarked (at p. 176):

> Unfortunately, statutory protection for the *bona fide* purchaser has developed in a piecemeal and haphazard fashion, and some of the relevant provisions have been so drafted and interpreted as to make their application depend not on principles of equity or justice but on fine technicalities which have little rhyme and less reason.

Such damning words ought to ring some warning bells with you. The law in this area is difficult and complex without a doubt and some hard concentration is necessary if you are to master the various principles and be able to apply them. Additionally, this chapter will cover a large amount of ground, normally covered in two or three chapters in the textbooks. We must repeat our view that this book is not a substitute for the reading of textbooks and other materials; it is to be read in conjunction with them. It follows, therefore, that we shall focus only on more difficult points which arise in the context of the topics under discussion.

Substantive difficulties

Seller's or supplier's duty to transfer good title

Section 12(1) of the Sale of Goods Act 1979 (see also the equivalent provisions in ss. 2 and 7 of the Supply of Goods and Services Act 1982) implies an obligation (condition) on the part of the seller that, in the case of a sale, he has the right to sell the goods, and in the case of an agreement to sell, he will have such a right when the property is to pass. This seems a relatively straightforward and reasonable provision, but some serious anomalies have arisen in the limited amount of case law. In addition, there are implied warranties (s. 12(2) to the effect that the goods are free from encumbrances not disclosed or known to the buyer before the contract is made and that the buyer will enjoy quiet possession of the goods. These two warranties are clearly linked to the implied condition, and breach of the right to sell provision will normally amount to a breach of warranty under s. 12(2) (or its equivalent under the 1982 Act).

A number of issues require comment.

(a) Any attempt to exclude the above terms in a sale of goods contract is declared void by s. 6(1) of the UCTA 1977. Likewise, s. 7(3) of that Act prevents exclusion of the similar implied terms in, e.g., work and materials contracts, namely, contracts covered by s. 2 of the 1982 Act. By way of contrast it should be noted that an attempt to exclude the terms as to title implied in a hire contract by virtue of s. 7 of the 1982 Act is subject to a reasonableness test (s. 7(4) 1977 Act).

(b) Section 12(1) uses the words 'right to sell' which suggests that the seller himself need not have title to the goods. So long as he can in some way ensure that title is passed to the buyer, s. 12(1) will be satisfied for example, he may be authorised as agent by the owner to sell. On the other hand, even if the seller owns the goods, he may be in breach of the subsection where, for example, a third party has the right to stop the sale because of an infringement of a trademark (see *Niblett* v *Confectioners' Materials Co.* [1921] 3 KB 387).

A further point under this heading concerns the position where the seller does not have title, but the buyer acquires a good title in law under one of the exceptions to the *nemo dat* rule, discussed below. If the buyer has title in this way, does he have a claim for a breach of s. 12(1)? The better view is that there is a technical breach but that the buyer has suffered no damage (see Atiyah at p. 71).

(c) As s. 12(1) is classified as a condition, then normally a buyer will be entitled to repudiate the contract and/or claim damages. *Rowland* v *Divall* [1923] 2 KB 500 suggests that the buyer can reject the goods and claim back the *whole* of the price paid, without any deduction for use in the meantime. The basis of this appears to be that the buyer has not got what he paid for, namely, title to the goods. There has been fierce criticism of this case (see Atiyah p. 74, the Law Reform Committee (1966, Cmnd. 2958, para. 36) and the Law Commission, Working Paper No. 85 (1983), p. 109). The rather absurd nature of the rule has also been highlighted in other cases (see *Karflex Ltd* v *Poole* [1933] 2 KB 251 and *Butterworth* v *Kingsway Motors* [1954] 1 WLR 1286). The main criticism appears to be that a buyer can reject and claim back the whole price even where there is never likely to be a claim by the true owner of the goods. Despite these criticisms the Law Commission in the 1987 Report could see no simple way to amend the law. The confusion likely to result in any change was such that the Commission decided against it (see paras 6.1-6.5).

(d) It is possible for a seller to contract to sell a limited title, in the sense that he is merely transferring such title or interest in goods which he or a third party might have (s. 12(3)). In such a case, the implied terms are the more limited warranties as to freedom from encumbrances and quiet possession as set out in subsections 12(4) and (5) of s. 12. One point to be wary of is that concerning any attempt to exclude s. 12(1) by use of an exemption clause. As we have pointed out any such clause would be void (see s. 6(1) UCTA 1977), but could it be argued that such a clause shows an intention by the seller merely to convey such title as he has, thus avoiding any breach of s. 12(1)? It is thought that this argument would be unsuccessful, as it would be tantamount to allowing indirectly the exclusion of the implied condition. Presumably, it would require much more to suggest that the seller was only purporting to transfer a limited title.

(e) The warranty of quiet possession is a continuing one and will provide a buyer with a remedy against a seller, where his possession is lawfully interrupted by a third party, as in *Microbeads AG* v *Vinhurst Road Markings Ltd* [1975] 1 All ER 529; where the third party acquired patent rights in the goods after the sale. Consequently, there was no breach of s. 12(1), but the buyer could recover damages under s. 12(2) under the warranty for quiet possession.

(f) In practice, it may be that claims under s. 12 are more theoretical than real. Often the seller will be a rogue or person not worth suing and so the buyer has a paper remedy, or alternatively the buyer may succeed in establishing one of the exceptions to the *nemo dat* rule, as mentioned earlier. We thus have our cue for discussing that rule and its numerous exceptions.

Nemo dat rule

We have already referred to the criticism of the Crowther Committee concerning the excessive technicality and injustice which has arisen in this particular area of the law. The problem is how to choose between the owner who has lost his property as a result of fraud, and the innocent third party who has acquired the goods directly or indirectly from the rogue. Despite a well-known dictum from an eminent judge, Devlin LJ (as he then was) in *Ingram* v *Little* [1961] 1 QB 31 to the effect that there should be some way of apportioning the loss between two innocent parties, the law still takes an all or nothing approach. Either the *nemo dat* rule applies in its stark simplicity, namely, a person cannot give a better title than he himself has, thus favouring the owner, or one of the exceptions to the rule is found, favouring the *bona fide* purchaser. This contest is traditionally summed up by quoting Denning LJ in *Bishopsgate Motor Finance Corpn. Ltd* v *Transport Brakes Ltd* [1949] 1 KB 332, at pp. 336-7 as follows:

> In the development of our law, two principles have striven for mastery. The first is for the protection of property; no-one can give a better title than he himself possesses. The second is for the protection of commercial transactions: the person who takes in good faith and for value without notice should get a better title. The first principle has held sway for a long time, but it has been modified by the common law itself and by statute so as to meet the needs of our times.

A student, on reading this statement, might be forgiven for thinking that the progression of the law in this area has been orderly; in truth it has been a haphazard and piecemeal development which seems to base the result of any case upon arbitrary and unjust distinctions, for example, the rule in market overt and the requirement that sale must be between sunrise and sunset for it to be a valid exception to the *nemo dat* rule. Indeed, after reading and coming to the end of the chapter on *nemo dat* in any text book, a student's impression might be that the adherence to the *nemo dat* rule is purely historical. One might wonder whether the rule exists in any real sense nowadays. It surely is a case of the rule proving the exception? By now you should have gathered that this area of law may well be one which examiners delight in exploring in examination questions, hedged as it is with difficulty and seemingly arbitrary rules. In addition, there is a considerable overlap with material previously studied, possibly in your torts course, i.e., conversion and trespass to goods. A good understanding of this area is important to an understanding of the *nemo dat* rule (see chapter 12 of our SWOT, *Law of Torts*, on interference with goods). The discussion which follows should only be regarded as a commentary on certain aspects of the law relating to the various exceptions. It assumes that students have done the basic reading of cases and textbooks on the *nemo dat* rule.

Estoppel   Section 21 of the Sale of Goods Act 1979 sets out the basic rule of *nemo dat*, but itself goes on to spell out two possible exceptions, agency and estoppel. We propose to consider the estoppel exemption only here. It is worth remarking that it is thought that there are two types of estoppel:

(a)   that established by words or conduct, whereby the owner is precluded from denying the seller's authority to sell; and
(b)   that where there is a negligent failure to act, which again results in the owner being unable to deny the seller's authority to sell.

Estoppel by words or conduct is clearly recognised and well established and it is not proposed to discuss the detail here. However, it is a common mistake to assume that by merely allowing another person to have possession of goods which he does not own, this operates as estoppel (see *Central Newbury Car Auctions Ltd* v *Unity Finance Ltd* [1957] 1 QB 371).

Estoppel by negligence is a much more interesting, though as we shall see restricted development, and one upon which an examiner might wish to test you. The major point to recognise is that the notion of estoppel by negligence is dependent upon establishing that a duty of care is owed by the party to the person alleging estoppel. Just how difficult this may be is shown by the approach of the House of Lords in the leading case of *Moorgate Mercantile Co Ltd* v *Twitchings* [1977] AC 890. In that case it was held by a majority, that there was no duty upon a member of H. P. Information Ltd to register hire-purchase agreements with that organisation, even though in practice there was heavy reliance by members and non-members upon information held by that company about vehicles subject to hire-purchase agreements. The failure to register in this case had resulted in the defendant's buying a vehicle subject to a hire-purchase agreement. The plaintiffs were not estopped because the House decided that they did not owe a duty to register in the first place, whether to members or non-members. The rules of the company have now been altered to make it compulsory on members to register agreements. This will give members as between themselves a contractual action, but probably does not alter the position of the non-member. This would seem to be anomalous, bearing in mind the substantial reliance placed upon H.P. Information Ltd by all in the motor and finance trades.

It should be remembered that the application of estoppel is limited to those who are privy to it, and those claiming under them. This means that an estoppel cannot operate against a person claiming under title paramount. For example, a car is stolen by B from A, B sells it to C, who in some way becomes estopped as against D. C is prevented by the estoppel from asserting any claim to the car as against D or those claiming under D. However, the estoppel cannot operate as against A, the original owner. This point is often overlooked. It has also recently been held that s. 21 and estoppel may only operate where there has been a sale as opposed to an agreement to sell (see *Shaw* v *The Commissioner of Metropolitan Police and Natalegawa* [1987] 1 WLR 1332).

Mercantile agents   We shall now turn to a very complex and technical area of the *nemo dat* rule, that concerning 'mercantile agents'. We emphasise that we shall be commenting only on the difficult and noteworthy points and will assume that you have sufficient knowledge of the basic elements of this exception to the rule. In particular, we assume that you are familiar with the wording of s. 2 of the Factors Act 1889 which sets out the 'mercantile agent' exception to the *nemo dat* rule.

The issue as to whether a person is such an agent has its difficulties. Section 1(1) of the Factors Act 1889 (see also s. 26 of the Sale of Goods Act 1979) defines such a person as:

> a mercantile agent having in the customary course of his business as such agent authority either to sell goods or to consign goods for the purpose of sale, or to buy goods, or to raise money on the security of goods.

It seems that a person may be such an agent even though he does not carry on the business of a mercantile agent, and even though he has never acted as one before.

Such a person must actually be in possession of goods or of documents of title to goods with the 'consent of the owner'. The meaning of the latter phrase has caused some difficulties where the owner has been persuaded to give up possession as a result of fraud. It was argued that in such circumstances the agent was not in possession with the owner's consent, but it appears from the Court of Appeal decision in *Pearson* v *Rose & Young Ltd* [1951] 1 KB 275 that such argument was laid to rest.

Further, the agent must be in possession of the goods with the consent of the owner for a purpose which is in some way connected with the business of the agent as mercantile agent. For example, a car handed over to the garage for repair would not fall within this exception, even if the garage in question dealt in the sale of cars. Of course, the *bona fide* purchaser may have no idea of the purpose for which the goods were entrusted to the garage; nonetheless, he or she will be affected by the fact.

It should also be noted that the mercantile agent exception only applies where the sale is in the ordinary course of business. As Atiyah points out (p. 284) this cannot be taken literally, as a sale without the authority of the owner can hardly be 'in the ordinary course of business'. However, the correct interpretation is probably that the sale must 'appear' to be in the ordinary course of business. Anything which puts the third party purchaser on notice or gives an indication that takes the transaction out of the ordinary, will presumably take the situation outside the scope of this exception. In *Pearson* v *Rose & Young* (above) the Court of Appeal held that a sale without a registration book would not be a sale within the ordinary course of business. This particular decision seems to fly in the face of the practical realities, as it is quite common for a transaction of a motor vehicle to take place without the registration document.

This particular exception to the *nemo dat* rule is riddled with technicalities. The crucial point here is that the third party's rights are dependent on such technicalities. This point was recognised by the Law Reform Committee in their Twelfth Report (*Transfer of Title to Chattels*, Cmnd. 2958, para. 18). However, the particular recommendation (paras. 30-31) which would have improved the position of the purchaser of goods on retail premises have regrettably not been enacted. Thus, the 'mercantile agent' exception may still operate in its rather arbitrary fashion.

Sales in market overt   Another *nemo dat* exception which operates in a similar way is that relating to 'sales in market overt'. The historical reasons for this rule may have originally been acceptable, but nowadays there is little justification for such a rule operating as it may do in an arbitrary manner. The ridiculous nature of the exception is perhaps best shown in the decision in *Reid* v *Commissioner of Metropolitan Police* [1973] QB 551, where it was said that the sale must be between the hours of sunrise and sunset. The Law Reform Committee (para. 31) recognised the capricious nature of the rule and recommended its abolition or extension to cover retail sales off trade premises as well as sales by auction. Neither of these steps has been taken. The extraordinary aspect of this exception is that the title of the original and true owner can be completely extinguished according to whether or not the sale took place a few inches within a recognised market and a few seconds before sunset or after sunrise.

Seller in possession/buyer in possession   There are two other exceptions to the *nemo dat* rule contained in the Factors Act 1889, ss. 8 and 9, although these are to some extent duplicated in the Sale of Goods Act 1979 (see ss. 24 and 25). This duplication of itself may cause some confusion for students; in addition, as with the mercantile agent exception, the sections themselves are far from straightforward.

(a)   *Seller in possession*   This exception relates to the situation where A has sold goods to B, but has retained possession (rightly or wrongly, as the case may be). A subsequently sells or agrees to sell (or otherwise dispose) of the goods to C, a *bona fide* third party. If the goods or documents of title are delivered or transferred to C by A, then C will have acquired title under this section. A, of course, will be in breach of contract to B, but this has no effect whatsoever on C's position. It should be noted that it does not matter that the disposition to C is only an agreement for sale, as opposed to a sale, C will still be protected. Nor does it matter that the disposition by A is outside the ordinary course of business (c.f., the mercantile agent exception).

(b)   *Buyer in possession*   This is, of course, the reverse situation of that discussed immediately above, namely, a person who has agreed to buy goods is given possession of the goods or of documents of title, although the property has not yet passed to him. He then sells the goods to a *bona fide* third party. Provided the requirements of s. 9 of the Factors Act 1889 are satisfied, the third party will obtain good title as against the original seller. It should be noted immediately that a purchaser under a hire-purchase agreement is not a person who has 'bought or agreed to buy goods', and nor is a buyer under a 'conditional sale' agreement regulated by the Consumer Credit Act 1974 (see *Helby* v *Matthews* [1895] AC 471 and s. 25(2)(a) of the Sale of Goods Act 1979). Nonetheless, as we shall see below, there are special provisions in relation to motor vehicles being purchased under hire-purchase or conditional sale agreements. Further, it should be noted that the buyer must be in possession of the goods or documents of title with the consent of the seller, before the innocent third party is protected. We have already discussed the meaning of 'consent' in the context of the 'mercantile agent' exception above. The only other comment we wish to make on this particular exception focuses upon the rather curious wording of s. 9 as compared with s. 8 (seller in possession). A disposition by a buyer under s. 9 is to have the same effect 'as if the person making the delivery or transfer were a mercantile agent in possession of the goods or documents or title with the consent of the owner'.

You should note the extremely narrow interpretation placed on this wording by the Court of Appeal in *Newtons of Wembley Ltd* v *Williams* [1965] 1 QB 560, where it was said that it had to be shown that the sale by the buyer in possession was 'in the ordinary course of business of a mercantile agent'. This would have the effect of making this particular exception subject to the qualifications relating to the 'mercantile agent' exception under s. 2 of the 1889 Act. The better view seems to be that the disposition by the buyer is to be treated merely as if he were a mercantile agent (see Atiyah, pp. 301-2).

Part III of the Hire-Purchase Act 1964   The final exception we propose to discuss was referred to briefly above in the context of the 'buyer in possession' exception. From a practical point of view it is probably the most important and interesting of the exceptions, thus constituting a favourite topic for any commercial law examiner. The exception is that created by Part III of the Hire-Purchase Act 1964 (as re-enacted in the Consumer Credit Act 1974, Schedule 4), whereby a *bona fide* purchaser of a motor vehicle held under a hire-purchase or conditional sale agreement by the 'seller' may acquire a good title to the vehicle as against the creditor/owner. As we have seen the person in possession of the vehicle under a hire-purchase agreement, or a conditional sale agreement (within the Consumer Credit Act 1974) is not a person who has 'bought or agreed to buy goods' under s. 9 of the Factors Act 1889. However, s. 27 of the 1964 Act creates a specific exception to the *nemo dat* rule in respect of motor vehicles held under such agreements.

The main point to note about this exception is that the benefit of the protection is only extended to those who may be regarded as 'private purchasers', namely a purchaser other than a 'trade or finance purchaser'. This does not mean that a business purchaser cannot get the protection: trade or finance purchaser means a dealer in motor vehicles or a person providing finance for the acquisition of vehicles under hire-purchase or conditional sale agreements. The philosophy behind this restriction is that a trade or finance purchaser should be in a better position to protect his own interests, e.g., by making a search of H.P.I. Ltd. You should be aware of the impact of the decision in *Stevenson* v *Beverley Bentinck Ltd* [1976] 2 All ER 606 which focusses precisely on this particular distinction between private and trade or finance purchasers. According to the Court of Appeal it is the status of the third party buyer which is to be considered, not the capacity in which he is making the particular purchase. The purchaser in that case carried on business as a part-time car dealer; it was held that he was a trade purchaser, despite the fact that the vehicle was being acquired for his own, private use.

One final point that is worth noting on this exception concerns the meaning of 'disposition' by the hirer or buyer. It appears that this can be an outright sale, an agreement to sell and a hire-purchase agreement. So if, for example, the innocent third party were to enter into a hire-purchase agreement with the hirer or buyer, then, provided he was a private purchaser, he would fall within this exception.

Passing of property and risk

So far we have considered the position where it turns out that the seller happens to have no or an inferior title to goods. We have seen what the buyer from that seller may be able to do about it if there is a breach of s. 12 of the Sale of Goods Act 1979. We have also seen that, in a significant number of instances, a buyer may be able to establish title under one of the *nemo dat* exceptions. We must now turn to the situation where the seller does have title, or property in the goods. The issues that arise here all too frequently concern the issue as to when the property, if at all, passes to the buyer and, in the meantime, who shall bear the risk of accidental loss or damage to the goods in question. This is another area which is far from straightforward. Indeed, the standard textbook, Atiyah, spends more time discussing this topic than the *nemo dat* exceptions, although some of this discussion focusses on whether there is a distinction between 'property' and 'title' in goods. Atiyah comes to the conclusion (at p. 217) that the only way to understand what is meant by this 'peculiar legal conception' is to consider the consequences which flow from the mere passing of property and contrast these with the consequences which follow when the buyer has acquired full title which binds both parties. The main consequence so far as we are concerned here of the passing of property in goods, is that *normally* risk of accidental loss passes with property (s. 20 SOGA 1979). The Sale of Goods Act 1979 contains a series of complex rules designed to decide the issue as to when property is to pass under a contract for the sale of goods. These rules are contained in ss. 16-18 of the Act and we assume you are familiar with these provisions. We propose to confine our comments to a number of important points. The rules start with the basic premise that property passes when the parties intend it to pass. As usual, there will often be little express indication of their intention and, consequently, s. 18 sets out five rules provided to govern the property issue in different situations.

Secondly, the application of the rules is dependent on the fundamental distinction between 'specific' and 'unascertained' goods. You should ensure that you fully understand this distinction, but be warned, as Atiyah points out, the meaning of specific goods does not appear to be consistent throughout the 1979 Act (see discussion on s. 13 and, in particular, *Beale* v *Taylor* (above)).

We propose to make only a few comments about the rules in s. 18. A word of warning is essential: remember that these rules may be displaced by a contrary intention, which may be gathered from the terms of the contract, the conduct of the parties and the surrounding circumstances (see s. 17(2)). Rule I is concerned with an 'unconditional contract for the sale of specific goods in a deliverable state' and states that property passes when the contract is made, irrespective of matters of time of payment and delivery. Straightaway we meet the problem of what is meant by 'specific goods', to which we referred earlier. There is little authority on what is meant by 'unconditional' or 'in a deliverable state'. The former may merely mean that the contract must not be subject to either a condition precedent or subsequent. The latter does not seem to be concerned with issues of quality despite s. 61(5) of the Act which says that goods are in 'a deliverable state' in circumstances where the buyer would under the contract be bound to take delivery of them. In *Underwood Ltd* v *Burgh Castle Brick and Cement Syndicate* [1922] 1 KB 343 it was held that property in an engine could not have passed until it had been detached from the floor to which it was cemented. Apart from that case there has been little litigation on the point.

As to when Rule 1 might be displaced by contrary intention, you should be aware of the important statement of Diplock LJ in *R. V. Ward Ltd* v *Bignall* [1967] 1 QB 534 (at p. 545) where he suggested that in modern times very little evidence is needed to rebut the inference that property passes on the making of the contract. This is extremely useful in the context of a consumer sale as it is highly likely that a court would infer that property did not pass until delivery.

Rules 2 and 3 raise few difficulties and appear relatively straightforward. Rule 4 deals with goods on approval or sale or return terms, common enough in practice. Most of the litigation has been concerned with the circumstances in which a buyer on sale or return is taken to have done some 'act adopting the transaction'. There is here some overlap with problems arising in the context of reservation of title (Romalpa) clauses, which you should appreciate. You should also note the other situations in which property will pass in a sale or return contract, namely, where after a fixed or reasonable time the buyer retains the goods without giving notice of rejection. The case of *Poole* v *Smith's Car Sales (Balham) Ltd* [1962] 2 All ER 482 is often a useful one to know in questions of this type.

Rule 5 often presents more problems in practice, dealing as it does with the passing of property in unascertained goods. With mass-produced goods most contracts will be for unascertained goods. Note that property cannot pass until the goods became ascertained (s. 16). Rule 5 then comes into its own and frequently provides the way of deciding whether property has passed. You will see, when reading this rule, that it refers to an 'unconditional appropriation' and this is the major element within it. A useful illustration of what this means can be seen in the case of *Healy* v *Howlett & Sons* [1917] 1 KB 337. The leading case, however, is *Carlos Federspiel & Co. SA* v *Charles Twigg & Co. Ltd* [1957] 1 Lloyd's Rep 240, a case to be aware of if you are expecting to answer a question on passing of property. You should pay particular regard to the clear statement by Pearson J, where he talks of the appropriating act being normally the last act to be performed by the seller.

As was indicated at the outset the major consequence of the passing of property is that the risk of accidental loss or damage to the goods normally passes also. This transference of risk is laid out in s. 20 of the 1979 Act. It is important to note that this may be affected by contrary intention in circumstances where it is clear that a person is intended to bear the risk although the property is not vested in him (see, e.g., *Sterns Ltd* v *Vickers Ltd* [1923] 1 KB 78). The impact of insurance cannot be ignored in this context. Indeed, Atiyah (at p. 250) observes: 'The question of who should bear the risk of accidental destruction, . . ., boils down in modern conditions to who should be required to insure them.' This may have nothing at all to do with the passing of property.

One further point is that we are here only talking about the risk of accidental loss or damage and the normal rule will not apply where loss or damage has arisen through the fault of one of the parties (see s. 20(2) and (3)).

Risk, whilst connected to some extent with the frustration of contract principle, must be distinguished from it. If applicable, frustration discharges the parties from future obligations, as you will no doubt recall from your contract law classes. You will also remember that the frustration principle at common law is extremely narrow in its scope. The 1979 Act (s. 7) provides that a contract for specific goods where property has not passed may be frustrated if the goods perish, without fault of either party. You should note that the Law Reform (Frustrated Contracts) Act 1943 does *not* apply to contracts frustrated by virtue of the provision in s. 7. Therefore if s. 7 does apply to a contract, the common law rule that the loss must lie where it falls will be applicable.

Section 7 is very narrow in its scope. It will only apply where the property has not already passed to the buyer and, as we are here concerned with specific goods under s. 18 Rule 1, this will normally happen at the time the contract is made. Would the common law principle apply to other contracts for the sale of goods, other than those for specific goods? As you know the common law principle is itself very restricted, and there will be very few occasions indeed where a contract for unascertained goods will be adjudged frustrated. One example might be where there is a contract to sell a quantity of unascertained goods from a *specific* source (see *Howell* v *Coupland* (1876) LR 1 QBD 258) and the source is subsequently destroyed. That type of situation apart, a seller is unlikely to be successful in relying upon frustration as excusing non-performance of his obligation to deliver where the goods are generic in nature. One final warning is perhaps needed; remember, do not confuse the situation where goods perish *before* the contract is made (mistake as to existence of the subject matter, see s. 6, 1979 Act) and situations where the goods perish *after* contract.

Reservation of title by unpaid seller

The issue of passing of property has spawned a large amount of litigation in the last decade in the context of reservation of title clauses (Romalpa). You are no doubt well familiar with what is meant by this type of clause which first raised its head in this form in the well-known case of *Aluminium Industrie Vaasen BV* v *Romalpa Aluminium Ltd* [1976] 1 WLR 676. We would anticipate that a question on this area might well be popular with examiners of commercial law for some time to come. However, you should be clear as to whether this topic is within the syllabus. Some law schools may well include this topic in company law, insolvency law or even equity syllabuses! We do not propose to go through the case law to any extent as often the issue is one of a drafting nature. Whether a clause is effective to reserve title to the seller as against the buyer's receiver depends upon the skill of the lawyer drafting the appropriate clause.Where the clause is seeking to reserve title in raw materials which may become incorporated in a finished product, there are strict requirements if the clause is to be successful. In appropriate cases a seller may have to register a charge under the Companies Act (see *Re Bond Worth Ltd* [1980] Ch 228 and *Re Peachdart Ltd* [1983] 3 All ER 204). There are a number of other cases on this topic and you will need to be familiar with the majority of them if you are to answer a question with any degree of success.

In conclusion we can see that the areas of law considered in this chapter are technical and complex within themselves; the interrelationship between issues of title, passing of property and risk further complicate the picture. In our specimen examination question below we cannot hope to cover all or any where near all the matters discussed above. However, we imagine that the question may well be representative of its type and may enable you to approach some aspects of this highly technical area with a little more confidence.

Illustrative question

On 1 April Ossie, the hirer of a car on hire-purchase from Easimoney Ltd, returned it to Tottenham Motors, the dealer in the original transaction. He informed the dealer that he could no longer keep up the payments. The dealer did not inform Easimoney Ltd and ten days later the car was sold to Ricci for cash, the dealer having told Ricci that the car had been on hire-purchase but was no longer so. Tottenham Motors continued to pay the instalments under Ossie's agreement with Easimoney Ltd.

On 1 May Ricci, having carried out some repairs to the car, sold it to Stamford Motors, the latter having checked with H.P. Information Ltd which stated that it had no record of any outstanding agreement in respect of the vehicle. A few days later Stamford Motors sold the vehicle to Cushy Credit Ltd (which did not bother to contact H.P. Information). Cushy Credit Ltd in turn let the car on hire-purchase to Glen.

Tottenham Motors stop paying the instalments on the original agreement and the car is traced to Glen. Advise him.

Commentary

At first sight this may appear to be a difficult and complex question. Often first impressions are correct. This is not an easy question because it contains a number of transactions and parties. Although you are asked to advise Glen, in order to do this you must trace through the various dealings to ascertain their validity (if any). In an examination context, this problem might produce some panic in the minds of most students and might therefore be passed over in favour of something which appears more straightforward and less demanding. However, as we and other authors in this series have said, no doubt many times, any difficult problem is capable of being mastered sufficiently well, if the approach is right. Some careful organisation may transform the problem into a manageable one and at the same time impress your examiner with your clarity of thought. The only useful way to approach this question is to go through the various transactions in chronological order. As we are asked to advise Glen he will presumably want to know:

(a)   Can I insist on keeping the vehicle or am I obliged to return it to Easimoney Ltd?
(b)   If I have to return it, have I any rights against any other person in respect of my loss?

Ossie and Easimoney Ltd

The issues as between these two parties are straightforward. We are told the agreement is a hire-purchase agreement and consequently property, ownership or title, whatever you wish to call it, does not pass to Ossie, he merely has a right to possession with an option to purchase. It might be possible to argue that Ossie has voluntarily terminated the hire-purchase agreement at common law, or, if it is a regulated agreement under the Consumer Credit Act 1974, under s. 99 of that Act. On the facts this seems unlikely, as it appears he has struck some kind of deal with Tottenham Motors. Whatever the arrangements are, Ossie is clearly in breach of the hire-purchase agreement. In any event, whether it is regarded as voluntary termination (see chapter 10) or breach of contract, Easimoney Ltd are entitled as against Ossie to recover the vehicle, subject to the Consumer Credit Act 1974 (see chapter 10).

Easimoney Ltd and Tottenham Motors

The question to be resolved here is whether Ossie has in some way transferred title to Tottenham Motors, even though he himself does not have title, under one of the *nemo dat* exceptions. Ossie is not a 'buyer in possession' within the Factors Acts 1889 (see *Helby* v *Matthews* [1895] AC 471), nor is it likely that the deal between himself took place in market overt.

In any event Tottenham Motors are hardly *bona fide* third parties, a normal requirement of all of the exceptions. Part III of the Hire-Purchase Act 1964 is of little use for that reason, as well as the fact that Tottenham Motors are obviously a trade purchaser. Therefore, if we were to freeze the picture at this stage, Easimoney Ltd would have an action in conversion against Tottenham Motors and would be able to recover the vehicle from the latter.

Easimoney Ltd and Ricci

There would seem to be only three possibilities, two of which are somewhat remote, of Ricci being able to establish title as against the finance company. The first of these is the market overt exception. On the facts we cannot answer this as we are not told when and where the transaction took place, i.e., was it a recognised market, did the sale take place between sunrise and sunset? This rather arbitrary exception to *nemo dat* will only arise infrequently and it is not likely to help Ricci here.

One of the other possibilities is Part III of the Hire-Purchase Act 1964. Despite the fact that Ricci is told, falsely as it happens, that the vehicle was the subject of a hire-purchase agreement which had been paid off, this will not of itself prevent him from being 'a private purchaser' within the provisions of the legislation (see *Barker* v *Bell* [1971] 1 WLR 983). However, for this exception to apply the disposition of the vehicle under the hire-purchase agreement must normally be carried out by the hirer, i.e., Ossie. It is clear that Easimoney Ltd have not consented to Tottenham Motors being in possession, nor can their consent be inferred. However, s. 27(3) of the 1964 Act does provide for this situation, stating that in circumstances such as these a private purchaser may take the benefit of the exception where a trade or finance purchaser is the first purchaser. As pointed out earlier Ricci must be a *bona fide* private purchaser wihout notice and as long as he has no reason to suspect what he is told by Tottenham Motors, he will get good title under this exception. This would mean that so long as all the other intermediate purchasers bought without notice and were *bona fide*, Glen's title to the vehicle would be established.

The final possibility is that the transaction between Tottenham Motors and Ricci is a sale by a mercantile agent. The major problem facing Ricci would be the question as to whether it could be said Tottenham Motors were in possession of the vehicle with the consent of the owner, Easimoney. Clearly there is no express consent. Of itself would the fact that Tottenham Motors Ltd were making the repayments amount to implied knowledge and thus consent? It seems highly unlikely.

So it seems that there is a reasonable possibility that Ricci has obtained good title under the 1964 Act. However, we are not in possession of all the facts and this is one of those occasions when you should proceed further on the assumption that he does not get good title.

Easimoney Ltd and Stamford Motors

We have assumed so far that Ricci is a private purchaser. If we continue to make that assumption, which seems justified on the facts, is there any way in which Stamford Motors can claim that they have acquired title through Ricci? Clearly the mercantile agent provision cannot apply. The 1964 Act will not aid them as they are trade purchasers. Ricci may be a buyer in possession, but this is of little use because all that he can transfer under that exception would be the title of Tottenham Motors, which was only possessory at the time. In any event such title as Tottenham Motors had would have passed to Ricci under s. 18 of the Sale of Goods Act 1979 (Rule 1). This latter point should bring home to you the very important point that the notion of the title (ownership) is a relative one. In other words, a person normally only has to show that he has a better title than the person claiming against him.

Stamford Motors might perhaps try to argue estoppel as against Easimoney Ltd. Estoppel to be successful here would be estoppel by negligence, i.e., omission, a failure to register the agreement with HPI, unless both Easimoney and Stamford Motors were both members of HPI. In this latter case Stamford would have a contractual action for damages or at least be able to set up an estoppel against Easimoney, as the rules of HPI now require members to register. However, if either or both parties are not members, Stamford must establish that they are owed a duty of care, that there was a breach of duty which caused their loss. They are likely to fall down on the first point in that the House of Lords was reluctant to extend the duty relationship in this type of situation (see *Moorgate Mercantile Credit* v *Twitchings* (above)). It would seem, therefore, that Stamford Motors would be in no position to establish that they had anything other than a mere possessory title which would not succeed as against Easimoney Ltd.

Easimoney Ltd and Cushy Credit Ltd

As between these two which will have the better title? Cushy Credit will naturally look to the exceptions to establish title. Which (if any) are likely to assist them? The only realistic prospect would appear to be the sale by mercantile agent exception, but their problem would be very similar to that of Ricci discussed earlier. It would surely not be possible for them to show that Stamford Motors, mercantile agents or not, were in possession of the vehicle with the consent of the owner. Quite the reverse, Easimoney would clearly not consent in such circumstances. Cushy Credit Ltd would probably not be able to establish title and would be liable in conversion to Easimoney (this assumes, of course, that Ricci did not get good title under Part III of the 1964 Act, discussed earlier).

Easimoney Ltd and Glen

We have at last reached the person who requires the advice. As mentioned earlier if Ricci did get good title, then all those following, provided they were in good faith, would get title, including Glen. However, assuming that not to be the case, what are Glen's prospects of being able to establish a right to keep the vehicle as against Easimoney Ltd? We can answer this in a fairly straightforward way. His chances are extremely poor. The only possibility would be Part III of the 1964 Act, but his problem here would be that if Ricci failed to get title, being the first private purchaser, because he had notice or was not in good faith, it seems that *no subsequent* purchaser may obtain title under Part III of the Act of 1964 (see s. 27(3)). In these circumstances we consider that Glen would not be able to establish title as against Easimoney.

We now need to consider Glen's contractual rights (if any) against Cushy Credit Ltd, even if he has in some way acquired a title under Part III or not. If he has such title, it is obviously not as marketable as the title he should have had, because the car is subject to a hire-purchase agreement. So even though Easimoney may not be able to recover the vehicle, prospective purchasers who have notice of the agreement will not get a good title through Glen. His opportunity, for resale will, therefore, be limited. Can he claim against Cushy for breach of contract? The answer now lies in Schedule 4 to the Consumer Credit Act 1974 which contains the implied obligations in hire-purchase agreements. There is an implied condition as to title in Schedule 4 (which cannot be excluded, see s. 6 Unfair Contract Terms Act 1977), and it is clear that Cushy Ltd will be in breach of this. If Easimoney have established they are entitled to the vehicle, then clearly Glen can recover any monies paid under the hire-purchase agreement with Cushy, together with any foreseeable consequential losses. If, however, he has been able to establish title against Easimoney Ltd he may wish to repudiate the hire-purchase agreement and again recover any monies paid under that agreement and consequential loss. On the other hand he may wish to keep the vehicle and claim damages from Cushy to reflect the difference in value of the car as it is, with a defective title, and as it should have been if Cushy had had the right to sell.

That concludes our commentary on the question. You will have realised that this is an extremely tricky area of sale of goods law and one which is frequently misunderstood. If you are to answer a question successfully, you need a good understanding of the notions of title, property and risk. It is really little use having very good knowledge of, say, title on its own. We hope that we have made this area a little more intelligible and have given you more confidence when tackling a question on these topics.

SEVEN

DEFECTIVE GOODS AND SERVICES: LIABILITY IN TORT

Introduction

In this chapter we propose to examine the legal position of those persons who fall outside the doctrine of privity of contract and whose action for any injury, loss or damage caused by 'defective' goods or services will lie only in tort — usually in the tort of negligence. Students will be aware that hitherto the benefit of the statutory reforms concerning the quality of goods and services, dealt with in our earlier chapters, have largely been confined within the privity rule. Purchasing consumers are, in a very real sense, a privileged minority by comparison with the vast majority of persons at risk from defective goods and services who have no contractual claim. This larger body of people includes members of the purchaser's own family (see *Preist* v *Last* [1903] 2 KB 148; *Daniels and Daniels* v *White & Sons and Tarbard* [1938] 4 All ER 258). Where goods which are subject to 'latent defects' (i.e., defects not discoverable by reasonable skill and care) are used to provide a service to the public and cause injury or damage, the injured person's only action may well be in tort against the manufacturer of the goods. (See *Davie* v *New Merton Board Mills Ltd* [1959] AC 604. Although the effect of the decision has been reversed with regard to injured employees by the Employer's Liability (Defective Equipment) Act 1969, it still holds good in the general area of product liability.) The negligently performed car repair may put at risk not merely the life of the unsuspecting driver but also the lives of many other road users (see *Stennett* v *Hancock and Peters* [1939] 2 All ER 578). No contractual action will lie in respect of the injurious side effects of drugs which are obtained by way of prescription under the National Health Service (see *Pfizer Corpn.* v *Ministry of Health* [1965] AC 512; *Appleby* v *Sleep* [1968] 1 WLR 948).

One would have difficulty in refuting the proposition that the public at large is more at risk from defective goods and services in circumstances in which the only claim in respect of any injury, loss or damage sustained, will lie in tort. Despite its practical significance the law of tort has remained in an unacceptable state for many years. The inadequacies of the fault-based system were most forcefully demonstrated by the Thalidomide tragedy which led to the establishment of the Royal Commission on Civil Liability and Compensation for Personal Injury (Cmnd. 7054) (The Pearson Commission). Almost ten years after the publication of the Commission's Report, some important changes in the civil law are at last imminent with the proposed introduction of so-called 'strict liability' under Part I of the Consumer Protection Act 1987. The nature and effect of the major provisions in Part I of the Act are central to this chapter. Other matters however, also need to be dealt with in order to convey an appreciation of the wider application of tort law, of which the new Act is but a part, albeit a most significant part.

First, a knowledge of the common law principles of negligence and an understanding of their application to particular situations will remain important. This is so not merely as a prerequisite to understanding the importance of the changes brought about by the Act. The new statutory regime is limited in its scope and there will remain a number of situations in which a plaintiff may have to rely upon his rights under the common law which are unaffected by the Act.

The more obvious of these limits is that strict liability is imposed by the Act only upon a 'producer' of defective goods which result in death/injury or damage to the property of a consumer where the damage exceeds £275. Clearly the Act does not cover damage to 'business' property. Nor does the statutory regime enable the recovery of pure economic loss (i.e., loss which is not consequential upon injury or damage to property) irrespective of the status of the plaintiff. Such loss may however be recoverable to a very limited degree under the common law.

Whilst an importer may be regarded as a 'producer' under the Act (see s. 2(2)(c)) it is by no means inconceivable that a statutory claim against a 'producer' may be worthless, where for example a defendant company may have gone into liquidation. The plaintiff may however succeed under the common law against some other person in the chain of distribution, provided of course he can establish negligence. Similarly, in certain circumstances the limitations period applicable to an action under the common law may be more favourable than that which applies to a statutory claim. Finally, we should recognise that the 1987 Act has no application to the producers of 'defective' services. In that respect the law of torts now repeats the distinction which exists in the law of contract, namely, some form of strict liability applies with respect to defective goods but liability for defective services remains firmly rooted in negligence. In the light of these observations we have approached the substantive difficulties arising from the broad issue of tortious liablity for defective goods and services under three heads.

Substantive difficulties

Personal injury and damage to property: The common law

At common law a manufacturer of goods may be liable for injury or damage under the principle enunciated by Lord Atkin in *M'Alister (or Donoghue) (Pauper)* v *Stevenson* [1932] AC 562 (at p. 599). Potential liability extends not merely to the user of goods but also to 'bystanders' (see *Lambert* v *Lewis* [1979] RTR 61: *Stennett* v *Hancock and Peters* (above)). In subsequent cases the principle has been extended and applied to persons in the chain of distribution other than the manufacturer (see *Fisher* v *Harrods Ltd* [1966] 1 Lloyd's Rep 500; *Watson* v *Buckley, Osborne, Garrett & Co. Ltd and Wyrovoys Products Ltd* [1940] 1 All ER 174).

The statistics contained in chapter 22 of the Pearson Commission Report (paras. 1201-1202, 1218) show that under the present law manufacturers appear to shoulder surprisingly little legal responsibility for injury/damage caused by defective products. The Commission considered that the present law was ineffectual as a means of providing compensation and had little if any measurable effect upon raising quality standards. This situation is the result of numerous interrelated, practical, procedural and substantive difficulties. Certain of these difficulties may be isolated and placed on one side, for they are not within the province of this book. The less than generous Legal Aid system for example, is believed to be an important reason why claims may not be pursued with the vigour they merit.

The difficulties which students experience in gaining an understanding of the law and how it operates stem to some degree from the conceptualised nature of the law of negligence itself. The complex concepts of duty, breach, causation and remoteness of damage, which have been developed in the wider law of negligence, have to be applied to the particular factual situations which arise in the context of the production and distribution of goods. Understanding the interrelationship between these various concepts is made the more difficult in a branch of law 'which is bedevilled by slovenly terminology'. Where for example a consumer injures himself using a product which he knows to be defective, is the decision against the imposition of liability upon the manufacturer based upon the absence of duty or causation (see *Street on Torts*, 7th ed. at p. 170; contrast *The Diamantis Pateras* [1966] 1 Lloyd's Rep 179 at p. 188)? In our experience a number of students, under examination conditions, tend not to demonstrate the depth of analysis required of a good answer. This seems to hold true in both problem and essay questions. This remains a matter of some surprise (and disappointment) to us, given that most students will have previously studied the principles of negligence within a Law of Torts syllabus.

Certain students appear to have a blinkered view of the potential liability which may fall upon a manufacturer. They often fail to show any real appreciation that liabliity in negligence may arise not merely as a result of a physical or functional defect in the product itself (either a manufacturing or design defect), but also, for example, from a failure to adequately warn or advise as to the use of the product (see *Vacwell Engineering Co. Ltd* v *B.D.H. Chemicals Ltd* [1971] 1 QB 111 CA). Perhaps more important than this is the fact that many students seem to be incapable of communicating a clear grasp of the limits of a manufacturer's liability even in those cases involving an alleged defect in the product itself. It is something of a truism to say that the mere fact that a product causes foreseeable harm may not of itself render the manufacturer liable. The present fault-based system substantially reduces such a potentially wide liability. Examination questions on this topic will naturally require students to show an understanding of the process of restriction which occurs via the concepts of duty, breach, causation and remoteness, together with the possible defences such as assumption of risk or contributory negligence, all of which are shaped to some degree by considerations of policy.

The principle which is applicable is that stated by Lord Atkin in *M'Alister (or Donoghue) (Pauper)* v *Stevenson* [1932] AC 562 at p. 599. We believe it useful to reproduce it here, not because it should be treated and interpreted as a statutory provision, but because key phrases in that statement point out some of the substantive issues with which students experience difficulty. In that sense it provides a useful structure for our observations on those issues.

A manufacturer of products, which he sells in such a form as to show that he intends them to reach the consumer in the form in which they left him with no reasonable possibility of intermediate examination and with the knowledge that the absence of reasonable care in the preparation or putting up of the product will result in injury to the consumer's life or property, owes a duty to the consumer to take reasonable care.

We can see from this statement that a duty of care exists in tort with regard to 'defective goods'. Students, however, quite often fail to explain that the concept of a defective product employed here is substantially different from the notion of unmerchantable goods employed in sales law. It seems reasonably clear from Lord Atkin's reference to 'injury to the consumer's life or property' that the duty in tort is confined to goods which are dangerously defective and does not extend to goods which are safe but shoddy. A claim that goods are merely lacking in quality is still regarded as sounding in contract rather than in tort. Only in special circumstances will it be possible to recover from a manufacturer the value of safe but shoddy goods or other pure economic losses. This matter is considered further on p. 134.

The questions as to whether goods are defective in this narrow sense and whether the manufacturer or other distributor has exercised reasonable care are often inextricably related. We have, however, indulged in a degree of artificial separation for the sake of exposition.

Defective goods   Strictly speaking under the common law it has not been necessary to define when products are dangerously defective. This nettle has however been grasped in s. 3 of the 1987 Act, a matter which is considered below. Many students appear not to appreciate the relative nature of this difficult concept. The mere fact that a product has caused foreseeable injury to a consumer may not be sufficient to render it defective in the eyes of the law, for 'it is difficult to think of a product which is totally incapable of causing harm when it is misused' (Miller and Lovell, *Product Liability*, at p. 187). In attempting to come to terms with this notion of defective goods it is absolutely essential to recognise certain basic distinctions which are embodied in the case law. For example goods which are obviously dangerous *per se* (knives, explosives, etc.) may not be defective as such. Whether these and other goods are regarded as being defective will depend to a considerable extent upon the judicial perception of the necessity for, and adequacy of, warnings. This issue is considered further (together with the effect of knowledge which might be acquired by intermediate examination) in the context of causation below.

Of more immediate concern is the broad distinction drawn between 'manufacturing defects' and 'design defects'. The term 'manufacturing defect' is used to describe a defect in a product which results from some failure in the production process itself. Such defects may arise in the context of the actual making or assembly of the product, or through contamination by extraneous material. In so far as such defects are not eliminated prior to distribution, that is seen essentially as a failure of the manufacturer's system of quality control. The goods are in such cases obviously not in the state which the producer intended them to be (see cases such as *M'Alister (or Donoghue)* v *Stevenson* (above); *Grant* v *Australian Knitting Mills Ltd and Others* [1936] AC 85; *Hill* v *James Crowe (Cases) Ltd* [1978] 1 All ER 812).

By contrast the term 'design defect' is used with regard to goods which are in the state the producer intended them to be. The allegations as to the defectiveness here may relate to the basic design of the product, the material from which it is constructed, or that warnings or user instructions were absent or inadequate (see cases such as *Walton and Walton* v *British Leyland Ltd* (1978) unreported, but extracted in Miller and Harvey, *Consumer and Trading Law, Cases and Materials* at p. 159; *Vacwell Engineering Co. Ltd* v *B.D.H. Chemicals Ltd* (above)).

Students generally fail to appreciate the significance of this dichotomy — that the truly contentious substantive issues are likely to vary according to the category into which a particular case falls. For example students quite often make unqualified statements as to the difficulty of proving negligence in product liability cases. Such bold statements disregard the fact that the nature of a manufacturing defect is often such as to allow an inference of fault to be easily drawn (see *Grant* v *Australian Knitting Mills Ltd* (above) per Lord Wright, at p. 251: 'If excess sulphites were left in the garment, that could only be because someone was at fault.'). Nor will the defendant easily rebut such an inference (see *Hill* v *James Crowe (Cases) Ltd* [1978] (above) in which Mackenna J. refused to follow the much criticised decision in *Daniels and Daniels* v *White & Sons and Tarbard* (above)).

By way of contrast, the difficulty of establishing that a defect existed in the product prior to distribution by the manufacturer is more likely to arise in cases involving 'manufacturing defects'. The decision in *Evans* v *Triplex Safety Glass Co. Ltd* [1936] 1 All ER 283 illustrates, *inter alia*, that particular difficulty.

The duty of reasonable care   One essential feature of the concept of defectiveness which may be distilled from the case law is that it does not require absolute safety — the producer or distributor is required to exercise reasonable care. If a court were to conclude that a defendant manufacturer has exercised such care he will not be liable notwithstanding that the product has in fact caused foreseeable harm to a consumer. The generality of the principle of 'reasonable care in all the circumstances' is immediately obvious. In seeking to apply that principle the courts may take into account a wide range of factors. An exercise which demonstrates the involvement of the courts in what is clearly a cost/benefit analysis of considerable complexity which involves consideration of factors such as the likelihood and seriousness of harm; the practicability and cost of obviating or reducing the risk; the social utility of the product in question. Students by and large manage to identify the relevant factors and indeed cite cases in support. The major difficulty which students face lies in assessing the relative weight to be accorded to each of those factors and reaching a conclusion as to the side on which the balance might or should fall. Students should be reassured to learn that examiners do recognise the difficulty in arriving at definitive conclusions on matters such as these.

An examiner might well however seek to establish whether or not students recognise that the courts appear not to apply this cost/benefit analysis with equal rigour between the 'manufacturing' and 'design' defect cases. For example the Privy Council in *Grant* v *Australian Knitting Mills Ltd* (above) were unimpressed by evidence of the low probability of risk (the defendants had previously produced almost five million pairs of underpants without a single complaint of dermatitis). It may well be that in the light of that evidence the court perceived that the economic impact resulting from the imposition of liaiblity was likely to be minimal. By contrast, the economic implications of holding, for example, that a particular model of motor vehicle (of which many thousands have been produced and sold) is negligently designed, may be such as to cause the courts to reflect upon their role in the promotion of safety standards, and to shy away from imposing liability. The issue is then left to Parliament to deal with. An attitude clearly reflected in the decision in *Budden* v *BP Oil Ltd and Another, Albery-Speyer* v *Same and Same* [1980] 124 SJ 376, Court of Appeal (concerning the permitted level of lead in petrol).

There are certain other issues associated with the question of the standard of care required of manufacturers which are frequently misunderstood by students. People generally are required only to guard against foreseeable probabilities rather than fantastic possibilities (see *Bolton* v *Stone* [1951] AC 850). However it must be recognised that 'foreseeability' in this context 'involves a hypothetical person, looking with hindsight at an event which has occurred' (*McLoughlin* v *O'Brian and Others* [1983] 1 AC 410 per Lord Wilberforce at pp. 420-421). Given this degree of hindsight the test is likely to require defendants to guard against risks other than those which were foreseeable at the relevant time. Two very important but distinct points need to be made here. The first is that a defendant's conduct is measured in the light of the then current state of knowledge. The dictum of Lord Wilberforce does not mean that knowledge is attributed to a defendant retrospectively (see *Roe* v *Minister of Health* [1954] 2 QB 66). In the context of product liability cases this is often referred to as the 'state of the art of defence'. Students should be clear that although the matter is one of *defence* under the 1987 Act, under the common law the plaintiff bears the burden of proving that the current state of knowledge was such as to render the accident foreseeable.

This issue is often confused with a quite separate point concerning the relative standard of safety required of products. If a product marketed in 1974 was not defective according to the acceptable standards obtaining at that time, that product would not become defective merely by reason that by 1980 manufacturers had generally improved their specifications and standards.

The question of a plaintiff consumer's sensitivity to products is perhaps more appropriately considered in the context of the relative standard required of manufacturers rather than in the context of causation. In our experience students often do not fully understand this issue nor its relationship with the 'egg shell skull' rule (i.e., that the tortfeasor takes his victim as he finds him). Such points are likely therefore to be commonplace in examination questions.

Where the composition of a product (whether by design or adulteration) is such that an allergic reaction would be caused to people generally (see Grant's case above), the extra damage sustained by the abnormally sensitive plaintiff is recoverable (see *Smith* v *Leech Brain & Co. Ltd* [1962] 2 QB 405). This is so even though the additional damage is of a kind and/or extent which is not foreseeable, so long as it is in fact caused by the product in question.

Given the widespread use of detergents, cosmetics, drugs, etc., it is inevitable that someone, somewhere will be allergic to some products. Whether a manufacturer is held liable to an extra sensitive consumer (where the product does not harm users generally) will depend largely upon the number of such persons who are adversely affected by the product. Liability may arise provided such persons are not 'altogether exceptional' (per Denning LJ in *Board* v *Thomas Hedley & Co. Ltd* [1951] 2 All ER 431 CA, at p. 432). Provided the sensitivities of a small group are known or ought to have been known to the manufacturer, the question of liability would turn upon the factors considered above, including the seriousness of the likely injury and the practicability and adequacy of warnings or pre-user tests.

Causation and remoteness of damage Some students experience considerable difficulty with regard to the principles of causation and remoteness of damage and the application of those principles in the context of the production and distribution of goods.

We need to deal first with the issue of 'cause in fact'. The so-called 'but for' test which is applied is simply a preliminary test which eliminates from consideration those cases in which the plaintiff cannot show on a balance of probabilities that the defective product in fact caused (wholly or partially) the injury or damage which he has sustained. In *Grant* v *Australian Knitting Mills Ltd* (above) the Privy Council reversed the decision of the lower court on this very point, holding that there was sufficient evidence, albeit circumstantial, to establish that the plaintiff's dermatitis was caused by an excess of sulphites in the underpants manufactured by the defendants (see especially Lord Wright [1936] AC 85 PC at p. 96). Whilst the problems here will tend to be evidentiary rather than substantive, examiners may well include such issues in examination questions either expressly or by implication. Students may be well advised therefore to ensure that they understand how a plaintiff in such a case might be assisted by the decision of the House of Lords in *McGhee* v *National Coal Board* [1973] 1 WLR 1 together with the implications of the more recent decision in *Hotson* v *East Berkshire Area Health Authority* [1987] 2 All ER 909.

Assuming that cause in a physical sense is established the question arises as to whether the manufacturer is liable for all the damage which results from the defective product. Students should realise that the basic principles of remoteness of damage will apply, the manufacturer being liable only with respect to that type of harm which was reasonably foreseeable (see *The Wagon Mound (No. 1)* [1961] AC 388 PC). It is not necessary for the plaintiff to show that the extent of the damage or the precise manner of its occurrence was foreseeable (see *Vacwell Engineering Co. Ltd* v *B.D.H. Chemicals Ltd* (above); *Hughes* v *Lord Advocate* [1963] AC 837).

In the general law of negligence the concepts of causation and remoteness appear to be used interchangeably to determine the issue of responsibility where the negligence of two or more tortfeasors has led to indivisible damage to the plaintiff. An individual defendant's share of responsibility is decided by a less than scientific assessment of the 'causative potency' of his act or omission vis-a-vis the damage, together with the degree of fault on his part relative to that on the part of the other defendants (see for example *Clay* v *A. J. Crump & Sons Ltd* [1964] 1 QB 533).

In other circumstances the negligence of one defendant may be regarded as the sole cause of the plaintiff's damage, severing the causal link between the negligence of other defendants and the subsequent damage to the plaintiff (a *novus actus interveniens*, see *Knightley* v *Johns and Others* [1982] 1 WLR 349; *Taylor* v *Rover Co Ltd* [1966] 1 WLR 1491).

The prospect of an apportionment of responsibility as between co-defendants may commonly arise in at least two different ways in the context of the production and distribution of goods. First, where a manufacturer is really nothing more than an assembler of parts bought in, who is liable in the tort of negligence to the consumer who is injured as a result of a defect in a bought-in part? Secondly, what degree of responsibility does the law of tort impose upon persons in the chain of distribution other than manufacturers such as importers, wholesalers and retailers?

The quite separate issue of the apportionment of responsibility as between *manufacturer and consumer* may also have to be addressed. The action of the consumer in mis-using a product may amount to contributory negligence with a consequent reduction in damages awarded. Again, in extreme cases the consumer's negligence may be such that it amounts to a *novus actus interveniens*, the consumer then being regarded as the sole cause of his damage (see *Farr* v *Butters Bros & Co.* [1932] 2 KB 606).

Our attention is drawn to these matters through the statement of Lord Atkin in *M'Alister (or Donoghue) (Pauper)* v *Stevenson* (set out above at p. 121), where he contemplated that liability on the part of the manufacturer would only arise in the absence of a 'reasonable possibility of intermediate examination'. Lord Wright in *Grant* v *Australian Knitting Mills Ltd and Others* [1936] AC 85 at p. 105 took this to mean that 'the principle in *Donoghue* v *Stevenson* can only be applied where the defect is hidden and unknown to the consumer, otherwise the directness of cause and effect is absent'.

The question of the legal effect of what is or ought to be known to an intermediary and/or a plaintiff consumer is complicated by the conceptualised nature of the tort of negligence. The issue may raise arguments as to the existence or discharge of a duty of care, causation and remoteness, as well as defences such as assumption of risk or contributory negligence. The principles applicable in other areas apply equally here, except with regard to issues raised by the prospect of an intermediate examination.

In cases where no warning has been given (e.g., the manufacturing defect cases such as *Grant* and *Donoghue* (above)), it seems fairly clear that the manufacturer will not escape liability unless the defect would have been discovered by an intermediate examination which can be reasonably expected of the intermediary. The mere possibility of such an examination will no longer suffice in this regard (see *Griffiths* v *Arch Engineering Co. (Newport) Ltd* [1968] 3 All ER 217). However, it may be that the failure by a distributor to make an examination reasonably expected of him amounts to negligence on his part which appears automatically to sever the causal link between the manufacturers' original negligence and the plaintiff's damage, with the result that the distributor alone is liable. It seems therefore that a negligent manufacturer may be automatically excused by the mere failure to discover a defect rather than by a failure to prevent harm. In these respects the law appears to differ from that in other areas of negligence which is perhaps typified by the decision in *Clay* v *Crump* (above) in which an apportionment between the joint tortfeasors was preferred and which was upheld on appeal.

In the foregoing pages we have attempted to draw attention to those matters which cause difficulties to students in an academic sense. These issues are often the same ones which pose problems in real life for potential litigants — the interest of your lecturers and tutors in such issues is an obvious one. It would be as well to bear this in mind when considering Part I of the 1987 Act, for one would imagine that examiners would be seeking to establish the student's understanding of the extent to which the difficulties associated with an action in negligence have been alleviated by the new legislation.

Strict liability for personal injury and property damage under the Consumer Protection Act 1987, Part I

We do not intend to rehearse the arguments for and against the movement away from a fault-based system towards some form of stricter liability.

Students should be aware of those arguments. Numerous sources may be consulted to that end including, The Law Commission's Report No. 82, Liability for Defective Products, Cmnd. 6831, 1977; The Pearson Commission Report (above) Cmnd. 7054, 1978, chapter 22. Nor shall we concern ourselves with root and branch of the Act. Our intention is to select and concentrate upon those issues which we believe students are likely to have difficulty understanding, or those, the importance of which might be overlooked. In so doing we have not surprisingly focused upon the issues which point out both the differences and similarities between the common law and statutory regime. As we suggested earlier this approach may well be adopted by your tutors since it draws attention to the requirements of the two different sets of rules, both of which are important.

Students will readily appreciate that interpreting new statutes can be a little like forecasting the weather. In coming to terms with this problem, guidance (as well as some differing opinions) will be forthcoming from the plethora of publications which will no doubt accompany the new Act. Furthermore, a valuable insight into the difficulties associated with this form of stricter liability may be gleaned from USA case law, useful extracts of which will be found in Miller and Harvey, *Consumer and Trading Law, Cases and Materials*, chapter 4. One exercise which we believe students will find particularly helpful is that of reconsidering the decisions in earlier common law cases in the light of the statutory provisions.

Our selective consideration of the provisions is structured under the following heads:

(a) The scope of Part I.
(b) The concept of defective products and the meaning of strict liability.
(c) The 'state of-the art' defence.

The scope of Part I of the Act   Under this head we draw attention to a number of provisions which severely limit the scope of the Act and thereby emphasise the continuing importance of the common law. The points raised are not likely to require any great depth of academic analysis and this is reflected in our treatment of them. These points are nevertheless of crucial importance and are just the kind of points which students so often overlook.

(a) *Who may be liable under Part I?*   Strict liability is imposed upon 'business producers' who are defined in ss. 1(2) and 2(2), so as to include those who provide raw materials or parts to industry as well as those who are in effect nothing more than assemblers of bought-in parts. Particularly noteworthy are the provisions in s. 2(2) which also treat as 'producers' those non-manufacturers whose brand names appear on goods (e.g., St Michael

— Marks and Spencer plc). Similarly included is the first importer of goods into a member state of the EEC. Note that this may or may not be the first importer into the United Kingdom. Section 2(3) further adds to this list by drawing in any business 'supplier' (e.g., a retailer) who fails to comply with a request from an injured consumer to identify the person who supplied the goods in question to, e.g., the retailer.

It is thus clearly possible that two or more persons may be jointly and severally liable (see s. 2(5)) as 'producers'. The matter of their respective contributions is left to be dealt with under the existing law as contained in the Civil Liability (Contribution) Act 1978. The respective degrees of responsibility of the defendants will presumably continue to be calculated on the basis of the 'causative potency' of their tortious acts together with the relative degree of fault on the part of the various defendants. Nothing in the Act prevents a court from reaching the conclusion that the causal link between a breach of duty by a producer and the plaintiff consumer's damage has been severed by a *novus actus interveniens* as in cases such as *Taylor* v *Rover Co. Ltd* [1966] 2 All ER 181.

(b)   *Actionable damage*   The damage actionable under the Act is, by virtue of s. 5, confined to personal injury and damage to consumer property.

(i)   Personal injury is actionable irrespective of the plaintiff's status, i.e., injury caused to a sole trader or a partner by a defective product used for business purposes is actionable.

(ii)   The damage actionable includes 'consumer property' but not 'business property'. Students might be well advised to ensure that they understand the definition of 'consumer' under s. 5 and how that differs from the concept employed in s. 12 of the Unfair Contract Terms Act 1977. This is the kind of issue which might well be raised in a mixed tort/contract question which is by no means uncommon.

(iii)   Damage to 'consumer property' is only actionable to the extent that it exceeds £275. Furthermore, s. 5(2) specifically excludes from recovery damage to the defective product itself or damage to any product which has been supplied with the defective product in it, even if such damage exceeds £275. Traditionally such loss has been regarded as 'pure economic loss'. The fact that it is not recoverable under the Act emphasises the importance of the common law where, upon proof of negligence, some limited recovery may be possible (see below).

(c)   *Which products are covered by the Act?*   The products to which the Act relates are widely defined in ss. 1(2) and 45(1). The exclusion from the Act of game or agricultural produce which at the time of supply 'had not undergone an industrial process' is a matter of some controversy and the relevant provisions in ss. 1(2) and 2(4) are a source of considerable uncertainty. Given the fact that people injured by way of food poisoning may well not have the benefit of a strict liability action in contract (nor does the Food Act 1984 confer any right of civil action), the question as to whether food has or has not 'undergone an industrial process' could be crucial. This point serves to remind us yet again of the continuing importance of the common law and of course the difficulties of proving negligence.

When is a product defective?   Defective products are defined in general terms in s. 3 of the Act. Section 3(1) proclaims that a product is defective 'if the safety of the product is not such as persons generally are entitled to expect'. The provision goes on to explain that 'safety' is to be understood in the context of potential damage to property as well as risk of personal injury.

Section 3(2) specifies in more detail what persons generally are entitled to expect — that all the circumstances shall be taken into account, including:

(a)   the manner in which, and purposes for which, the product has been marketed, its get-up, the use of any mark in relation to the product and any instructions for, or warnings with respect to, doing or refraining from doing anything with or in relation to the product;

(b)   what might reasonably be expected to be done with or in relation to the product; and

(c)   the time when the product was supplied by its producer to another.

The subsection concludes by confirming that the product is to be judged according to the standards of acceptability prevailing at the time the goods were produced.

The definition of defective products is in our view the heart and soul of the new regime. The controversy concerning the state of the art defence (which we consider below) has served to distract attention from the fundamental importance of s. 3. Far more cases will turn upon the interpretation of this section than will be won or lost according to the success with which producers are able to maintain the state of the art defence.

Students must appreciate the relative nature of the standard required by s. 3. Strict liability does not mean absolute liability — far from it. The fact that the standard is no longer defined in terms of the manufacturer's conduct but rather in terms of the expectation of Joe Public should not be allowed to obscure this crucial point. Whilst the injured consumer need no longer establish that his injury was foreseeable, s. 3 clearly embodies a risk/benefit test which means that factors (such as the probability/seriousness of the likely harm, the cost of obviating/reducing the risk and the social utility of the product in question) will all continue to be relevant. The producer may be liable for unforseeable harm but only where the product is defective. Section 3 contains numerous specific provisions and 'weasel words' which will ensure that the boundaries of liability will not differ greatly from those which exist under the common law. In support of this view we would suggest students should give careful consideration to the following points.

(a)   Products which are inherently dangerous and are known to be so, clearly fall within the possible scope of s. 3. This appears at first sight to be a substantial departure from the common law. In reality, in the vast majority of cases, the section imposes nothing more than a duty to adequately warn, although the remote possibility that a court might take the view that some particular product ought not to be marketed at all cannot be totally disregarded.

(b)   Although the point is not entirely free from doubt, we have taken the view that the phrase 'such as persons generally are entitled to expect', in s. 3(1), probably relates to the expectation of the public at large rather than to that of producers. The phrase may be of considerable importance in confining liabilty under the Act. If a product is not harmful to the majority of users the general expectation may well be satisfied and the product is not 'defective'. This conclusion may be reached notwithstanding the fact that the product is known to be harmful to a small group of particularly sensitive consumers, the duty towards such persons being discharged by an adequate warning. Where the injury to the especially sensitive consumer is unforeseeable, the producer will probably need to rely upon the state of the art defence (see below).

(c)   The time at which the goods are put into circulation is relevant in two quite distinct ways. First, the producer is only liable where the goods are defective at the time the producer supplied them, the burden of proof in this respect is (unlike the common law) placed upon the producer (see s. 4(1)(d)). You may wish to consider whether *Evans* v *Triplex Safety Glass Co. Ltd* [1936] 1 All ER 283 would be decided differently under the Act. Time is also important in the sense that the product is to be judged according to the standards applicable at the time of production. Specific provisions is made in s. 3(2) (above) that the subsequent evolution of safer products is not of itself evidence that the product in question was defective. In this regard the Act again mirrors the relative standard of the common law.

(d)   Under the common law we saw that a manufacturer may escape liability completely where some distributor or the consumer is either aware of the defect or has failed to take the opportunity to carry out a reasonable examination which would have brought the defect to light (above at pp. 126-127). It has been said that the 'defence' of intermediate examination 'provides one of the largest loopholes in the "Donoghue" rule through which manufacturers and repairers have escaped getting wet' (*RMS Gibson*, (1974) 3 Anglo-American LR 493 at p. 512). As we indicated above, the decision in *Clay* v *A. J. Crump & Sons Ltd* [1964] 1 QB 533 may mark a turning point and the courts may be less willing to allow manufacturers to pass on responsibility to the extent which earlier cases appear to permit. In what way, if at all, does the Act affect this issue?

Section 2(1) states that a producer is liable where damage is caused 'wholly or partly' by a defective product. Thus the producer may be fully liable despite contributory fault on the part of a third party — either a distributor or the consumer himself. This liability is however subject to the producer's right to recover a contribution from a distributor under the Civil Liability (Contribution) Act 1978. The amount of damages awarded to a consumer may also be reduced under the defence of contributory negligence which is expressly preserved by s. 6(4) of the Act.

Any liability on the part of the producer will, however only arise when the product can be shown to be defective. Section 3 (above) in which defectiveness is defined, clearly takes account of any warnings and instruction which may accompany the product. In addition, 'what might reasonably be expected to be done with or in relation to the product' (s. 3(2)(b)), must also be taken into consideration in deciding whether the product is defective at all. The provision in s. 3(2)(b) (above) may be called in aid not only to deal with matters such as deliberate misuse, but also with respect to the question as to whether goods are defective, given the failure by a distributor or a consumer to heed warnings or to carry out some reasonable examination prior to resale or use. It remains to be seen whether the notion that liability under the Act is stricter will move the courts more in the direction of apportionment than has been the case under the common law.

The state of the art or development risk defence   Unlike the common law, the Act does not require the injured plantiff to show that his injury was foreseeable. The basic premise of a strict liability regime is that the producer should bear the responsibility for the unforeseeable injury to consumers. In reality the cost of that responsibility would ultimately be borne by consumers generally to whom it would be passed via the price mechanism. The inclusion of any provision which permits the producer to avoid that responsibility, even in terms of a defence, represents a substantial derogation from the fundamental principle of strict liability. Lord Scarman has suggested that the inclusion of any such provision 'would really be like a torpedo hitting a ship below the waterline' (see Hansard HL Deb 12 Nov 1980, vol. 414, col 1411). We would suggest that a careful analysis of the definition of defectiveness shows that this ship already has in it a number of holes.

We do not propose to rehash here the arguments for and against the inclusion of a state of the art defence. Those arguments are well covered in the legal literature and they will no doubt continue to form the substance of lively seminars and tutorials. We wish to concentrate upon certain basic points of difficulty which arise from the defence provision contained in s. 4(1)(e) of the 1987 Act.

The inclusion of any development risk defence is controversial, but the inclusion of this particular defence is especially so. The reason for this is that the wording of s. 4(1)(e) appears to be considerably wider than Article 7(e) of the Directive which the section is supposed to implement. At the time of writing, moves are afoot to challenge the legitimacy of s. 4(1)(e) which may result in litigation before the European Court of Justice even before the Act comes into force.

Article 7(e) of the Directive states simply that the defendant producer may escape liability if he can show, that the state of scientific and technical knowledge at the time when he put the product into circulation was not such as to enable the existence of the defect to be discovered. By comparison the wider and more convoluted wording of s. 4(1)(e) is to the effect that the producer is not liable if he can show:

> that the state of scientific and technical knowledge at the relevant time was not such that a producer of products of the same description as the product in question might be expected to have discovered the defect if it had existed in his products while they were under his control.

The first thing students need to note is that any development risk defence represents a substantial step back to a negligence based regime, even where the burden of proof on the matter of foreseeability is placed upon the producer. The defence is only likely to arise in the context of claims alleging some compositional or design defect in new products. In this type of case it would seem that the provisions of both the Directive and the Act would excuse the producer not only in circumstances where the defect was scientifically undiscoverable, but also in cases where it was physically and objectively possible to discover the defect, but where it would be in some way unreasonable to expect him to have done so. With this in mind the points arising out of the provision in s. 4(1)(e) to which students should give careful attention include the following:

(a) Where an entirely new product is alleged to be defective the discoverability (or effort towards that end) is to be judged by reference to 'a producer of products of the same description'. Where will such a producer be found? Is he a hypothetical 'reasonable' producer?

(b) The defence appears to rest upon the subjective ability of this hypothetical producer to discover the risk which subsequently manifests itself, or a subjective assessment of his efforts to that end. Might this mean the differential treatment of producers according to their resources relative to the cost of discoverability?

(c) It is important to keep the defence separate from the definition of defectiveness contained in s. 3. If a risk is discoverable or even known, the product may not be defective given that it is to be judged, *inter alia*, according to the standards of acceptability prevailing at the time the product is put into circulation — the Act expressly prevents retrospective judgment (see s. 3(2)).

The development risk defence on the other hand can only be invoked where the defect is allegedly undiscoverable — but at what time? Section 4(1)(e) is somewhat confusing on this. The date at which the state of knowledge is tested is the date of supply by the producer (see s. 4(2)(a)), whereas the date to which discoverability by the hypothetical producer relates is the time the goods were 'under his control'. This could be taken to suggest that the producer will need to show that a defect was not discoverable after the date of supply perhaps until recall is no longer reasonably practicable. This is all rather odd since the only scientific and technical knowledge which can be taken into account is that which was, or ought to have been, possessed at the date of supply.

Pure economic loss: Liability in tort

Under this head we consider the extent to which such loss is recoverable in tort where such loss results from the supply of defective goods or services. Pure economic loss is, in general terms, financial loss which is not consequent upon injury to the plaintiff nor damage to the property of the plaintiff. Precisely which losses fall within this category in the context of the provision of goods and services is considered below. What must be grasped at this stage is that certain of the losses so categorised are not recoverable at all, whilst others are only recoverable in exceptional circumstances. Although such losses are generally recoverable in contract (subject to the relevant rules of remoteness of damage) the position in tort is not unimportant. Such losses may be sustained by many people outside privity of contract. Furthermore an action in contract may, for other reasons, be impossible or pointless, as illustrated in three recent cases: *Lambert* v *Lewis* [1980] 1 All ER 978 CA and [1981] 1 All ER 1185 HL; *Muirhead* v *Industrial*

Tank Specialities Ltd [1985] 3 WLR 993; *M/S Aswan Engineering Ltd* v *Lupdine Ltd* [1987] 1 WLR 1.

Pure economic loss is not recoverable under Part I of the 1987 Act and this includes further loss or damage to the product itself caused by a defective part comprised in it (see s. 5(2)). The position under the common law is less straightforward and we need to recognise the possibilities which may arise not only from the actual supply of defective goods and services, but also from statements associated with their supply. Before outlining the various possibilities it is necessary to gain some idea of what is regarded as purely economic loss in this context. This can be a difficult question and one which tends to catch many students off balance.

Under the common law where a product itself sustains damage or deterioration due to some inherent defect such loss has traditionally been regarded as purely economic. Where the plaintiff purchases goods in containers and the containers prove to be defective with the result that the goods are rendered useless, is that loss purely economic for the purposes of a claim in tort against the manufacturer of the container? In the *Lupdine* case (above) Lloyd LJ was of the view that this constituted damage to property rather than pure economic loss. (See [1987] 1 WLR 1 at pp. 18-21. Contrast the views of Nichols LJ (*ibid.*) at pp. 28-29.) As was indeed recognised in the case itself, there is here an important type of loss, the precise categorisation of which (and the rules governing recovery) is extremely uncertain.

The decision in *Muirhead* (above) illustrates that business losses which result solely from a hold-up in production rather than from any delay in cleaning or repairing production equipment are purely economic (see also *Spartan Steel and Alloys Ltd* v *Martin & Co.* [1973] QB 37 CA).

Clearly the value of the product itself if claimed in tort is regarded as pure financial loss, as is any attempt by a retailer to claim an indemnity from a manufacturer for damages payable by the retailer to persons injured by an unmerchantable product: see *Lambert* v *Lewis* (above).

As we indicated earlier the consequence of a loss falling within this ill-defined category of 'pure economic loss' is that it is recoverable only in the following exceptional circumstances.

(a)   Where a manufacturer responds to a specific request and gives an assurance as to the quality of his goods which are then purchased by the plaintiff from a retailer, such assurance may amount to a collateral warranty. In this type of situation any action will lie not only where the goods prove to be dangerously defective (see *Andrews* v *Hopkinson* [1957] 1 QB 229), but also where the goods are safe but shoddy (in the sense that their performance does not match up to the assurance given: see *Shanklin Pier Ltd* v *Detel Products Ltd* [1951] 2 KB 854; *Wells (Merstham) Ltd* v *Buckland*

Sands and Silica Co. Ltd [1965] 2 QB 170. Strictly speaking this is a contractual action which is not dependent upon proof of fault as such and confers the possible additional benefit of allowing the plaintiff to claim expectation losses (rather than reliance losses which would be recoverable in a tort action).

(b)   Where the goods supplied are discovered to be dangerously defective and pose a threat of injury or further damage to the product itself or damage to other property, the cost of obviating that risk may be recovered in tort from a negligent manufacturer under the principle in *Donoghue* v *Stevenson* itself (see *Dutton* v *Bognor Regis Urban District Council* [1972] 1 All ER 462, per Lord Denning MR at p. 474; per Sachs LJ at pp. 480-481).

(c)   Where there exists no threat to person or property certain economic losses may still be recoverable in tort against the negligent manufacturer or other supplier of goods or services. If the negligence lies in advice or information given about a product then liability may be established under the principle in *Hedley Byrne & Co. Ltd* v *Heller & Partners Ltd* [1964] AC 465, provided a specially close proximate relationship exists between the parties. In *Lambert* v *Lewis* (above) the House of Lords refused to rule out the possibility that a retailer might recover an indemnity from a manufacturer in this way. In the context of the provision of services, the decisions in three cases which allowed the recovery of pure economic loss in tort seem unquestioned (see *Ministry of Housing and Local Government* v *Sharp* [1970] 2 QB 223 CA; *Ross* v *Caunters* [1980] Ch 297; *Yianni* v *Edwin Evans & Son* [1982] QB 438). The 'contract fallacy' (i.e., that a person performing a contractual duty owed no duty in tort) was demolished with regard to injury and damage to property by the decision in *Donoghue* v *Stevenson* (above). The three cases mentioned above explode the fallacy with regard to pure economic loss.

That point is confirmed by the decision of the House of Lords in *Junior Books Ltd* v *Veitchi Co. Ltd* [1983] 1 AC 520 in which recovery was allowed in negligence for losses resulting from a defective floor laid by the defendant sub-contractors at the plaintiff's premises, despite the absence of any allegation that the floor constituted a threat to the safety of persons or property. The case was decided very much on its facts, which demonstrated a relationship between the parties which was so close that it was in the words of Lord Roskill, 'as close as it could be short of privity' (at p. 546). The majority were at pains to point out that their decision was not to be taken as authority that a duty of care is owed by manufacturers to consumers with regard to the value of safe but shoddy products. The majority were at one in their concern that any such claims would undermine established sales law, though very different technical explanations were proferred as to why such claims would not succeed. Contrast the views of Lord Roskill (lack of reliance); Lord Fraser at p. 533 (lack of proximity and difficulty of setting appropriate standards); and Lord Keith at p. 537 (policy).

In the absence of some specially close relationship between manufacturer and plaintiff, economic loss resulting solely from the supply of defective goods will not be recoverable in tort unless it represents expenditure incurred in obviating a risk to person or property.

In his leading judgment in *Junior Books*, Lord Roskill employed the 'two stage approach' advocated by Lord Wilberforce in *Anns* v *Merton London Borough Council* [1978] 2 All ER 492 at p. 498. In a number of more recent cases in the general law of negligence, the expansionist effect of that approach has been regarded with great concern. So much so that the existence of even a *prima facie* duty of care is not only dependent upon the existence of the requisite degree of proximity, but it must also be 'just and reasonable' to impose such a duty (see, e.g., *Governors of Peabody D.F.* v *Parkinson* [1985] AC 210; *Curran* v *Northern Ireland Co-ownership H. Ass.* [1987] 2 All ER 13 HL; *Business Computers Ltd* v *Registrar of Companies* (1987), *The Times*, 1 July; *Yeon Kun Yeu* v *Attorney-General Hong Kong* [1987] 2 All ER 705 PC).

All the above-mentioned cases were concerned with economic loss and, since so little of this kind of loss is recoverable in tort against a manufacturer, these cases appear to have little relevance here. There is however a possibility that this more restrictive approach may also be applied to property damage resulting from defective products (see the *Lupdine* case (above) per Lloyd LJ [1987] 1 WLR 1 at p. 23).

Illustrative question

A consignment of 10 tonnes of Egyptian potatoes was imported into the United Kingdom by Murphy Ltd. Unknown to Murphy Ltd a proportion of the potatoes had been accidentally contaminated by a highly toxic pesticide. The pesticide was odourless, tasteless and colourless and the contaminated potatoes were not distinguishable from the rest by visual inspection.

Two tonnes of the potatoes were sold to Bigga Pies Ltd who used them in the production of vegetable pies which were then sold to Healthy Supermarkets Ltd.

Mrs P purchased a number of these pies which bore the Healthy brand name, and placed them in her freezer. One of the pies was eaten by her husband who was fatally poisoned by it.

Fred, a labourer employed in the warehouse of Murphy Ltd suffered an extremely rare form of dermatitis previously unknown in the United

Kingdom, as a result of contact with the potatoes. Bigga Pies Ltd has gone into liquidation.

Consider the tortious liability which may arise from the above facts. Assume that Part I of the Consumer Protection Act 1987 was in force at all relevant times.

Commentary

The choice of the type of question on this topic was not without difficulty. We finally opted for a problem question which will test the student's knowledge and understanding of a wide range of points arising under the Act and the common law. Our hope is that this illustrative exercise will be both beneficial in terms of technique and also serve to implant firmly in the minds of students at least some of the important points concerning the 1987 Act and its relationship with the common law.

We recognise that the rubric is somewhat artificial in assuming the 1987 Act to be in force, but this kind of assumption is often necessary in law examinations. Questions of this ilk will in all probability appear with some degree of frequency in the immediate future in examination papers the length and breadth of the country. We will forecast the even greater probability that, faced with such a question, there will be a number of students who answer solely on the basis of the Act and ignore completely the common law. Unless the rubric states otherwise, we would strongly advise students to ensure that their answers to such questions embrace both the common law and the provisions of the 1987 Act in so far as they are both relevant.

Next, a little logistical thinking: how best to structure an answer to such a question? No apologies whatever for repeating the need for a rough plan. The problem reveals a number of potential claims in respect of different types of damage under the common law and Part I of the 1987 Act. This is a typically complex scenario and it makes sense to devote a few minutes of your valuable time in examinations to sort out some kind of order in which to deal with the issues which you identify. It will be necessary in answers to such questions to refer to numerous sections of the 1987 Act. May we remind you yet again to avoid the unnecessary regurgitation of the detailed wording of the statutory provisions themselves. Students who are allowed copies of various Acts in examinations are particularly, but not exclusively, prone to this problem. We recognise that it may be necessary at times to focus upon the detailed wording of an Act, where much turns upon the fine interpretation of some word or phrase. Those situations apart it is infinitely preferable to summarise briefly the purpose and effect of the relevant provisions. In this commentary we have included quite a number of detailed references to the Act. We have done so because the essential feature of our commentary is that it is an exercise of instruction rather than a model answer.

Perhaps the way to begin an answer to our illustrative problem is by recognising that the 'defective goods' in question are agricultural products and that such produce is not covered by the Act, even if it is defective, unless and until the produce has 'undergone an industrial process' (see s. 2(4)). When the produce has undergone such a process the processor (producer) will only be liable if the 'essential characteristics' of the resulting product were attributable to that process (see s. 1(2)(c)). This latter requirement does not however apply to other persons who may be liable as producers, e.g., importers (s. 2(2)(c) or 'own branders' (s. 2(2)(b)), nor does it apply to other suppliers who may be strictly liable under s. 2(3) (i.e., by reason of refusal or inability to identify a producer or supplier).

The first question to try to answer therefore is whether, and at what stage, if any, the potatoes have been subject to an 'industrial process' so as to bring them within the Act. The wording of s. 2(4) differs significantly from the wording of Article 2 of the Directive, which proposed that agricultural products should be included once they have 'undergone initial processing'. Whilst this may well have included, e.g., the harvesting and bagging of potatoes, it is by no means clear that this operation is sufficient to constitute an 'industrial process' within the meaning of s. 2(4). If that activity were regarded as sufficient in that respect, then the potatoes would be caught by the Act and Murphy Ltd would be strictly liable (as the first importer into the EEC) under s. 2(2)(c) for the resultant damage. Murphy Ltd would be liable not only to the estate of Mr P (a user) but also to Fred their employee, for liability for personal injury is not confined to consumer use. That liability is however subject to any defence which Murphy Ltd might raise under the Act. The fact that the contamination may have been unforeseeable and undiscoverable by Murphy Ltd is irrelevant in a strict liability regime. The only defence which might be open to Murphy Ltd is that in s. 4(1)(e): the 'state of the art' defence. There is nothing in the facts of our problem to suggest this is in any way a reasonable prospect, such as would require or justify a detailed analysis of that defence. We have therefore merely acknowledged this as a possibility.

Is the question of foreseeability of the dermatitis sustained by Fred a relevant consideration? Is Fred an especially sensitive plaintiff and if so what is his position under the Act? It is by no means clear what rules of remoteness of damage will be applied to breaches of the statutory duty. Foreseeability may play a part on this issue in the way that it does in the present law of negligence. Were that to be the case then the harm sustained by Fred is likely to be regarded as being within the broad category of foreseeable harm (personal injury). In applying the Wagon Mound principle, decisions such as that in *Bradford* v *Robinson Rentals Ltd* [1967] 1 WLR 337 are, we would suggest, more likely to be followed than that in *Tremain* v *Pike* [1969] 1 WLR 1556.

If on the other hand the potatoes were not regarded as having undergone an 'industrial process' prior to their importation and subsequent supply by Murphy Ltd, then the only liability which that company might incur would be under the common law. On the facts of the problem the defect might well be regarded as 'latent', i.e., not discoverable by the exercise of reasonable care, with the result that there may well be no breach of duty by Murphy Ltd and consequently no liability in tort to either Fred or the estate of Mr P.

The probability that Fred has no claim against Murphy Ltd under the Employer's Liability (Defective Equipment) Act 1969 deserves a brief mention. Section 1 of that Act renders an employer strictly liable to employees injured by defective 'equipment provided by the employer'. It is upon this phrase that Fred's claim would flounder. Whilst this has been held to include a 91,650 tonne bulk tanker on which the employee worked (see *Coltman* v *Bibby Ltd, The Derbyshire* [1986] 1 WLR 751), it does not include the employers 'stock in trade', i.e., potatoes (see, e.g., *Yarmouth* v *France* (1887) 19 QBD 647 per Lindley LJ at p. 658).

The use of the potatoes by Bigga Pies Ltd in the production of vegetable pies would almost certainly constitute an 'industrial process'. However it is vital to note that Bigga Pies Ltd would only be liable as a producer, if in addition it can be shown that the 'essential characteristics of the product' result from that process (see s. 1(2)(c)). It is generally expected that this provision will prove difficult to interpret and apply. One point which is reasonably clear and which deserves to be made, is that the Act does not require the establishment of any causal link between the process and the defectiveness of the product. Thus, in our problem, if the use of the potatoes by Bigga Pies Ltd is an 'industrial process' establishing the 'essential characteristics of the product' (and we believe it would be) then it does not matter that the defect is in no way physically caused by that process. In our view Bigga Pies Ltd would be strictly liable under the Act.

The fact that the company has gone into liquidation would probably render pointless any claim by the estate of P. This serves to draw attention to a matter of some concern upon which a student might legitimately and usefully comment in his or her answer — it is that the absence of any compulsion of producers, etc., to insure against their potential liabilities and the possibility of trading through dispensable companies with few assets may substantially undermine the Act.

We turn next to consider whether or not Healthy Supermarkets Ltd might incur any liability under the Act or indeed under the common law. So far as the latter possibility is concerned we would very much doubt whether on such facts Healthy Supermarkets Ltd could be regarded as being negligent. The defect is in all probability a latent one, not discoverable by the exercise of care. Given that Mr P is outside the 'privity rule' the only remaining possibility would be to establish liability under the 1987 Act. Students could well pick up the odd mark by explaining that whilst the Food Act 1984 imposes criminal sanctions upon those who supply food which is unfit for human consumption, a breach of that statutory duty does not confer any civil right of action (see *Square* v *Model Farm Dairies Ltd* [1939] 2 KB 365).

Healthy Supermarkets Ltd could incur a 'secondary' liabiity under the Act if they fail or refuse to identify Bigga Pies Ltd as the supplier of the pies in question (see s. 2(3)). More important is the possibility that Healthy Supermarkets Ltd could be liable as an 'own-brander' under s. 2(2), i.e., that although the company is not the manufacturer of the pies, the company may be regarded as a producer, if the company name is put on the product in such a way as to 'hold out' Healthy Supermarkets Ltd 'as the producer of the product'. In view of the limited facts in the problem this would require a degree of speculation on the part of the student as to whether or not the name of Bigga Pies Ltd also appeared on the product as its manufacturer. If it did then the probability is that Healthy Supermarkets Ltd would not incur any liability under the Act to the estate of Mr P.

The final substantive issue which merits some discussion concerns the position as between Murphy Ltd and Healthy Supermarkets Ltd on which two distinct matters need to be considered. First, we need to note that any claim by Healthy Supermarkets Ltd in contract against Bigga Pies Ltd in respect of any defective pies still held in stock or, for an indemnity for any damages payable to P's estate, would be effectively frustrated by the liquidation of Bigga Pies Ltd. Can Healthy Supermarkets Ltd claim either of these losses from Murphy Ltd? No such claim can be maintained under the 1987 Act, since neither the value of the defective pies nor any financial liability (incurred to P's estate) constitutes actionable damage within s. 5. So far as the common law is concerned, it seems reasonably clear that the value of the defective pies themselves would not be recoverable (see *Junior Books, Muirhead* and *Lupdine* (above)), even if Murphy Ltd could be shown to be negligent. What may be recoverable in principle is the expense, if any, incurred by Healthy Supermarkets Ltd in disposing of the remainder of the defective pies *and* the cost of warning consumers and recovering any other pies which had been sold (see *Dutton* v *Bognor Regis Urban District Council* [1972] per Lord Denning and Sachs LJ above at p. 136). However, on the facts as given, it is unlikely that Murphy Ltd could be shown to be negligent. Any attempt by Healthy Supermarkets Ltd to obtain from Murphy Ltd an indemnity in tort (for any damages payable to the estate of P) would probably fail for the same reason. That claim might also be unsuccessful on the additional ground that the relationship between the parties was not sufficiently close to give rise to a duty of care, see *Lambert* v *Lewis* (above). The final matter which arises as between these parties is the question of their respective contributions in the possible event that both were liable to the estate of P under the Act. The plaintiff is favoured by the fact that defendants are jointly and severally liable under the Act. The matter of contributions as between defendants is still dealt with by the Civil Liability (Contribution) Act 1978, apportionment being on a 'just and equitable' basis.

We would advise students to make every effort to round off examination answers by way of a short succinct conclusion which should draw together the main points in their answer. A conclusion to an answer on our illustrative question would briefly indicate the apparent low prospect of success of most of the possible claims, highlighting the limited change brought about by the Act and the restrictive requirements of the common law. There is, we believe, also an important point of technique here: it is equally important to explain why a claim might fail as it is to show why an action might succeed.

EIGHT

CLASSIFICATION OF CONSUMER CREDIT AGREEMENTS AND JOINT AND SEVERAL LIABILITY

Introduction

This is the first of three chapters devoted to discussion of some of the provisions of the Consumer Credit Act 1974. We say only some of the provisions because the Act is extremely long with over 190 sections and several schedules and we cannot realistically hope to cover all the details. In addition the Act has many enabling provisions and the delegated legislation alone which has already issued forth would fill a book on its own. The Act followed in the wake of the Crowther Committee Report (1971, Cmnd. 4596) on Consumer Credit, which recommended wholesale changes in regulation of the credit industry. The major complaint of the Committee was that hitherto the law had looked at the form of the various types of credit transaction rather than their substance; the law had often concerned itself with technicalities without considering the practical realities. Indeed, in this first chapter we shall see how the draftsman of the Act has, to some extent successfully, achieved the reform of the law envisaged by the Crowther Committee.

In these chapters we shall be considering in the main only the civil law provisions of the Act, namely those regulating the position between the creditor and the debtor, and sometimes, the supplier of goods and services. The scope of the Act goes much further than just the regulation of individual credit agreements, but also creates a monolithic licensing system and numerous criminal offences. Regulations have been made in relation to advertising of credit and quotations which seek to regulate the pre-contractual behaviour of the potential creditor and others, backed up by criminal sanctions. We shall not be concerned with these in the discussion which follows, but you ought to be aware of their existence.

Consumer credit is a serious and important business nowadays and we consider that most consumer law and many commercial courses will have some part of the syllabus devoted to it. While there is hardly a large amount of case law upon the 1974 Act, it does give the student the opportunity to exercise his other skills of statutory interpretation. Our experience has shown that if you are prepared to sit down and painstakingly master the

'consumer credit is a serious and important business nowadays'

classification of agreements introduced by the draftsman, this effort will be rewarded at examination time. One practical point you should check is whether or not you will be provided with a copy of the Act in the examination room. If you are so provided, however, please be warned that this does not mean that you need devote less time to revision of consumer credit. We consider this to be a fallacy: you must be able to find your way through this Act and this cannot be done for the first time under examination conditions. Prepare this area as carefully and methodically as any other topic.

In this chapter we shall consider first the classification of consumer credit agreements. We shall then go on to discuss the liability of the creditor and supplier for the latter's misrepresentation and breach of contract where the debtor has entered into some form of credit agreement for the acquisition of goods and services. We consider that this topic is suitable for inclusion at this stage as it follows up and reinforces the importance of the classification of agreements. As you will see this classification appears complex, convoluted and cumbersome at first sight; it is only by considering some of the later provisions in the Act that an understanding of the classification provisions is obtained.

The other two chapters, 9 and 10, will be concerned with withdrawal, cancellation and termination of consumer credit agreements.

Substantive difficulties

Classification of consumer credit agreements

The first point we need to make may already be evident from what we have said above. Tha language of the Act may be something of a barrier to many students. 'Debtor-creditor-supplier' and 'debtor-creditor' agreements are hardly explicit expressions of what they are designed to convey. Likewise, the distinctions between 'unrestricted-use' and 'restricted-use' credit agreement are not that obvious from the language.

Secondly, you need to appreciate some basic distinctions between the various forms of credit which were recognised in law long before the 1974 Act appeared. The Act, despite its revolutionary approach to credit law, has not dispensed with the need for you to know a hire-purchase agreement as distinct from a personal loan. Many students, and qualified lawyers as well, do not fully appreciate precisely what goes on in the traditional 'triangular transaction'. We would add that the layperson rarely appreciates this at all, unless and until it is carefully explained to him or her. We use two diagrams below in our attempt to explain the possibilities. These are not to be confused with the cartoons!

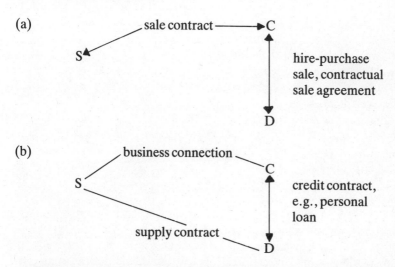

(a)   sale contract ———►C
      S◄   │ hire-purchase
                         │ sale, contractual
                         │ sale agreement
                         ▼
                         D

(b)   business connection
      S   C
                     │ credit contract,
                     │ e.g., personal
                     │ loan
      supply contract ▼
                     D

In diagram (a), although the debtor (D) may well appear to and believe he is contracting with the supplier (S), there is no formal agreement between them. S, in law, is deemed to sell the goods to the creditor (C), who in turn sells by credit or conditional sale, or lets on hire-purchase to D. Remember that it is the form of the agreement between C and D which determines what goes on in the triangular transaction. It is essential to identify the form of that agreement — if you do not, then mistakes will follow. For example, if the agreement between C and D, as in (a) above, is hire-purchase, credit sale or conditional sale, then as far as the law is concerned C is both the supplier of the *goods* and the credit in one and the same agreement. Of course, C will probably never physically possess or deliver the goods to D. This will normally be done by S, but you should not let this obscure what is really going on, in a legal sense. If, for example, the goods were unmerchantable, then D's claim in this type of situation is against C *not* S. It is a mistake to issue proceedings against S, but a mistake often made. By way of contrast, in diagram (b), what really goes on in this triangular transaction is more closely connected with what appears to go on. If the credit agreement between C and D is a personal loan agreement, for example, then that is a legally separate contract from the supply contract between S and D. If the goods or services supplied are unmerchantable or below the requisite standard, then normally D's claim is in contract against S under some implied or express term of that contract. As we shall see, however, if it can be shown that there is some 'business connection' between S and C, the 1974 Act may link the two agreements and not treat them in isolation as has happened in the past. A number of unfortunate debtors have been faced with paying a creditor in respect of goods which have turned out to be defective, or goods or services which have not been supplied, because of S's insolvency. This aspect of the Act will be explored fully later in this chapter.

We feel it necessary to emphasise just how important it is to identify correctly the type of agreement between C and D, because as you should now appreciate in the light of the above discussion, the form of that agreement dictates, in a legal sense, the nature of the transactions between the three parties, D, C and S. It follows from this that a debtor should never be advised without your being able to see a copy of the relevant agreement. It is not safe to rely on the debtor's possibly mistaken belief as to the nature of the agreement.

Is the agreement regulated by the Act? We find students do have some difficulty in deciding whether an agreement is one that is regulated by the Act. Some assume that it is without showing why that is the case. The concept of the regulated agreement has been described as the key to an understanding of the Act, because it is only the regulated agreement, in the main, which is caught by the provisions of the Act. There seem to be three elements in making a decision as to whether any particular credit agreement is regulated:

(a)   Is the credit advanced £15,000 or less?
(b)   Is the debtor an individual?
(c)   Is the agreement exempt by virtue of the provisions in the Act?

As far as the first issue is concerned, some of you have difficulty dealing with fairly straightforward calculations. Remember it is the *credit advanced* with which we are concerned here, not the overall amount that the debtor is to pay or has paid. From the overall figure you should deduct any deposit/part exchange allowance and interest charges.

As to the second issue, in a somewhat roundabout fashion, the Act provides that only where the debtor is an individual can the agreement be regulated. The important point to note here is that businesses may be debtors under regulated agreements, so long as they are not incorporated. This point is often overlooked. Remember that if the debtor under the credit agreement is described as Limited or plc, then the agreement is not regulated, irrespective of the amount of credit advanced. The third point relates to the provisions in s. 16 of the Act and orders made thereunder. Broadly, they provide that credit agreements falling into a number of categories are exempt from the majority of the Act's provisions, although they would otherwise be regulated. You should make yourself familiar with those broad general categories, but it is unlikely that you would be tested on the precise detail of the provisions.

If the appropriate answer is given to the three questions above, then the agreement is regulated. Nearly all the provisions we propose to discuss in this and the next two chapters are concerned primarily with regulated agreements.

There are a number of other classifications in ss. 11 to 19 of the 1974 Act with which you should be fully familiar. Of these, the three most important are:

(a)   restricted and unrestricted-use agreements;
(b)   debtor-creditor and debtor-creditor-supplier agreements;
(c)   linked transactions.

These classifications are crucial to the operation of many of the later provisions in this Act and careful study and understanding of them now should pay a dividend in the long run.

Restricted and unrestricted-use credit   The first distinction to be made is that to be found in s. 11 of the Act, namely, 'restricted-use' and 'unrestricted-use' credit. 'Restricted-use credit' is where either the creditor and supplier are one and the same person, as in hire-purchase, credit sale and conditional sale agreements, or where the creditor and supplier are separate entities and the creditor pays the credit direct to the supplier. Into this latter category would fall a personal loan agreement in which C sent a cheque representing the amount of the credit direct to S, or a credit card agreement such as Access or Barclaycard where the creditor pays the supplier direct, less commission, on receipt of a voucher signed by the debtor. 'Unrestricted-use' credit is where D is able to get his hands on the money and physically use it for some purpose other than that for which it was intended. Credit is still unrestricted use where D is in breach of contract with C if the loan is expressly stated to be used for the original purpose (see s. 11(3)). So, for example, if D goes to his bank to arrange for a personal loan to purchase a car, and the arrangement is that the bank credits his account with the amount of the loan, enabling D to draw a cheque, the credit is unrestricted because D could direct the money elsewhere other than for his original purpose.

Debtor-creditor and debtor-creditor-supplier agreements The second important, and some would say fundamental, distinction is that between a debtor-creditor-supplier (d-c-s) agreement and a debtor-credit (d-c) agreement. This is possibly the most radical change adopted by the draftsman of the 1974 Act. The object of this particular classification is to achieve recognition of what the Crowther committee called 'connected lenders' and 'unconnected lenders'. The 'connected lender' situation arises where there is some business connection between creditor and supplier, referred to earlier. Where there was such a connection this had been traditionally ignored in law. The recognition of this connection is achieved through the medium of the d-c-s agreement, whereby D is given more protection if his credit agreement falls into the d-c-s category. The most important source of that protection can be seen shortly in the context of the discussion of ss. 56 and 75 of the 1974 Act.

Unfortunately, whilst you may readily appreciate the underlying reasons for and the purpose of recognising the connection between supplier and creditor, the language by means of which the objective is achieved is far from readily comprehensible. Sections 12 and 13 are the relevant provisions, but s. 12 is the principal one as s. 13 in reality states that anything not falling within s. 12 is a d-c agreement within s. 13 itself. It is perhaps best to proceed by considering the three types of d-c-s agreement. The s. 12(a) d-c-s agreement category covers the situation where the creditor and supplier are one and the same person, namely, hire-purchase, credit sale or conditional sale agreements. Whilst it might seem odd to give this the name of d-c-s implying that there are three parties involved, nonetheless it makes sense to call it that, especially if we remember that in this instance the creditor is supplying the goods as well as the credit. You should note that *only* these three types of agreement — hire-purchase, credit sale and conditional sale — can be s. 12(a) d-c-s agreements. Remember this and it will save you problems later.

Other types of credit agreement may be a d-c-s agreement within s. 12(b) or (c), provided the relevant provisions are complied with. For an agreement to be d-c-s under s. 12(b), it must be a restricted-use agreement (c.f. s. 12(c) below). In addition, it must be shown that there is a business arrangement between the creditor and supplier. Remember this is a situation as in diagram (b) earlier, where on the face of it we have two separate contracts, the supply contract between S and D, and the credit contract between C and D. Under s. 12(b) the form of business connection may be 'pre-existing arrangements', or something 'in contemplation of future arrangements' between supplier and creditor. 'Arrangements' here must mean something less than a contractual arrangement. It has been suggested that it may only involve supplying the supplier with a stock of finance proposal forms.

For example, D goes to S and agrees to buy an item worth £4,000. He requires a loan for £3,000. S introduces him to C Ltd and the latter agrees to the loan and pays S direct.

This is a restricted-use agreement (i.e., the credit agreement) and probably will fall within s. 12(b). In this instance it may be the first time that S introduces a person such as D to C Ltd. Nonetheless, this will suffice to make it a 12(b) d-c-s agreement.

If an agreement is for unrestricted-use credit then it can only be a d-c-s if the conditions specified in s. 12(c) are fulfilled. These are that there are 'pre-existing arrangements' and, in addition, the creditor is aware of the purpose for which the loan is sought. This provision is in one sense more stringent than s. 12(b), in that if S refers D to C in 'contemplation of future arrangements', this will not be adequate. There must be 'pre-existing arrangements'. This stricter requirement is justified under s. 12(c) as we are dealing with unrestricted-use agreements (c.f. s. 12(b)). We can see, therefore, that the business connection sufficient to create a d-c-s agreement is different under s. 12(b) and (c). Why does the draftsman put us through the hoop in trying to distinguish between s. 12(b) and 12(c) d-c-s agreements? He has done this because, as we shall see in the next chapter, a debtor under a 12(b) d-c-s is marginally better protected than his counterpart under a 12(c) agreement.

If an agreement cannot be placed into one of the three categories above, then it is a d-c agreement, namely, an unconnected loan. One particular agreement, the regulated credit card agreement illustrates this point. In fact this type of agreement is what is shown as a 'multiple agreement' (see s. 18).

It falls into more than one category. If it is used to pay for goods and services supplied by a person who agrees to accept that card, it is a 12(b) d-c-s agreement. However, if used to obtain cash from a bank, it is in that instance being used as a d-c agreement.

We feel that we cannot emphasise too strongly the importance of grasping this crucial distinction. You will get some practice on this in the question discussed in the next chapter. However, the importance of the distinction will be fully considered in the remainder of this chapter.

Linked transactions   The other important type of classification under the Act is that called the 'linked transaction'. Where there is a d-c-s agreement under s. 12(b) or (c) there is also a supply transaction financed by the credit agreement. The fate of such a transaction is bound up with that of the credit agreement and thus is called a 'linked transaction' (see s. 19(1)(b)). In addition, other ancillary contracts may be linked, as it may be a condition of the credit agreement that such a contract be entered into by the debtor or a relative of his, e.g., a maintenance contract (see s. 19(1)(a)). Transactions may also be linked if the requirements in s. 19(1)(c) and (2) are satisfied, assuming these provisions have any meaning! The main objective of establishing that an agreement is linked to the credit agreement is that cancellation of the latter will normally automatically cancel any linked transaction. The importance of this should be self-evident. You should also note the effect of s. 19(3) which states that a linked transaction entered in to before the making of the credit agreement has no effect unless and until that agreement is made. Beware, however: some forms of linked transaction, principally insurance contracts, are exempt from the operation of s. 19(3).

Joint and several liability of creditor and supplier

We have decided to discuss here two of the most important sections of this Act so far as the individual consumer is concerned. We are talking here of ss. 56 and 75 of the 1974 Act. These two sections between them are without doubt a major improvement in the rights of a debtor under credit agreements. Broadly, they make the creditor in appropriate circumstances, liable for things said or done by the supplier vis-à-vis the debtor. In this part of the chapter we shall confine ourselves to a few general comments about these sections, because, as you will see, we have selected an essay question on these two sections as a specimen examination question. In our suggested answer we shall be focusing on the detail.

What these sections do is not to confer any additional substantive rights on the debtor, but rather allow him or her to pursue his or her existing rights against some other person, namely, the creditor. They are merely providing the debtor with another target if things go wrong with the supply of goods and services.

Secondly, you should remember that there are differences in the applicability and operation of these two sections, although there are some overlaps. The detail of this will be explored in our commentary on the question below.

Thirdly, the impact of these two sections as a whole cannot be overestimated. Some sections of the credit industry, particularly the credit card section, do not take too kindly to ss. 56 and 75 and have sought to explore possible loopholes in the terminology of the provisions.

Fourthly, as we shall see shortly, there is much misunderstanding of the scope of the sections. What little case law there has been fully demonstrates that confusion in the judicial mind is no exception to this.

Fifthly, we have chosen an essay question because this is the way we have tended to examine these two important sections. However, a problem question might easily be set which might overlap with other topics, particularly those discussed in chapters 3 and, possibly, 4.

Illustrative question

To what extent do ss. 56 and 75 improve the position of the debtor under a credit agreement?

Commentary

Introduction By the time you reach the second or third year of your legal studies you should be capable of resisting the temptation to write down everything you know about these two sections, without any thought being given to the structure of your answer. More importantly if you merely regurgitate your knowledge, you will fail to answer the question. The words 'to what extent' are asking you to make some evaluation of the merits of these two important provisions. Indeed, it is perhaps a good practice to get into to start your answer by giving an indication of your critical thoughts upon their respective merits. You might usefully start your answer by stating that, taken together, ss. 56 and 75 represent a massive step forward in the improvement of the debtor's rights. Broadly speaking, they give to the debtor an alternative source of remedy by making a creditor liable for things said and done in certain circumstances by a supplier of goods and services. As between the sections themselves, in view of some of the limitations on the applicability of s. 75, to be gone into shortly, s. 56 may have the advantage of being a much wider and more beneficial provision on the whole.

In the above brief discussion we have indicated our views in response to the question and pointed out in advance the direction which the subsequent detailed discussion will take.

The middle and largest part of the essay will be devoted to a discussion of the detailed provisions of the two sections, drawing comparisons as appropriate. You should remember, however to try to step back from the detail and consider at various points how your detailed comments relate to the question. Finally, in your conclusion you may perhaps summarise the advantages and disadvantages of ss. 56 and 75. To round off your essay you can finish where you started by repeating the views expressed in the short introduction.

Rationale underlying ss. 56 and 75

Having stated as we have done above, in fairly brief terms, the impact of these two sections, it might at this stage make sense to consider the rationale for the introduction of such an extension of liability in the 1974 Act. The underlying reasons for this are, of course, to be found in the Crowther Committee Report on Consumer Credit. Some reference to this and a brief discussion of the reasoning behind the two sections should impress even the hardest of examiners. In para. 6.6.22 the Committee referred to their view that 'to a considerable extent the finance house and the dealer are engaged in a joint venture'. The Report goes on:

> The finance house controls the contract documents used by the dealer in his instalment credit business . . . When business is slack, the finance house will continually press the dealer to increase the volume of transactions put through. In every sense, therefore, the finance house relies on the dealer as a medium for promoting its own business and it cannot be equated with a wholly independent lender such as a bank approached by the borrower himself.

This, in a nutshell, is the rationale for making the creditor liable for the supplier's defaults. We can see here the link between this and the search for the 'business connection' which has to be established if there is to be a d-c-s under s. 12(b) and (c) discussed earlier. Once the details of ss. 56 and 75 have been discussed, it might be possible for you to come back to this underlying rationale and discuss whether the provisions actually achieve their supposed purpose.

So far we have briefly stated the impact of the sections and considered the apparent reasons for their implementation in the legislation. We must now turn our attention to the detail of the two sections. This is your opportunity to show your knowledge. You should not, however, rush straight into a descriptive, and possibly unimaginative, account of the sections. You should particularly avoid writing out the sections in full where a copy of the Act is provided for your use in the examination room. As examiners we would expect you to explore anomalies and loopholes in the sections and would invite a comparison of their respective merits as a method of protecting the debtor. You might also comment on whether there is any overlap between the two sections.

Section 56

It is perhaps worth pointing out that the section is also important in connection with the cancellation provisions which we shall consider in the next chapter. Section 56(2) is the all important provision for it states that negotiations conducted by certain persons are deemed to be conducted by those persons in the capacity of agent of the creditor as well as in their actual capacity. This 'deemed agency' provision, which may make a creditor liable for things said or done by the supplier, is thought necessary because of the reluctance of the common law to infer an agency relationship between the supplier and the creditor. Indeed, the approach of the common law was often neutral, sometimes ambivalent, where it held that the supplier in some instances was to be regarded as the agent of the debtor, in others the agent of the creditor. Generally, however, the law refused to accord such a relationship in law to the dealings between the parties. Section 56(2) seeks to get round this difficulty by imposing an agency relationship in the circumstances outlined in s. 56(1). 'Negotiations' by a person mentioned in that subsection attract the deemed agency provision in subsection (2). This includes the supplier (dealer) who is a credit broker and who sells the goods in question to the creditor before they form the subject-matter of a s. 12(a) d-c-s agreement, in other words, hire-purchase, conditional sale and credit sale agreements (see s. 56(1)(b)). Therefore the dealer/supplier in the triangular transaction represented in diagram (a) earlier in this chapter is the 'negotiator' for these purposes and the agency provision will apply to him.

Section 56(1)(c) also makes it clear that the dealer-supplier in a situation giving rise to a s. 12(b) or (c) d-c-s agreement is in a similar position. Negotiations by him are deemed to be conducted by him as agent for the creditor.

Antecedent negotiations   There are a number of significant points to be observed upon the scope of this provision. The meaning of 'negotiations' or, more correctly, 'antecedent negotiations' requires some explanation. At the outset it can be said without qualification that the Act attributes an extremely wide meaning to this phrase. Section 56(4) states that such negotiations begin when the negotiator and the debtor first communicate (including advertisements). It seems plain from this that a creditor may be bound by anything said in a poster or advertisement put out by a dealer who falls into either of the categories in s. 56(1)(b) or (c). As Goode points out (*The Consumer Credit Act, A Student's Guide*, para. 595), it is virtually impossible for a regulated agreement to come into being without some prior communication. In addition, s. 56(4) refers to 'any other dealings between them [i.e. the debtor and negotiator]' and includes these within the meaning of 'antecedent negotiations'. Goode (at para. 698) suggests that this would seem to encompass any act by the negotiator involving the proposed credit agreement. This might, therefore, include the delivery of dangerous goods and thus render the creditor liable in negligence to third parties who suffer personal injury or damage to property caused by those goods (see *Andrews* v *Hopkinson* [1957] 1 QB 229).

Another interesting feature of the 'deemed agency' provision is the fact that it does not matter that the acts of the negotiator were wrongful, or have been expressly forbidden by the creditor. Indeed, s. 56(3) makes the agency relationship non-excludable. There are some qualifications, however, upon the scope of s. 56. It seems that by definition 'antecedent negotiations' cannot cover post-contractual statements, and, in addition, it is thought that s. 56 can only be relied upon where a concluded credit agreement is made. Once that position is reached then, in a sense, s. 56 operates retrospectively to make the creditor liable for what passes in the 'antecedent negotiations'. Also, s. 56, unfortunately, only applies to regulated consumer credit agreements, and not to regulated consumer hire agreements. Such agreements cannot be d-c-s agreements under s. 12 and therefore fall outside the scope of s. 56(1)(b) and (c).

The final point on s. 56 concerns the precise legal status of any statements made by the dealer-supplier in the antecedent negotiations. If you recall your general contract law at all, you will remember that factual statements made in the precontractual period may be representations or terms of the contract, depending upon the intention of the parties. Consequently, if s. 56(2) applies, those statements may be representations or terms of the contract in relation to the creditor. Likewise, it should be recalled that any description applied to goods by the dealer/supplier may be relevant in assessing the merchantability or fitness for particular purpose of those goods. In a s. 12(a) d-c-s situation, such statements will be attributed to the creditor by virtue of s. 56(2) and may well affect his liability for the quality of the goods under the relevant implied obligations.

Section 75

This section, on the face of it, appears far more radical than s. 56 in its scope. The latter section had at least been foreshadowed by s. 16 of the Hire-Purchase Act 1965, although it must be accepted that the ambit of s. 56 is much wider. Section 75 clearly breaks new ground in its attempt to extend the notion of joint and several liability as between the supplier and creditor for the former's misrepresentation and breach of contract. The section recognises the nature of the joint venture between the two parties and its applicability depends on the establishing of the relevant business connection between supplier and creditor so as to constitute the credit agreement as a d-c-s under s. 12(b) or (c).

The impact of this section would appear to be such that certain sectors of the credit industry have made numerous attempts to restrict its scope and we shall discuss some of these points later. However, the section itself contains a number of points which require some clarification.

Like claim First, s. 75(1) talks of the debtor having a 'like claim' against the creditor if he has a claim against the supplier of goods or services for misrepresentation or breach of contract. You should consider precisely what the words 'like claim' signify. Already in one reported case, *U.D.T.* v *Taylor* 1980 SLT 28, the Sheriff's Court took the rather extreme view that if the debtor is entitled to rescind the supply contract, he is also entitled to rescind the credit contract. The better view is that 'like claim' refers to a 'monetary' claim. So, for example, if the claim against the supplier is for damages representing the cost of the repair to an item, then the debtor has a like monetary claim against the creditor for the amount in question. If the creditor is owed money by the debtor, then the latter has a right of set-off in respect of his s. 75 claim. He may deduct the amount of the claim from the balance outstanding under his agreement with the creditor. On the other hand, if the claim against the supplier is for rescission or repudiation, then the claim is still a monetary one, namely, the return of the price paid. In such circumstances the debtor has a 'like claim' against his creditor. It may well be that the amount of the 'like claim' will be equal to or more than the amount owed under the credit agreement, in which case the situation will be tantamount to rescission of the credit agreement. It should be remembered that the creditor is liable for the whole amount for which the supplier is or would be liable, irrespective of the amount advanced by way of credit. The seriousness of this should not be lost on the creditor, as he may find himself liable for consquential losses going far beyond the amount of his loan, particularly where personal injuries or damage to property are caused by unmerchantable goods supplied by the dealer.

Joint and several liability   Secondly, joint and several liability means that the debtor need not pursue or exhaust his remedies against the supplier; he may, if he so chooses, go straight to the creditor and sue him, or exercise his right to set-off mentioned above. This is a tremendous advantage to the debtor, particularly where he knows the supplier is insolvent or otherwise reluctant to meet his claim. In a sense the law is providing the debtor with another target. The creditor, in this context, may be seen as an insurer; after all he should be able to exercise some degree of control over those suppliers with whom he chooses to associate. Indeed, s. 75(2) provides the creditor, subject to any agreement between them, with a right of indemnity against the supplier, if the creditor is obliged to meet the debtor's claim under s. 75(1).

Liability depends on general law   Thirdly, it should not be forgotten that the creditor's liability depends upon that of the supplier. This liability is not governed by the 1974 Act, but by the general law of contract, the law relating to misrepresentation, and the provisions of legislation such as the Sale of Goods Act 1979 and the Supply of Goods and Services Act 1982. In this respect, however, s. 75 is less wide-ranging than s. 56, which as we have seen embraces liability in negligence, whereas s. 75 is limited to actionable misrepresentation and breaches of contract, whether of express or implied terms. Nor does s. 75, for example, extend to a supplier's breach of an ancillary maintenance contract unless the credit is being used to finance this contract also.

Section 12(b) and (c) d-c-s agreements   Fourthly, s. 75, despite judicial authority to the contrary (see *Porter* v *General Guarantee Corpn.* [1982] RTR 384) does not apply to s. 12(a) d-c-s agreements, i.e., hire-purchase, credit sale or conditional sale agreements; liability for the quality of the goods transferred under such agreements rests, in any event, with the creditor as far as the debtor is concerned. The creditor may well be able to claim indemnity from the supplier under the contract of sale, or under a 'recourse' agreement, namely, a separate agreement made between creditor and supplier whereby the latter agrees to indemnify the former in respect of claims made against the creditor by debtors. Under a s. 12(a) d-c-s agreement the creditor supplies the goods as well as the credit, whereas s. 75 only operates in circumstances where creditor and supplier are separate entities, though there is a business connection to satisfy s. 12(b) or (c).

Exceeding credit limit   Fifthly, s. 75 applies even in circumstances where the debtor has exceeded his or her credit limit under the agreement, or where some other term of the agreement has been broken. So, for example, if the debtor pays by credit card for an item worth £500, but his agreed credit limit is only £400, s. 75 will still apply.

Exclusions from section 75   However, there is one important qualification upon the usefulness of s. 75, contained in s. 75(3). This states that the section does not apply to non-commercial agreements, but, perhaps, more significantly, it imposes financial limitations upon its applicability. Section 75 is stated as not applying where the claim relates to any single item to which the supplier has attached a cash price not exceeding £100 (originally £30) or more than £30,000 (originally £10,000). For example, if the debtor buys two items each costing £75 and pays by using a credit card regulated under the Act, then as the cash price of each separate item does not exceed £100, s. 75 will not apply. The phrase 'single item' might give rise to some difficulty where a debtor bought, say, 150 items for £1 each. The answer as to whether s. 75 would apply might well depend upon whether the contract could be regarded as divisible or severable (see chapter 4). The lower limit may also provide a trap for the unwary. Remember that it is the cash price of the item which dictates whether the section applies, not the amount of credit used up. For example, A agrees to go on a holiday the total price of which is £500. He pays £50 deposit by Access. Section 75 will apply here, because the relevant figure is £500.

As to the £30,000 figure, it should be remembered that an agreement may still be regulated even though the cash price payable is £30,000 or more. Provided the credit advanced is £15,000 or less, then the credit agreement will be within the Act. However, there will be no joint and several liability where the £30,000 ceiling is exceeded. Presumably, the policy justification for such liability runs out where such large amounts are concerned.

Those are the major points arising under the provisions of s. 75. You might wish to refer to some of the attempts of the credit card industry in particular to get round the imposition of liability under s. 75. One of the early attempts related to the date of the coming into force of the regulated agreement provisions of the Act, namely, 1 April 1977. Creditors argued that credit cards issued before that date were not regulated agreements and not therefore within the section. As Goode points out (para. 675) every time the card is used a distinct contract is generated and so long as this was after the relevant date, s. 75 applies. The matter was resolved by agreement between the Office of Fair Trading and the credit card issuers on a voluntary basis. The strength of the argument obviously diminishes with time, but is a good illustration of the dislike of the type of liability created by s. 75. One other possible argument is that once the credit advanced has been repaid, s. 75 no longer applies to that particular transaction. This seems to be justified on the dubious basis that the debtor is no longer strictly a 'debtor' under the agreement in question.

Conclusion

We have now considered the detail of the two sections and at this stage we perhaps need to assess the relative merits of the two sections and conclude on their contribution to the improvement of the debtor's rights as a whole. On the face of it s. 56 would seem to be wider in its scope than s. 75. As mentioned earlier it includes 'any other dealings', whereas s. 75 is limited to misrepresentation and breach of contract claims. In addition s. 56 applies to hire-purchase, etc., agreements and is also not subject to the financial limitations in s. 75(3). There is some duplication between the two sections, particularly with regard to misrepresentation by the supplier-dealer in appropriate situations.

Overall, in conclusion, one can say without hesitation that these two sections have been significantly instrumental in enlarging the consumer's rights, by recognising the obvious links between suppliers and creditors in their so-called joint venture.

NINE

CONSUMER CREDIT: CANCELLATION AND WITHDRAWAL

Introduction

In this second chapter on the complex topic of consumer credit, we propose to consider the rights of a debtor to withdraw from or cancel a regulated consumer credit agreement. It has long been recognised that consumers, under pressure, will often sign documents agreeing to take items on hire-purchase or by some other means of credit. This is particularly thought to be the case where the pressure is face to face, i.e., the so called 'door-step sale'. The previous hire-purchase legislation to some extent provided for this, by allowing a right of cancellation during a 'cooling-off period'. The consumer could cancel an agreement for whatever reason during this period.

This right has been only given in restricted circumstances hitherto and, as you will no doubt be aware, does not apply to contracts in general. As we shall see the right of cancellation of a regulated consumer credit agreement is itself only available in very restricted circumstances under the 1974 Act. By way of contrast the right to withdraw from an agreement is available generally in the law of contract, in the sense that, at common law, an offeror is always able to withdraw or revoke his offer before acceptance. This is obviously different from a right of cancellation where an agreement has actually been concluded between the parties. As we shall see, the Act recognises the right of withdrawal of an offer to enter into a regulated agreement and contains some important provisions relating to that right.

This particular area is of great practical importance to the consumer/debtor who has been persuaded against his or her better judgment to sign credit proposal forms. Surprisingly, perhaps, there has been virtually no case law on the previous provision in the Hire-Purchase Act 1965. We are, therefore, thrown upon the provisions of the Act, which as you might expect by now, are often complex. It is again the case that fairly straightforward objectives are not easily achieved.

Questions on withdrawal and cancellation would seem to be popular for those examining consumer credit, whether in a consumer or commercial law context. We have found that the student who is prepared to devote some painstaking study to the topic usually finds that marks are more easily available on this topic than some others in this book.

Substantive difficulties

Withdrawal

The first point to note has already been briefly touched upon in the introduction. Withdrawal is a general common law right available to any person who has made an offer, provided there has not been a valid acceptance of that offer. We should not have to go through the basic principles of offer and acceptance for you, but do feel that some repetition is necessary. There is often confusion in the layperson's mind as to when he or she made a binding agreement, it being assumed that once a person has signed a document a contract has been made. However, in a situation where the prospective debtor has visited a dealer's premises with a view to buying an item on credit, often it will be the case that he or she has only made an offer to enter into a credit agreement. A credit agreement proposal form may have been completed by the dealer and debtor and even signed by the latter, but normally there will not be a concluded agreement at that stage. To use the terminology of the Act, the agreement is likely to be 'unexecuted' because it has not yet been signed by or on behalf of the creditor. It is unlikely that the dealer in the usual triangular transaction will have the authority to make a binding agreement. Indeed, he will normally have to send the proposal, for that is what it is at this stage, to the creditor for approval. Amongst other things the creditor may well wish to check the creditworthiness of the prospective debtor at this point. When will there be a concluded contract? When the creditor 'executes' the agreement and communicates his acceptance of the debtor's offer. Remember that the postal acceptance rule may well apply here. Prior to this time, however, the prospective debtor has the right to withdraw, despite what the dealer's or creditor's view might be on this.

This is, of course, a common law right but it was thought necessary to include some provisions in the Act concerning the method of withdrawal from a prospective regulated agreeement and the consequences of such withdrawal. It should be noted that a withdrawal need not be in writing (c.f. cancellation) and does not have to be in any specific form, as long as the intention is clear (s. 57(2)). The withdrawal must, however, actually be communicated (c.f. cancellation). Note also that s. 57(3) deems certain persons to be the agent of the creditor for the purpose of receiving notice of withdrawal and that this may include a person acting on behalf of the *debtor* in negotiations for the agreement, as well as the dealer/supplier (see s. 56(1)).

Withdrawal from land mortgages

Withdrawal from land mortgages is governed by special rules in s. 58 specifying the procedure to be adopted by the prospective creditor under such an agreement. Broadly, a prospective debtor is given a period of reflection before signing such an agreement. There is thus no right to cancel an agreement once it is made, but the protection for the prospective debtor lies in the procedure set out in s. 58 which is designed to give him or her a pressure-free period for thought before deciding to proceed or not, as the case may be. The effect of a failure to observe the special copy and isolation rules in ss. 58 and 61 will be that the agreement (if any) entered into by the debtor is improperly executed. What this involves will be discussed below.

Consequences of withdrawal

The consequences of valid withdrawal of an offer at common law are obvious: there is no contract between the parties. In the context of a prospective regulated credit agreement, there may be other consequences provided for by s. 57(1) of the Act. You should note that a withdrawal is deemed to have the same effect as if the agreement were cancelled under ss. 68-73. The various provisions governing the return to the position the parties were originally in will be discussed below in the context of cancellation. The point to note here is that these consequences follow a valid withdrawal also. In particular, linked transactions or offers to enter into such transactions are rescinded or withdrawn automatically.

One final point on withdrawal is that if the agreement is executed, i.e., signed by both debtor and creditor, then withdrawal is probably out of the question. Attention must then be turned to the possibility of the agreement being cancellable under s. 67 of the Act.

Cancellation

The first point to remember has been made before: the right to cancel, if applicable, gives a debtor the right to rescind for whatever reason an agreement which would otherwise be binding upon him or her. It is consequently a restricted and jealously guarded right. Section 67 lays down the specific requirements if an agreement is to be capable of cancellation. Assuming that the agreement in question is regulated, there are two questions to be answered:

(a)   Where was the agreement signed?

(b)   Were there any oral representations made face to face by the creditor or his representative ('the negotiator' — see chapter 8) to the debtor during antecedent negotiations (see s. 56(4))?

For the agreement to be cancellable there must be face to face discussions; telephone and other forms of communication will not suffice. However it does not seem to matter where these oral representations take place. They could occur at the creditor's or dealer's business premises; that fact will not prevent the agreement from being cancellable so long as the debtor does not also *sign* the agreement there. 'Oral representation' seems to mean almost anything said as long as it is in some way connected with the making of the agreement. As long as the debtor does not sign at the business premises of the creditor, any party to a linked transaction (other than the debtor or his or her relative), or those of the negotiator, i.e., the dealer/supplier, then the agreement may qualify as being cancellable.

Not all agreements are cancellable, so be careful. As we said above, s. 67 only applies to regulated agreements, so those exempt under or by virtue of s. 16 are outside the cancellation provisions, as are agreements secured on land as mentioned above in the discussion on withdrawal from land mortgages. Small agreements (see s. 17) for restricted-use credit where the credit does not exceed £50 (e.g., credit sale, *but not* hire-purchase or conditional sale agreements) are not within s. 67, nor are non-commercial agreements.

Formalities

Given that an agreement is cancellable in accordance with the provisions discussed above, it is essential that you should be fully aware of the intricate formalities to be observed by the creditor with regard to copies and notices of cancellation rights (ss. 62, 63 and 64). If these are not strictly observed an agreement will be regarded as improperly executed and unenforceable as against the debtor. In the context of cancellable agreements the copy and notice provisions also provide us with the starting and finishing points for the statutory 'cooling-off period', during which time the debtor must cancel if he so wishes.

The exact procedure to be adopted by the creditor depends on whether the agreement is 'executed' or 'unexecuted' when the debtor signs it.

Executed   In these circumstances the debtor must be given there and then a copy of the executed agreement which, if the agreement is cancellable within s. 67, must contain in accordance with s. 64 a notice of cancellation rights in the prescribed form. Failure to supply the copy or to include the notice renders the agreement unenforceable as against the debtor (s. 65). Whereas under s. 127 the court has power to allow enforcement where the debtor is not prejudiced, it *cannot* do so where there is a failure to comply with s. 64. If this section is not strictly adhered to, the agreement will be unenforceable as against the debtor indefinitely.

The second step to be taken where the agreement is executed concerns the sending of the reminder of his rights to the debtor. Section 64 requires that within seven days of the making (i.e., in this case, execution) of the agreement, the creditor must send by post to the debtor a separate notice of cancellation rights. It is the receipt of this separate notice which signals the commencement of the final five day 'cooling-off' period (s. 68).

Unexecuted   In these circumstances, the debtor must be given there and then a copy of the unexecuted agreement which, in the case of a cancellable agreement must include a notice under s. 64. In addition, a second copy, but this time of the *executed* agreement, must be given to the debtor within the seven days of the *making* of the agreement. Be careful here, because s. 63(2) talks about 'making' the agreement, not execution. If the unexecuted agreement, having been signed by the debtor, is sent to the creditor for signature, the agreement is not made until (a) it is executed by the creditor, *and* (b) his acceptance is communicated to the prospective debtor, or the postal acceptance rule applies. Thus it is only when the agreement is *made* that the obligation to send the second copy arises. Normally, this will be done at the same time as the letter of acceptance/approval is sent by the creditor. Again, this second copy must contain the appropriate notice under s. 64, if it is a cancellable agreement.

Students often confuse these two differing procedures. In the case of the second set of circumstances it is the receipt of the second copy which triggers the 'cooling-off' period under s. 68.

You should remember that the five day period commences the day after the receipt of the separate notice or second copy, as the case may be. Notice of cancellation by the debtor must be written, but can be delivered by hand. If posted however, you should note the effect of s. 69(7) which makes it effective at the moment of posting, even if it goes astray and never arrives. As with notice of withdrawal, notice of cancellation may be given to the negotiator (the dealer/supplier), or even the agent of the debtor (see s. 69(6)).

Consequences of cancellation

So far we have looked at the rather detailed mechanics involved in withdrawing from or cancelling a regulated agreement. We must now turn our attention to the impact of a valid withdrawal or cancellation. We have often found that students spend considerable time discussing the cancellability of an agreement and the mode of cancellation, but then they tend to forget to deal with the important consequences which may follow the decision to cancel. They should not be forgotten; after all the Act devotes four whole sections in an attempt to restore the *status quo ante* (see ss. 70-73). Our specimen question, as you will see, requires you to consider the consequences of cancellation with regard to a number of issues.

Recovery of monies paid

There is often misunderstanding concerning the effect of ss. 70-73 and there are a number of points to look for. Remember that payments made under a cancelled agreement, or any linked transaction are normally recoverable from the person to whom they were originally paid. This will include deposits and any other payments made by the debtor.

However, s. 70(3) does provide for joint and several liability between S and C, but *only* where the credit agreement is a d-c-s under s.12(b). This is a point commonly overlooked by students. Similarly misunderstood are the provisions concerning any part-exchange goods accepted by the dealer. The Act merely provides that if such goods are not returned to the debtor in substantially the same condition as when delivered to the dealer within 10 days of cancellation, then the debtor is entitled to recover from the dealer the part-exchange allowance (s. 73(2)). The Act does not entitle the debtor to insist on return of his goods. Any such right will depend on the terms of the agreement between dealer and debtor. Note also that joint and several liability for the part-exchange allowance only extends to s. 12(b) d-c-s agreements (see s. 73(3)).

Repayment of credit

Another important consequence of cancellation concerns the repayment of any credit advanced. Section 71 provides that in the case of an unrestricted-use d-c-s, despite cancellation, the agreement continues so far as it relates to repayment of credit and payment of interest. In the d-c-s restricted use agreement, of course, the debtor has never had his or her hands on the money and so there is no question of the debtor having to repay anything to the creditor. This ties in with the rules in s. 70(3) to the effect that payments made are recoverable from the person to whom they were originally paid. That means in a restricted-use d-c-s the creditor must recover the amount of credit from the supplier/dealer.

In the agreements covered by s. 71 there is an obligation on the debtor to pay back the credit advanced plus interest. However you should note the provisions of s. 71(2) which may penalise a creditor quite severely if the debtor pays back the amount of the credit either within a month of cancellation or before payment of the first instalment under the credit agreement. Section 71(3) provides for the situation where the debtor does not repay the credit under s. 71(2), which involves a recalculation of the instalments. We shall see this provision in operation in our examination question below.

Duties in relation to goods supplied

The two remaining issues to which we would like to draw your attention relate to any goods obtained from the dealer, where the agreement is a d-c-s restricted-use agreement (s. 12(a) or (b)) or under a linked transaction (which will naturally include situations where the credit agreement is a 12(c) d-c-s). Remember the nature of the duties owed by the debtor in respect of any goods, i.e., duty to take reasonable care for 21 days after cancellation, duty to retain possession and deliver them up at the written request of the other party (normally the dealer). Note also the other issue, namely, that the possessor of the goods (normally the debtor) has a lien over those goods with regard to any monies owed to him under s. 70(1), or in respect of part-exchange goods or allowance under s. 73(2) (see s. 70(2) and 73(5) respectively). This is a valuable protection for the debtor. Under no circumstances should he or she give up possession of the goods until the monies, etc., have been repaid. The lien is lost by the voluntary surrender of possession.

That concludes our discussion of the consequences of cancellation. We now propose to turn our attention to a rather full examination-type question. As you will see and appreciate, we would not expect so much from a student in 30-35 minutes. However, we believe that this is a useful question to illustrate a number of points discussed above and in the previous chapter.

Illustrative question

On 1 April P signed an agreement to purchase a new caravan from S Ltd. P paid a deposit of £500 and S Ltd agreed to take his old caravan in part-exchange. As S Ltd only dealt on a cash basis P was referred by S Ltd to C Credit Ltd to obtain a loan to provide the balance of the purchase price.

At P's request a representative of C Credit Ltd called at P's home on 5 April and following discussions, P signed a loan agreement which provided for the repayment of £6,500 by monthly instalments over a three year period. P was given a copy of the agreement together with a cheque for the requisite amount. P endorsed the cheque and handed it over to S Ltd the next day when he took delivery of the caravan. S Ltd took possession of P's caravan.

On 12 April P took the caravan on a trip to Cleethorpes and discovered that his car was not powerful enough to tow the caravan safely despite an assurance from S Ltd's salesman that it would be. P returned home on 20 April to find a second copy of the agreement had been sent to him by post.

Advise P.

Commentary

Introduction   As you are asked to advise P, he presumably will be seeking some way out of the agreements into which he has entered. You should be able to see on reading through the facts that there are two possible avenues to pursue.

(a)   cancellation or withdrawal;
(b)   actionable misrepresentation or breach of contract.

Classification of the agreement

Before following up one of these possible lines of enquiry, it is essential that you should correctly classify this particular agreement. This step done now will save time and avoid possible confusion later on. It also gives your answer an introduction and thus a structure of sorts.

Classification of agreement

The agreement signed by P on 1 April is a sale of goods contract between himself and S Ltd and as such will be regulated by the common law and the Sale of Goods Act 1979. However, as we shall see, if it is a linked transaction it may also be affected by the Consumer Credit Act 1974. To discover whether it is or might be linked we need to ascertain the status of the other contract made between C Ltd and P. This is clearly a personal loan agreement. It is within the financial ceiling of £15,000, P is an individual and there are no indications that it is an exempt agreement (see ss. 8, 9 and 16). It is therefore a regulated consumer credit agreement. There are two further categories which we must consider, i.e., restricted or unrestricted-use and debtor-creditor-supplier or debtor-creditor. Our discussion at this point is of fundamental importance, because any conclusions reached at this stage on the classification of this credit agreement will have implications for our advice to P and the remedies available to him.

Restricted or unrestricted-use?

First, let us consider s. 11 and restricted/unrestricted-use categories. We can tell immediately that, as this is not hire-purchase, credit or conditional sale, the agreement is not a restricted-use agreement within s. 11(1)(a). Nor is it a refinancing arrangement within s. 11(1)(c), so the only category available is s. 11(1)(b). The answer to this question lies in s. 11(3) and the fact that in the problem P endorsed the cheque given to him by the representative of C Credit. This strongly suggests that the cheque was made payable to him, i.e., P; otherwise why does he endorse it over to S Ltd? Section 11(3) provides that if the debtor, P, is provided with credit in such a way as to leave him free to use it as he wishes, then the agreement is not within s. 11(1) and is therefore an unrestricted-use agreement. We can be fairly certain about this on the facts. It does illustrate the need for you to pay close attention to the facts in problems of this kind.

D-c-s or d-c agreement?

The next step is to decide, if possible, whether the agreement is a d-c-s or d-c agreement. However having decided that the agreement is one for unrestricted-use credit, we can see that the only possibility for this agreement to fall into the d-c-s category is by showing that it satisfies the requirements under s. 12(c). If this is not possible this is merely a d-c agreement, i.e., in the language of the Crowther Committee an 'unconnected loan'. What are the requirements of s. 12(c)? There must be shown to be 'pre-existing arrangements' between S Ltd and C Ltd and knowledge on the part of the latter that the credit is to be used to finance a transaction between S Ltd and P. It would seem highly unlikely that C Ltd, through their representative were unaware of the purpose for which the loan was required. The question of what constitutes 'pre-existing arrangements' and whether on the facts there is anything of that nature is a little more complex. Section 187(1) attempts to define 'pre-existing' arrangements as arrangements previously made between supplier and creditor, which is not very helpful at all. It seems that the word 'arrangement' is to be given a wide meaning and does not have to be a legally binding agreement between creditor and supplier. On the facts of our problem we are told that S Ltd only deals on a cash basis. It may therefore be the case that C Ltd have indicated in the past that persons referred to them by S Ltd would be financially accommodated by them and this might be sufficient to raise the necessary business connection within s. 12(c). It is difficult and probably dangerous, however, to be categorical on this point. In any event whether the agreement is a d-c-s under s. 12(c) or moreover a d-c under s. 13, we must now go on to consider the issue of cancellation or withdrawal.

Cancellation

To be cancellable an agreement must, as indicated in our earlier discussion, fall within the provisions of s. 67. Withdrawal is, of course, something different in that this is the common law right of an offeror to withdraw his or her offer before acceptance. As we shall see withdrawal does not appear possible on the facts of the problem. However, the agreement would appear to be potentially cancellable. We are told that 'discussions' take place between C's representative and P on 5 April. These would almost certainly constitute 'oral representations' made face-to-face as is required under s. 67. In addition, P signs the agreement at home. We can safely conclude, therefore, that the agreement is cancellable. However, whether P is still in a position to cancel on 20 April is not quite so clear. We need to establish what formalities have to be observed by C Ltd and whether these have been complied with. This in turn will enable us to decide the issue of cancellation on P's return from his holiday.

Executed or unexecuted?

In order to do this, it is necessary to consider whether the agreement signed by P on 5 April was executed or unexecuted following his signature. Close attention to the facts is required here. Would C Ltd's representative have handed over the cheque representing the credit if the agreement was unexecuted at that stage? As this is a most unlikely sequence of events, we can assume with some certainty that the agreement was executed at that time. This rules out the possibility of withdrawal as there is a binding agreement at this point.

Formalities

We are told that P is given a copy of the agreement, along with the cheque. This copy must be a copy of the executed agreement (s. 63(1)) and, what is more, this being a cancellable agreement, that copy must contain a notice of cancellation rights in accordance with s. 64(1)(a). It is worth pointing out that if this requirement is not satisfied, then the agreement is unenforceable as against P. The court has no power (see s. 127(4)) to allow enforcement, thus giving P an indefinite right to cancel.

Assuming the copy does comply with ss. 63 and 64, then according to s. 64(1)(b) a notice of cancellation rights must also be sent by post within 7 days following the making of the agreement. We are told that a second copy of the agreement had been sent by post to P and this he discovered on his return from holiday on 20 April.

There seem to be two points on this. First, was the second copy sent by post 'within seven days' after the making of the agreement, i.e., 5 April? Section 64 does not say it has to be received within seven days, so presumably if it was posted on 11 April, s. 64(1)(b) would be satisfied on that account. The copy may have arrived on 12 April after P had left for his holiday. It must be assumed that the onus would be on C Ltd to show that the second copy was posted within the seven days and that it was correctly stamped and addressed. The second issue raised by the facts concerns the point that C Ltd have sent a second copy of the agreement (which we shall assume contains a notice of cancellation rights). Section 64(1)(b) talks of a 'notice' being sent by post, presumably meaning a separate notice of cancellation rights. Would the sending of a full copy fall foul of s. 64? Remember the dire consequences for C Ltd if this were the case. Technically, there would appear to be a breach of s. 64. Would C Ltd be penalised for doing more than they were legally obliged to do? On the other hand, if a second copy of the agreement is sent, the debtor is less likely to be reminded of his cancellation rights than if a separate notice was sent. We shall assume for the present purposes that a court would not regard the sending of a full copy as a breach of s. 64.

The sending of either a second copy or notice of cancellation rights under s. 64 has a dual purpose. Not only is it meant to be a reminder to the debtor of his or her cancellation rights, but it also serves to set a time limit for the 'cooling-off period' (see s. 68). The period is stated to be five days following the day on which the copy or notice was received. The difficulty facing P on the facts is whether the five day period will run from the moment he discovers the copy at his home on 20 April, or is he deemed to have received it at some earlier time? This earlier time might be when it would normally have arrived in the usual course of post, i.e., 12 or 13 April. If this latter interpretation were to be accepted, then cancellation is out of the question on 20 April. However, it might be strongly argued that s. 68 is intended to indicate in clear and finite terms just how long a debtor may have in which to cancel. To introduce the notion of a 'deemed' receipt may involve uncertainty as to the start and finish of the 'cooling-off' period. We shall again make an assumption, i.e., that P still has the right to cancel on 20 April.

It should be pointed out that he has until the fifth day, excluding 20 April, in which to cancel. So if he cancels before midnight on 25 April, this will be effective, provided it is in writing and is served upon one of the persons specified in s. 69(1). If our agreement is a d-c-s this may mean (see s. 69(6)) that service of notice of cancellation on S Ltd will be valid. There is no strict form of wording to be observed so long as the debtor's intention is clear. If P posts his notice then it will be effective from the moment of posting, whether or not the notice is ever received or is received outside the 'cooling-off' period (see s. 69(7)).

Effects of cancellation

The effect of the notice is to cancel the credit agreement, whether it is a d-c or d-c-s. If the agreement in the question is a 12(c) d-c-s agreement, then by virtue of s. 19(1)(b), the supply agreement made on 1 April between P and S Ltd is a linked transaction and this will also be cancelled automatically.

Recovery of deposit

We have also to advise P, in the event of a valid cancellation, as to the further consequences with regard to payments made by him, repayment of the credit advanced, the part-exchange and his rights and liabilities in respect of the new caravan. If the agreement is a d-c-s, then the issue of P's deposit of £500 will arise. Section 70(1) provides that any sum paid under a linked transaction shall become repayable and according to s. 70(3) it is recoverable from the person to whom it was originally paid. Here this means that P is entitled to recover his deposit from S Ltd and S Ltd *only*. There is no joint and several liability here because that only applies where the agreement is restricted-use d-c-s under s. 12(b).

Recovery and repayment of credit

Secondly, P endorsed the cheque representing the credit over to S Ltd, so it would appear that s. 70(1) and (3) apply in the same way as with the deposit. However, s. 71(1) provides that on cancellation of a regulated agreement, other than a restricted-use d-c-s, the credit is repayable to the creditor including interest. As our agreement may be a 12(c) d-c-s or a d-c, then this provision will apply. However, s. 71(2) provides that no interest is to be paid on any amount repaid by the debtor within one month of cancellation, or where instalments are payable, before the first instalment is due. As far as P is concerned he must repay the credit and interest; if he does so quickly, then he may escape payment of all or some of the interest due. If he is unable to pay all or any of the credit, then he is not liable to repay any credit until he receives an appropriate request in writing in accordance with s. 71(3).

Part-exchange goods or allowance

Thirdly, we must consider the position with regard to the part-exchange goods or allowance. Section 73 of the Act provides that unless those goods are returned to P in substantially the same condition as when delivered to S Ltd (assuming S to be a negotiator, i.e., there must be a d-c-s agreement, see s. 56), then S Ltd will be liable for the part-exchange allowance. Note once again that there can be no joint and several liability, unless the agreement is a 12(b) d-c-s (restricted-use). This point is frequently overlooked (c.f. s. 75).

Lien

It should be noted also that in respect of monies owed to P by S Ltd, whether the deposit, credit advanced or the part-exchange goods or allowance, P will have a lien on the new caravan if it is still in his possession until such time as those items are paid or handed over by S Ltd (see ss. 70(2) and 73(5)). This leads us on to the rights and liabilities of P with regard to the new caravan. Section 72 sets out the duty to take reasonable care for 21 days after cancellation, the duty to restore, subject to any lien, to the other party (S Ltd). In the problem, it would seem that P will be in a strong position as against S Ltd because of his lien. He can refuse to part with possession until his claims under ss. 70 and 73 are satisfied, and his duty of reasonable care expires after 21 days from cancellation. It probably then becomes a duty not to wilfully damage the goods, but it is in P's interests in any event to keep the goods in good condition so as to protect his lien. A lien over worthless goods is of little value. It is perhaps worth pointing out that P need not deliver the goods to S Ltd's premises but he is under a duty to retain possession of them. There is nothing in the Act which permits P to sell the goods so as to recoup his monies.

If the credit agreement was a d-c agreement, then the transaction between S Ltd and P would be unaffected legally by P's cancellation of the credit agreement, unless it could be argued at common law that the supply contract was conditional upon the making of a credit agreement. Even so, if P cancels the credit agreement, it could still be argued that he must proceed with the supply contract in any event. It could be said that the condition had been fulfilled, or that it was P's action which caused it to be unfulfilled.

Misrepresentation or breach of contract of supplier

The other possibility raised by the facts concerns the assurance of the salesman employed by S Ltd about the towing capability of P's car in relation to the caravan. This could amount to an actionable misrepresentation, or conceivably a breach of s. 14(3) of the Sale of Goods Act 1979. Whilst the statement appears to concern the towing capacity of P's car, which was not the subject of the sale, it is still essentially a comment about the caravan's fitness for P's particular purpose, namely, the ability of his car to tow it. If P does rely on this and S Ltd fails to show the reliance was unreasonable, then S Ltd would be liable for misrepresentation and/or breach of s. 14(3). This would entitle P to rescind or repudiate the contract of supply and recover his money back from S Ltd. He would, however, on the face of it still be obliged to pay the creditor under the agreement. If S Ltd does pay P all his money back P will have little difficulty in that he will be able to repay the credit more or less straightaway. However, his difficulties may start if S Ltd refuses to refund the money paid, or even worse has gone into liquidation. If the credit agreement is a d-c, there is nothing further P can do. However, if the agreement is a d-c-s, under 12(b) or (c), there are two possible lines of action. Section 56(2) will make the creditor liable for statements of S Ltd's salesman, because S Ltd will be a credit broker and thus a negotiator within s. 56(1)(c). Alternatively, s. 75 will render C Ltd jointly and severally liable for the misrepresentation or breach of contract by S Ltd. Furthermore, the much criticised decision in *UDT* v *Taylor* (above) seems to suggest that rescission or repudiation of the supply contract entitles the debtor to do the same to the credit agreement. As was pointed out in our earlier discussion, the words 'like claim' must relate to a monetary claim. Even so the effect is likely to be the same, in that the monetary claim by P against S Ltd is likely to exceed or equal the amount owed under the credit agreement. Therefore, by exercising the right of set-off P will effectively wipe out the credit agreement.

Conclusion

We can see in this question two possible avenues of escape for P from his predicament, i.e., cancellation of the agreement, or rescission/repudiation for misrepresentation or breach of contract. The effect of either of these solutions as far as P is concerned will be broadly the same, except that if he successfully proves misrepresentation/breach of contract, he might also recover for any reasonably foreseeable consequential losses.

Finally, a brief word of comfort for those of you who might be concerned at the large number of points in the question discussed above. We suspect that an examiner might, for example, not have brought in the possibility of an action for misrepresentation/breach. Indeed, when we first used this question, the phrase concerning the assurance by the salesman was omitted. This made the question a little more manageable in the context of the examination room.

TEN

CONSUMER CREDIT: TERMINATION

Introduction

In this, our third and final chapter on consumer credit, we propose to consider the various ways in which a credit agreement may be terminated. Most credit agreements end in the way both parties intended, i.e., by payment of the appropriate sums over the time period agreed. However, a credit agreement may come to a premature end in one of a number of ways. The 1974 Act gives the debtor two distinct and separate methods of terminating the agreement before it has run its full course. Section 94 entitles a debtor to settle early and earn a rebate calculated, according to a statutory formula, rather than being left to the whim of the creditor. Whilst this applies to all credit agreements its practical importance perhaps lies mainly in the context of the trading-in of motor vehicles which are the subject of hire-purchase agreements. We do not propose to discuss the detail of these provisions because, important though such a right is, it gives rise to little academic difficulty. It is therefore unlikely to figure to any great extent in an examination question.

The second method of bringing an agreement to an early end is given by ss. 99-100 of the Act, which enable the debtor under a regulated conditional sale or hire-purchase agreement to terminate voluntarily the agreement. The detail of how and when this right can be exercised and the consequences that follow will be discussed below.

The two methods of bringing an agreement to an end do not involve any element of default on the part of the debtor; they are steps which a debtor is lawfully entitled to take. The exercise of these rights needs no justification, as with the right of cancellation discussed in the previous chapter. *Remember not to confuse voluntary termination with cancellation.*

Termination where the debtor is *in default* is the other major aspect which needs to be considered in some depth. Whilst we recognise that default may take a form other than non-payment (e.g., wrongful disposal of goods on hire-purchase), non-payment appears to be the most common form of default and consequently it is upon that which we shall concentrate. One of the difficulties facing students here is that the Act does not contain a comprehensive set of rules to deal with the matter of default. It is therefore necessary for you to have a good understanding of what constitutes breach at common law and the basic common law principles on assessment of damages. This is an area of immense importance from both a practical and examination point of view.

Substantive difficulties

Voluntary termination

The present provisions in ss. 99-100 of the 1974 Act are likely to be fully understood only in the context of the development and use of so-called 'minimum payment' clauses in hire-purchase agreements. The essence of a hire-purchase agreement is that at common law the debtor has a right to terminate the agreement before it runs its full course; namely, it is a hiring of goods with an option to purchase. Creditors adopted this form of agreement principally to avoid certain exceptions to the *nemo dat* rule (see chapter 6).

In the event that the debtor exercised his right to terminate in this way, creditors inserted 'minimum payment' clauses in their agreements. Such clauses were designed to ensure that they received at least sufficient monies to cover any depreciation in respect of the goods returned to them. It was not uncommon to find clauses which went much further than this by insisting, for example, that on termination the debtor had to pay two-thirds of the total hire-purchase price. This amount was payable irrespective of the amount of depreciation in the goods and without any discount for early receipt of payment (see, e.g., *Campbell Discount Co. Ltd* v *Bridge* [1962] AC 600).

Where the debtor was in breach of contract under the common law such clauses could not be enforced on the grounds that they were penal in nature under the guidelines laid down by Lord Dunedin in *Dunlop Pneumatic Tyre Co. Ltd* v *New Garage & Motor Co. Ltd* [1915] AC 79 at p. 86 (see *Cooden Engineering Co. Ltd* v *Stanford* [1953] 1 QB 86). However, if the reason for the agreement being brought to an end was the debtor's own lawful voluntary termination, the rules on penalties were held to be inapplicable (see *Associated Distributors Ltd* v *Hall* [1938] 2 KB 83). This anomaly moved Lord Denning to observe upon 'the absurd paradox' that the law 'will grant relief to the man who breaks his contract but will penalise the man who keeps it' (*Bridge* v *Campbell Discount* at p. 629). This anomaly was only resolved at a factual level in *Bridge* and subsequent cases by treating the debtor's communications as confirming a breach of contract as opposed to a voluntary termination. This remains the position at common law and will apply to agreements which are not regulated.

Under the common law the right of voluntary termination is confined to hire-purchase agreements only. Under the Act, however, the statutory right of termination extends to both regulated hire-purchase and regulated conditional sale agreements which are assimilated for this purpose.

If a debtor under such a regulated agreement exercises the right of termination, the Act controls the maximum he may be required to pay, irrespective of what the agreement itself requires him to pay. This is the so-called 'fifty per cent rule'. The purpose of this rule is to ensure that debtors are not penalised when exercising their right, but it should not be thought of as providing a financially attractive solution for the debtor. The rule is that where the debtor has not yet paid 50% of the total hire-purchase price, then the maximum sum he can be required to pay is such sum as would bring his total payments up to the 50% figure. In calculating the amount payable, account needs to be taken of any arrears due at the time, these being recoverable under a separate head. In the position where the debtor has already paid more than 50%, he is only required to pay arrears (if any) of instalments at the date of termination. The following example illustrates how the rule would operate in a given situation:

50% of total hire-purchase price	$\dfrac{£5,000}{2}$	£2,500
Amount received by creditor at date of termination:		
Deposit plus instalments paid	£1,800	
Instalments in arrears (recovered)	£ 200	
	£2,000	£2,000
		£ 500

The application of the 50% rule would require the debtor to pay:

$$\frac{£5,000}{2} - £2,000 = £500.$$

The rule itself is quite arbitrary in that it takes no account of the value of the goods which have been returned to the creditor. If, for example, the goods returned (now second-hand) are worth less than £2,500, then in our illustration above the creditor would sustain a loss, in the sense that he would receive less than the amount he would have received if the agreement had run its full course. Conversely, the depreciation on the goods returned may be so low that the application of the 50% rule could result in the creditor making a profit over and above that which he would have made in the normal course of events.

The provision in s. 100(3) is designed to deal with this difficulty. It does so by giving the court a discretion to order the payment by the debtor of a lesser sum than that which would be payable under the 50% rule. The discretion, however, is limited to circumstances in which such a lesser sum would 'be equal to the loss sustained by the creditor'. The conventional view is that the creditor sustains a 'loss' if he receives anything less than the total hire-purchase price. Thus the debtor will almost invariably carry the burden of the whole of the depreciation up until the time of his voluntary termination. The discretion in s. 100(3) is therefore of limited value. Let us assume in our illustration above that the value of the goods in the creditor's hands is £1,000. Assuming there is no allegation that the debtor has failed to take reasonable care of the goods (see s. 100(4)), the 50% rule would prevent the debtor bearing the whole of the burden of the depreciation, but there is no scope for the Court exercising its discretion under s. 100(3).

In conclusion we think it important to re-emphasise that voluntary termination may only in rare cases be a financially attractive method of bringing an agreement to an end for the debtor in difficulties. There may in fact in many cases be little difference in the amount that the creditor receives whether he recovers a payment under s. 100 or at common law by way of damages for breach.

Breach

It is important to recognise that the Act does not actually define what amounts to a breach, or indeed what amounts to a repudiatory breach (which may automatically terminate the agreement or justify the creditor in doing so). These matters are, as we shall see, left entirely to the common law. The main provisions of the Act regulate the enforcement of the creditor's rights in the event that there has been a breach by the debtor. The protection afforded to debtors takes two different but related forms. The first is in the nature of procedural requirements, e.g., default notice or court order (see ss. 87-91), which the creditor is under a duty to observe before exercising his remedies. The second form of protection is contained in the wide powers vested in the court by ss. 127-135 (e.g., time orders).

From an examination point of view it is likely that the procedural provisions and the consequences of compliance and non-compliance may assume greater significance than the discretionary powers of the court. However, existence of these should not be overlooked. The relevance of these powers should be made clear to the examiner in the context of any discussion of the procedural requirements. For example, the issue of a default notice by a creditor triggers off the debtor's right to apply for a time order under s. 129.

Assuming that the debtor is in default and that the default is in the nature of non-payment of instalments, it is necessary to identify at some stage the precise status of that breach under the common law: i.e., is it repudiatory or non-repudiatory? We shall address the question first because the creditor's remedies vary accordingly and with it the action he is likely to take. This in turn will have implications as to the procedural requirements he needs to observe: e.g., if a debtor is in arrears with the first instalment under a hire-purchase agreement and the creditor is not seeking to terminate the agreement, he is not required by s. 87 to serve a default notice. Additionally, the amount of damages to which the creditor may be entitled will also vary according to the nature of the debtor's breach. It is perhaps helpful to students to approach the whole issue by looking first at the common law.

It is important that you should distinguish between the different categories of breach which may be committed by the debtor. First, the mere failure to pay instalments as and when due is in itself a breach and this is so irrespective of any express provision to that effect. The consequences of such a breach depend upon whether it amounts to a repudiatory or non-repudiatory breach. This is essentially a question of fact. You will no doubt recall that a repudiatory breach is one which entitles the creditor to terminate the contract and sue for damages, namely expectation losses. This will allow the creditor to recover not merely the arrears at the date of the breach but also the amount of future instalments less the resale value of the repossessed goods and discount for earlier receipt of monies (see *Yeoman Credit Ltd* v *Waragowski* [1961] 1 WLR 1124; *Overstone Ltd* v *Shipway* [1962] 1 WLR 117). In short, the creditor is to be placed in the financial position he would have been in had the contract been fully performed.

If, however, the debtor's breach is of a non-repudiatory nature, i.e., relatively minor, then (in the absence of any express term which makes such breach a repudiatory breach) the creditor will only be entitled to those instalments in arrears at the date of the breach (see *Financings Ltd* v *Baldock* [1963] 1 All ER 433, CA).

It should be noted that the mere failure to pay instalments on time or at all in itself may not amount to a repudiatory breach. The test is whether the debtor has evinced a clear indication not to carry out his future obligations under the agreement (see *Financings Ltd* v *Baldock* above and contrast *Yeoman Credit Ltd* v *Waragowski* above). Any minimum payment clause which in these circumstances sought to make the debtor liable for more than the arrears would be struck down as penal (see our earlier discussion in this chapter and see *Financings Ltd* v *Baldock*).

The relatively simple position outlined above may be complicated by the fact that it is commonplace to find in credit agreements clauses which may allow a creditor to treat an otherwise minor breach as grounds for terminating the contract. Whether any such clause has that effect is a question of construction. If a clause does have that effect, then the creditor is entitled to repudiatory damages despite the fact that the debtor may in reality only be guilty of a trivial breach (see *Lombard North Central plc* v *Butterworth* [1987] 1 All ER 267, CA). This may be achieved by clauses which clearly make time of payment of the essence of the contract. The implications of this for the debtor may be quite serious. The facts of *Butterworth* (above) illustrate this succinctly. In that case the hirer who had committed a relatively minor breach found himself paying approximately £10,000 for the hire of a computer for 18 months. If he had completed the agreement as intended he would have only paid £11,700 for five years' use of the machine! This was a hire agreement; consider what would have been the position had it been a regulated hire-purchase agreement and he had exercised the right of voluntary termination.

We must now turn to the provisions of the Act. As we pointed out above these provisions do not determine what is or is not a breach, nor the precise status of such breach. They impose constraints mainly of a procedural nature upon the manner in which the creditor can enforce his common law rights as to termination of the agreement and repossession of goods (if any).

There are three provisions of which you should be aware and understand well. The first is the default notice procedure set out in ss. 87-89. You should know the circumstances in which a default notice is necessary (s. 87). You should be conversant with the major items which must be included in such notice. Whether or not you are required to know any detail contained in regulations is a matter of guidance from your lecturers or tutors. Finally, you should be aware of the consequences of compliance (s. 89) or non-compliance by the debtor. Perhaps more importantly you should be aware of the consequences if the creditor fails to carry out his statutory duty in this regard (see *Eshun* v *Moorgate Mercantile Co. Ltd* [1971] 1 WLR 722 on an earlier provision in the Hire-Purchase Act 1965). You should note from *Eshun's* case the insistence by the courts on strict compliance by the creditor with regard to the contents of default notices.

Secondly the provisions in ss. 90-91 are of great importance in that they create a category of goods known as 'protected goods'. You need to be sure you understand how to calculate the one-third aspect. Our experience shows that there will always be one or two students who seem unable to carry out this usually straightforward numerical calculation. Be particularly careful if there is an installation charge involved in the credit agreement.

The consequence of goods being protected is that the creditor cannot recover possession unless he obtains a court order. If the creditor does apply for such an order, this will trigger off the debtor's right to apply for a time order (s. 129). The prospect of the debtor in these circumstances applying for a time order may move creditors to recover possession by the alternative means permitted by the Act, namely, the consent of the debtor (see s. 173(3)). Case law on this issue under the Hire-Purchase Act 1965 suggests that the consent must be 'full, free and informed' (*Mercantile Credit* v *Cross* [1965] 1 All ER 577 and see, more recently, *Chartered Trust plc* v *Pitcher* (1987) unreported). We must emphasise yet again that the protected goods provisions apply only to regulated conditional sale and hire-purchase agreements.

The final restriction we wish to mention is of much wider application in that it applies to regulated conditional sale and hire-purchase agreements whether the goods are protected or not, and additionally to goods under regulated hire agreements. Section 92 requires a creditor or owner to obtain either a court order or consent to enter 'any premises' in order to recover possession of goods. It should be noted that the consent which will suffice under s. 173(3) must be consent 'given at the time'. Advance consent, e.g., in the agreement itself is not sufficient.

Illustrative question

In June 1985 D, a greengrocer, took possession of a new 'mobile shop' under a hire-purchase agreement with C Finance Ltd. The total hire-purchase price (including interest) of the vehicle was £20,000. D paid a deposit of £2,000, with the balance to be paid by 36 monthly instalments of £500.

D paid the first eight instalments as and when due. The ninth and tenth instalments were each more than two weeks late and were paid only after valid default notices had been served upon him by C Finance Ltd.

D again fell into arrears due to a downturn in business and wrote to C Finance Ltd to explain why he had failed to pay the latest instalment on time. In his letter D stated, 'It is unlikely that I will be able to maintain payments at the present level. Would it be possible to reduce the instalments and extend the period of credit?'

A few days later D received a valid default notice but failed to pay the arrears by the date specified in the notice. A week later a representative of C Finance Ltd called at D's home. D explained that he had lost his copy of the agreement and was not sure what to do. The representative advised him that he was obliged in law to allow him to repossess the goods. D allowed him to do so. The vehicle was subsequently sold at auction but realised only £8,000. The hire-purchase agreement contains a clause which gives C Finance Ltd the power to terminate the agreement if any instalment is more than 10 days in arrears. The clause also renders time of payment of the essence. D has now received a demand from C Finance Ltd for £5,000 by way of damages for breach.

Advise D.

Commentary

Your outline plans of an attempted answer to this question should identify the following issues:

(a)   Is the agreement regulated by the 1974 Act?

(b)   If so, has D exercised his right of voluntary termination? If he has done so, what are the consequences of that action?

(c)   If, alternatively, D is in breach, what constraints are there on recovery of possession of the goods: namely, are the goods 'protected'? The issue of consent would appear to be a crucial issue. What are the consequences of non-compliance with the 'protected goods' provisions?

(d)   Assuming there is no breach of these provisions, is D liable for the whole of the £5,000? This will involve a consideration of the nature of the breach in the light of the clause purporting to make time of the essence and also the case law on recovery of damages in such instances.

Certain points of advice made in previous chapters concerning the use of the Act in examinations are no less relevant here.

We shall approach the issues in the order listed above.

Is the agreement regulated?

Whilst it is fair to assume that your examiner would seek to ensure that hypothetical credit transactions fell within the Act, this does not preclude him or her from arranging facts so as to make you show that you understand why an agreement is regulated. In this particular case, whilst D is a greengrocer and therefore engaged in business, he is an 'individual' within s. 189(1) of the 1974 Act, unless he is trading as a limited company. We can safely assume on these facts that he is not. In addition, whilst the total hire-purchase price is £20,000, the agreement is likely to be regulated. First, it should be noted that D pays a deposit of £2,000 which must be deducted from the £20,000. Also the interest charges are likely to exceed £3,000 in an agreement of this nature lasting three years. In these circumstances the credit advanced, we would suggest, is not likely to exceed £15,000. Finally, there is nothing in the facts to suggest that the agreement is exempt under s. 16 or regulations made thereunder.

Voluntary termination

As the agreement in question is stated to be a hire-purchase agreement, you will appreciate that the debtor, D, has both at common law and under the statute (s. 99) the right to bring the agreement to an end before payment of the final instalment. This is a voluntary right which is exercisable unilaterally by the debtor for whatever reason.

On the facts, whilst there is a possibility of D's action being regarded as voluntary termination, it should be pointed out that it is not the strongest of possibilities. The question is one of construction which revolves around ascertaining D's intention. It is more likely that his letter would be construed either as a mere enquiry, or as a breach of contract. However, it is worth considering the issue of voluntary termination at the very least briefly. Assuming that the letter is so regarded, it is necessary to point out the following consequences and advise D accordingly. Voluntary termination involves the return of the goods to the creditor. This would not require the latter to obtain a court order or the consent of the debtor to retake possession, irrespective of whether the goods might be 'protected'. The financial consequences of which D should be made aware are determined by s. 100. In these circumstances D should be advised that he will be liable for the instalment in arrear at the date of the letter (£500). In addition D would be liable to pay, by virtue of s. 100(1), such sum as would bring his total payments up to 50% of the total hire-purchase price (i.e., £20,000/2 − £7,500 (total payments) = £2,500).

D would be obliged to pay this sum unless it could be shown that a lesser sum would satisfy the creditor's loss resulting from the termination of the agreement by D. Under s. 100(3) the court may award the payment of such lesser sum. On the facts of this problem the loss sustained by the creditor would in fact *exceed* the sum of £2,500 which D would be required to pay under s. 100(1). Had the contract run its normal course C Finance Ltd would have received £20,000. In the event however the creditor would only receive £7,500 (deposit and instalments) plus £8,000 (resale of vehicle), equalling £15,500. The additional sum of £2,500 would still leave the creditor with a 'loss' of £2,000.

The court has no discretion under s. 100(3) to *increase* the amount of the debtor's liability over and above that calculated in accordance with s. 100(1). Assuming that the debtor has taken reasonable care of the goods (and is thus not required to recompense the creditor under s. 100(4)), the total payments for which D will be liable, namely, £3,000 (£500 arrears plus £2,500), may be substantially less than the amount for which he would be liable if his conduct is regarded as a repudiatory breach. On the other hand if the breach is non-repudiatory, D may only be liable for the instalment in arrear at the time. We shall discuss these matters further below.

Breach of contract

Assuming that what D has done does not amount to voluntary termination, there is clearly a breach of contact. We propose to consider here the statutory procedures which a creditor is required to follow in these circumstances.

The first point to note is that the question specifically states that the default note is 'valid'. Do not waste time, therefore, considering the requirements of s. 88 or the consequences of non-compliance. The provisions which do require discussion are those concerned with 'protected goods', namely ss. 90, 91 and 173.

It will be necessary to show that the goods are 'protected' within s. 90 of the Act. This will involve a straightforward calculation of which students often rather surprisingly make a mess. The goods in question are protected since more than one third of the total hire-purchase price has been paid by D, i.e., £2,000 (deposit) plus £5,000 (10 instalments) equalling £7,000 (which exceeds £20,000 ÷ 3 = £6,666.66). We apologise for labouring the point.

It follows therefore that C Finance in order to lawfully repossess require a court order or, according to s. 173(3), the consent of the debtor 'given at that time' to repossession. It is clear from the facts that C Finance have not got a court order, but rather have sought to obtain D's consent to repossession. The issue is whether or not the consent is valid. In order to be able to advise on this point, it is necessary to consider the approach adopted in the case law on the old Hire-Purchase Act 1965. The consent must be real and to use the words of Willmer L.J in *Mercantile Credit Co. Ltd* v *Cross* [1965] 2 QB 205 at p. 214 it must be 'free and voluntary and . . . informed consent'. However, the Court of Appeal in that case was prepared to hold that constructive notice of his rights on the part of the debtor would suffice. The Court was substantially influenced by the fact that debtors did receive notification of their rights in copies of the agreement and concluded in that case that the consent was real.

It is at least arguable that this reasoning is inconsistent with dicta of Lord Denning MR in *United Dominions Trust (Commercial) Ltd* v *Ennis* [1968] 1 QB 54 where his lordship appears to suggest that *actual* notice by the debtor of his rights and obligations under the agreement is necessary (at least in the context of voluntary termination). In the most recent case, *Chartered Trust plc* v *Pitcher* (1987) unreported, on the peculiar facts the Court of Appeal expressed the view that the absence of information as to their rights meant that the consent of ther debtors was not 'informed'. To use the words of Kerr LJ the repossession was 'coercive' as opposed to 'consensual'.

The facts of our problem cause some difficulty. On the one hand both from the contents of D's letter and from the statement by C Finance's representative it could be argued that the consent was not free and informed. In *Pitcher* the Court of Appeal was clearly influenced by the fact that the debtors had expressed an interest in continuing with the agreement, as indeed D has on these facts. In addition, there seems to be an element of coercion in the statement of the representative that 'D is legally obliged to allow repossession'. It seems clear from *Pitcher's* case that the creditor's representative is under no obligation to explain to the debtor his rights, or the various powers of the court concerning repossession of the goods. However, on the facts of the problem the positive statement made by the representative of C Finance Ltd might arguably mislead D as to his rights, and may have the effect of vitiating any consent.

An examiner would expect a student to consider the alternative possibilities on this issue. If it were found that the consent was not real on the facts, the repossession would be unlawful. Section 91 of the Act would apply with the result that, far from having to pay all or any part of the £5,000 demanded by C Finance, D would be entitled to recover from them all payments made without any reduction for use and be under no further obligation under the agreement. For an illustration of the way this type of provision operated under the hire-purchase legislation, the student might refer to *Carr* v *James Broderick & Co. Ltd* [1942] 2 KB 275.

Liability

By way of stark contrast, if the consent to repossession is lawful, we need to consider the extent of D's liability for breach of the agreement which will essentially depend on whether the breach is repudiatory or non-repudiatory. We would suggest that the discussion might be approached in the following way.

If the conduct of D does not itself amount to a repudiatory breach, but the creditor treats it as grounds for terminating the contract, D's only liability would be for any instalments in arrears at time of termination (i.e., £500, see *Financings Ltd* v *Baldock* [1963] 2 QB 104). He will not be liable for any loss of the future instalments. Whether or not D's breach of itself constitutes repudiatory conduct is a question of fact. A mere failure to pay an instalment on time is most unlikely to be regarded, on its own, as such conduct. This is particularly so in the light of the terms of D's letter.

However, the decision of the Court of Appeal in *Butterworth's* case recognises the possibility that the creditor may, by making time for payment 'of the essence', render the failure to pay a single instalment within a specified date as a repudiatory breach. On the facts of our problem this appears to be the case. Accordingly, D would appear to be liable for the £5,000 claimed by C Finance Ltd. However, even if the decision of *Butterworth* were to be applied to the facts, the claim for £5,000 fails to take account of any reduction for the early receipt of monies by C Finance Ltd (see, e.g., *Overstone Ltd* v *Shipway* [1962] 1 WLR 117, a case on voluntary termination but relevant on this issue).

Despite any such allowance being made in D's favour, his resultant liability bears remarkable contrast with the position in the event of an unlawful repossession, or indeed, in the exercise of the right to voluntary termination. The net result would be that D would have in fact paid a total of £12,000 (less a relatively small amount of discount) for approximately one year's use of the vehicle.

This might be regarded as somewhat unjust and consequently provide the impetus to discover means by which the injustice might be avoided. The facts of this question have been deliberately chosen to prompt the discussion of one such possibility, namely, that of waiver. Although time of payment was initially of the essence, it might reasonably be argued that by accepting 'late' payments (i.e., more than 10 days in arrears), C Finance Ltd have waived the condition. Whether such is so is a question of fact namely, 'late' payment may have been accepted 'without prejudice'. The possible use of the waiver argument was specifically adverted to by Mustill LJ (at p. 275) in *Butterworth*, although little argument was directed towards it. A student who drew attention to this point would make a favourable impression. In view of the present uncertainty on this, all that one could reasonably expect from a student is some reference to the argument itself, rather than resolution of it.

A student ought, by way of conclusion, set out the financial consequences of the various possibilities outlined above, of which D would need to be advised.

ELEVEN

TRADE DESCRIPTIONS: CRIMINAL LIABILITY IN RESPECT OF FALSE STATEMENTS ABOUT GOODS

Introduction

In this and the following chapter we shall consider aspects of criminal liability arising from false or misleading descriptions of goods and services. Of necessity we shall treat offences relating to the supply of goods (s. 1, TDA 1968) separately from offences relating to the supply of services, accommodation and facilities (s. 14, TDA 1968), though many, if not all, of our introductory remarks apply equally to both areas.

There is a marked contrast between our discussion in the previous three chapters on consumer credit and the chapters on trade descriptions. A point we made in our comments on consumer credit concerned the fact that there was very little case law. However, as we shall see, there has been no shortage of appeal cases on the 1968 Act. This mixture of statute and interpretive case law tends to make this area more interesting to students who appear to find it easier to relate to the law.

It would perhaps be useful to begin by offering some observations on the volume of case law and associated questions of procedure with which the student may not be familiar. There are numerous reasons for the large amount of case law at Divisional Court level, which is the level at which cases are normally reported. These are appeals by way of case stated from decisions of either magistrates' courts (mainly) or Crown Court. It is useful for you to recall that case stated procedure is on a point of law only, as opposed to a full rehearing of the evidence. It is often therefore a relatively straightforward procedure. In addition, appeals by the prosecutor may be funded from local authority or central funds rather than from the aggrieved consumer's pocket. Likewise, since the Act is concerned with 'business crime', traders often have the necessary wherewithal to finance appeals despite the fact that fines tend to be relatively low. This may be in some way due to a fear of the effect of adverse publicity on their business (see, for example, *Manley* v *Marks and Spencers Ltd* (1981) 89 MR 212, where the defendants appealed against conviction despite an absolute discharge being granted).

The provisions of the Act themselves, as we shall see, are in many instances widely drawn. This was felt to be necessary in order to ensure that a wide variety of misleading practices were outlawed and that the purpose of the Act was not defeated by the ingenuity of business. The approach has not been without its difficulties. Judges on a number of occasions have expressed their concern as to where the boundaries of criminal liability lie. In seeking to restrict the potential liability there has been a tendency by the judiciary to resort to civil law concepts. This has not always been in line with the mischief at which the Act was originally directed. From an examination point of view there is a clear possibility that a single question may involve cases of civil and criminal liability and thus test a student's understanding of the interrelationship of the civil and criminal controls.

Finally, the nature of liability imposed by the various provisions of the Act is also noteworthy at this early stage. First, there is a point of difference between s. 14 of the Act and the other sections of the Act. That section, as we shall see in the following chapter, has a *mens rea* requirement. Other offences, including those in s. 1, are offences of so-called 'strict liability'. We would assume that students would be aware from their study of criminal law of the controversy surrounding this type of regulatory offence. For present purposes it should be noted that, whilst the *prima facie* offences under s. 1 do not require proof of *mens rea*, s. 24 of the Act provides the defendant with defences of 'reasonable precautions' and 'due diligence'. In reality, therefore, the offences under this Act will rarely be committed without some blameworthy conduct on the part of the defendant.

Substantive difficulties

We have chosen to examine here not only the substantive difficulties relating to s. 1 offences themselves, but also the issues arising from the possible use of 'disclaimers', the relevant defences and the 'by-pass' provision contained in s. 23. Our reason for so doing is that very often all these issues may be raised in a single question, whether it be a problem or essay question.

Section 1 offences

Section 1 is the offence-creating section in respect of misdescription of goods. Whilst it creates three separate offences, the core concept in each of these is the 'false trade description'. It is necessary to look beyond s. 1 itself in order to understand the meaning attributed to 'false trade descriptions' namely, ss. 2-6 of the Act. Students do have difficulty with some of the rather tortuous wording, particularly, in s. 3(2) and (3) discussed below.

What is a false trade description?

In order to answer this question, we must pass through the various stages set out in the Act.

We begin with s. 2(1) of the Act which defines a trade description in extremely wide terms as 'an indication, direct or indirect, and by whatever means given' as to a variety of matters listed in subparagraphs (a) to (j). Students ought to be conversant with the more important provisions in s. 2(1)(a) to (j), knowledge of which will no doubt be collected by reading the cases to which they have been referred. For example, from the abundance of cases concerning prosecutions relating to false mileometer readings, you should be aware of the relevant subparagraph (j), namely, an indication as to 'other history including previous ownership or use'. Whilst examiners are unlikely to be looking for encyclopaedic knowledge of the contents of these subparagraphs, it does, however, impress if you can indicate correctly, albeit in precis form, the relevant subparagraph and its content.

It is worth commenting that this list is meant to be exhaustive and perhaps most notably excludes the issue of the price of goods. The reason for this is that false or misleading price claims were dealt with by s. 11 of the 1968 Act (see now Part III of the Consumer Protection Act 1987). This separation has caused some difficulty in the past, see, e.g., *Cadbury Ltd* v *Halliday* [1975] 1 WLR 649.

We have already commented on the width of the statutory language and this is supported by judicial dicta as to the meaning of the word 'indication' (see, e.g., *Doble* v *David Greig Ltd* [1972] 1 WLR 703 per Melford Stevenson J. at p. 710). It seems that conduct and signs of many different kinds, including pictorial representation may constitute an 'indication' within the 1968 Act.

The meaning of 'indication' is deliberately widened even further by the provision in s. 3(3):

Anything which, though not a trade description, is likely to be taken for an indication of any of those matters [s. 2(1)(a)-(j)] and, as such an indication would be false to a material degree, shall be deemed to be a false trade description.

The provisions of ss. 2(1) and 3(3) are so broad that it is difficult to see where the boundary between them lies. This difficulty is perhaps reflected in the differing opinions in the Divisional Court in *Holloway* v *Cross* [1981] 1 All ER 1012. The case concerned an oral statement of opinion by a car salesman as to the probable mileage of a second-hand car. Two members of the Court thought that the statement was an indication within s. 2(1), whilst the other member thought it necessary to invoke s. 3(3) in order to bring such a statement within the statute.

Another enormously important provision is to be found in s. 3(2). The effect of this provision is that an offence may be committed where there is a trade description which, although not false, is misleading to a material degree. The importance of this provision can be seen in those cases where consumers are likely to be mislead by half-truths and ambiguities, for example, *R v Inner London Justices and another* [1983] RTR 425. In that case a vehicle had been described as having one previous 'owner'. The vehicle had in fact been owned by a leasing company who had leased it out to no less than five different keepers. In the circumstances the Divisional Court was of the view that such a description, though technically true, was arguably misleading, and clearly capable of being caught by s. 3(2). Other cases which illustrate the effect of this provision include: *Robertson v Dicicco* [1972] RTR 431 ('a beautiful car'); *Chidwick v Beer* [1974] RTR 415, DC ('car in excellent condition for year'); *Hawkins v Smith* [1978] Crim LR 578 ('in showroom condition throughout').

It needs to be remembered that by virtue of s. 3(1) and (2) the indication must be false or misleading *to a material degree*. This is no more than the statutory enactment of the so called *de minimis* rule, namely, the law is not concerned with trifling deviations. A good illustration, perhaps, is the case of *R v Ford Motor Co. Ltd* [1974] 3 All ER 489, in which it was held that to describe as 'new' a motor vehicle which had previously sustained relatively minor damage in the manufacturer's compound was not an offence. This conclusion was reached on the basis of the quality of repair which had been carried out and had rendered the vehicle 'good as new'. It is important to recognise that the provisions of the 1968 Act apply with equal force to descriptions of second-hand goods. In *Simmons v Ravenhill* (1984) 148 JP 109 a second-hand Reliant Robin ('plastic rat') was described as a de luxe model. Whilst certain of the necessary de luxe extras had been added to the basic model by the previous owner, some refinements were still absent. On those facts it was held that, although the description was false, it was not false to a material degree.

One point which is often overlooked by students and occasionally by the judiciary concerns the issue of reliance. In general it is quite clear from the case law that the prosecution need not show that anyone has actually been misled. It is sufficient to show that the trade description in question is likely to mislead the average consumer and this may well be the case, despite the fact that an individual consumer disregards the trade description in the context of a particular transaction (*Chidwick v Beer* (above)). It is perhaps appropriate here to ask whether any offence is committed by applying a description which is obviously false. The answer is of some practical significance in the context of car mileometer readings. It would now seem that the practice of zeroing mileometers is to be regarded as an offence under s. 1(1)(a) despite the blessing given to the practice by the dicta of Lord Widgery CJ in *Lill (K.) Holdings Ltd (trading as Stratford Motor Co.)* v *White* [1979] RTR 120, DC; see *R* v *Southwood* (1987) CA, *The Times*, 1 July.

One final comment on the wide impact of ss. 2 and 3 may be found in the decision of the Crown Court in *R* v *A. F. Pears Ltd* (1982) 90 Monthly Review 142, where the size and shape of a double-skinned container of cosmetics, which was only two-thirds full, was regarded as a false indication of quantity, despite the fact that the net weight of the contents was accurately stated on the outside of the container itself.

Applying a false trade description (s. 1(1)(a))

So far we have considered what amounts to a false trade description. We now need to turn to the first of the three offences under s. 1, namely, that of applying such a description to goods. Sections 4 and 5 (in respect of advertisements) give specific examples of ways in which descriptions may be applied to goods. Often there should be little difficulty where goods are advertised in newspapers, etc. We need only draw your attention to the special defence for publishers in s. 25.

There are, however, a few noteworthy points arising from the cases. First an 'applying' offence can only be committed where a supply of goods is in contemplation (see *Wycombe Marsh Garages Ltd* v *Fowler* [1972] 3 All ER 248). However, provided there is a supply transaction in contemplation, the offence is not 'confined to the parties' to that transaction (*Fletcher* v *Sledmore* [1973] RTR 371, DC). In *Hall* v *Wickens Motors (Gloucester) Ltd* [1972] 1 WLR 1418, it was held that s. 1(1)(a) applies to descriptions 'associated with' the supply transaction. This would appear to preclude statements made after delivery. The facts of *Fletcher* v *Budgen* [1974] 1 WLR 1056 provided a 'startling' result, according to Lord Widgery, in as much as it was realised that a person could be guilty of an offence under s. 1(1)(a) when *buying in* goods in the course of trade or business. In that case a car dealer stated that a car offered in part-exchange was only fit for scrap. After purchasing it for £2, he spent £56 on repairs and offered it for sale at £135. The Divisional Court allowed the prosecutor's appeal against the magistrate's decision of no case to answer.

The provision in s. 4(3) and the decision in *R* v *Ford* (above) illustrated the notion of 'impliedly applying' a false trade description, namely, where the customer in the context of negotiations asks for goods of a particular description and a supplier without qualification supplies goods which do not correspond with that description. A far more contentious example of 'impliedly applying' which is not specifically dealt with by any provision in the Act arose in *Cottee* v *Douglas Seaton (Used Cars) Ltd* [1972] 1 WLR 1408. We shall explore the facts of this case in more depth later, but it is worth mentioning Lord Widgery's view that it may be an offence 'to cause goods to lie about themselves', namely, where repair work of inferior quality is concealed. Whilst a clear distinction can be recognised between this type of case and the quality of repairs done in *R* v *Ford* (above), there are serious implications for persons whose business it is to repair and renovate goods, a point recognised by the Lord Chief Justice in *Cottee* itself.

Supply and offer to supply (s. 1(1)(b))

There are only a further three points to make here in respect of these two offences. The provisions in s. 6 which define 'offer to supply' as including 'exposing goods for supply, having goods in possession for supply' seek to avoid a well-known problem which arose in *Fisher* v *Bell* [1961] 1 QB 394, DC, and the section clearly rejects the civil law notion of 'offering' (see *Doble* v *David Greig* (above)). It is clear from s. 6 that goods bearing a false description stored in a warehouse and never having been exposed to the public gaze might fall foul of s. 1(1)(b).

There is one point specifically concerned with the meaning of the word 'supply' in s. 1(1)(b). This relates in fact to the question of time of 'supply' and the uncertainty surrounding this issue is best dealt with in the context of our discussion on disclaimers below.

The final point under this heading is that the offence of 'offering' or 'supplying' may be committed by the supplier where the false trade description has previously been applied by *some other person*. In that regard s. 1(1)(b) imposes on suppliers a strict duty to avoid 'passing on' false trade descriptions. Of course, this is subject to the statutory defences, in particular that in s. 24(3) discussed below.

'Trade or business' requirement

In chapter 3, p. 39, we indicated that phrases such as 'in the course of a trade or business' were to be found in a number of statutes in this area. We also indicated that a more restrictive interpretation appears to have been placed on this requirement in statutes creating criminal liability. In particular there seems to be a divergence between the civil and criminal law on the issue of supply of goods which have comprised the assets of a business. Under the Trade Descriptions Act the House of Lords in *Davies* v *Sumner* [1984] 3 All

ER 831 held that the sale of such an item would only be 'in the course of' a business if such sales were a regular and frequent occurrence in that business, as for example, in *Havering London Borough Council* v *Stevenson* [1970] 1 WLR 1375. By way of contrast in *Buchanan-Jardin* v *Hamilink* 1983 SLT 149, it was held that the sale of the assets of a farm was within the 'course of the business', and consequently, the implied term as to merchantable quality under s. 14 of the Sale of Goods Act 1979 applied to the cattle included in that sale.

In addition, we also pointed out in chapter 3 that this issue has two aspects. In some cases it has been necessary for the courts to decide whether there was in existence a 'trade or business'. There have been some less than satisfactory decisions, for example, *Blakemore* v *Bellamy* [1983] RTR 303, DC and *Eiman* v *London Borough of Waltham Forest* (1982) 90 Monthly Review 204. In practical terms the main area of importance is probably confined to the sale of second-hand cars whereby persons supplement their income by regularly purchasing vehicles at auction and reselling apparently as private sellers. It is the kind of practical example which an examiner may occasionally wish to explore. It will be seen to follow from this that the private individual cannot commit an offence under s. 1. However, as we shall see below, it is possible for such a person to be successfully prosecuted under s. 23.

By-pass procedure: s. 23

We think it useful to set out the text of this section:

> Where the commission by any person of an offence under this Act is due to the act or default of some other person that other person shall be guilty of the offence and a person may be charged with and convicted of the offence by virtue of this Section whether or not proceedings are taken against the first-mentioned person.

The purpose of this section is to allow the prosecution 'to get at' the *real* culprit. For example, if a manufacturer has applied a false trade description on the packaging of goods, resulting in an offence under 1(1)(b) by the retailer, s. 23 would allow a prosecution whether or not the prosecuting authority chose to pursue the retailer.

It will be noted that there is no mention of the 'act or default' taking place in the 'course of a trade or business'. Confirmation that a private person might be liable under s. 23 is to be found in the recent decision of *Olgeirsson* v *Kitching* [1986] 1 All ER 746. Whilst it was suggested in that case that prosecutions ought to be confined to cases where the private individual concerned had some guilty knowledge, on the facts, this was satisfied (deliberate 'clocking' of car by the defendant).

Given the wording of s. 23, namely, the reference to 'act or default', it is open to some doubt as to whether liability can be confined to cases in which there is an element of dishonesty. However, in *Lill (K.) Holdings Ltd (trading as Stratford Motor Co.)* v *White* [1979] RTR 120, DC, Wien J at p. 125 suggested that 'the act or default' must be in some way 'wrongful'. Quite what is meant by this is not clear. The case of *Meah* v *Roberts* [1977] 1 WLR 1187, decided on a similar provision (s. 113 Food and Drugs Act 1955), is an illustration that dishonesty may not be a requirement of this type of provision.

Whilst in many cases the 'causal link' between the 'act or default' and the later offence by, e.g., the retailer may be easily established, the facts of *Lill (K.) Holdings* v *White* (above) do illustrate a particular problem in the context of motor vehicle mileometer readings. Again, this is a point which might well be raised in an examination question.

One fundamental point to note about s. 23 liability is that it is conditional upon proof that A, the defendant, has caused a person B to commit a *prima facie* offence under one of the other sections of the Act, e.g., s. 1(1)(b). So long as this is established, it does not matter whether B has a defence under s. 24, or is even prosecuted. To establish a *prima facie* offence has been committed under s. 1(1)(b) it is not necessary for the *prosecutor* to show that B either knew that a trade description had been applied or that any trade description applied was false. The burden of proof in respect of both these matters is placed squarely on the shoulders of the defendant by the defence contained in s. 24(3). The decision to the contrary in *Cottee* v *Seaton* (above) is, we consider, incorrect on this point. An appreciation of this issue may well impress an examiner.

It follows that if B is not *prima facie* liable, then A cannot be convicted under s. 23. It should be remembered that it is possible in appropriate circumstances for both A and B to be convicted of the offence (see *Meah* v *Roberts* above).

Disclaimers

We should like to begin by saying that the use of the term 'disclaimer' is something of a misnomer in the context of criminal liability. The disclaimer concept is a judicial invention and is not specifically created by any provision of the Act. It is essential that students, by now accustomed to the notion of disclaimers in civil law, appreciate this point. In the criminal law the so-called 'disclaimer' is only effective in so far as it prevents an offence being committed. Such clauses cannot excuse criminal liability once it has arisen.

Some confusion on this point has plagued some of the criminal cases (see e.g., *Simmons* v *Potter* [1975] RTR 347, DC) and blurred the distinction between 'disclaimers' and the statutory defences. It should be made clear that the defences provided in s. 24 where appropriate *do excuse* a liability which has already arisen.

A disclaimer may be effective to prevent an offence arising in one of three ways. It may prevent an indication from being treated as a trade description under s. 2(1); or it may qualify a trade description in such a fashion that it is not false or misleading; or qualify it in such a way that it is not false or misleading to a *material degree*. The guidelines as to the effectiveness or otherwise of disclaimers, as evolved through the cases, are set out below. Before examining those, students would perhaps appreciate some examples of the different types of disclaimers: 'X brand sweaters — second hand'; 'Norfolk King turkeys — Danish' (when imported from Denmark); 'all sizes quoted are approximate'. It may be seen from some of these examples that there might be some argument as to whether a description is 'disclaimed' or whether a qualified description is being applied. Any such metaphysical debate has been largely avoided by the courts. The rough and ready test which has been developed is to consider the effect of the total message on the ordinary consumer.

The guidelines in this respect were laid down by Lord Widgery in *Norman* v *Bennett* [1974] 1 WLR 1229, and are as follows:

To be effective a disclaimer must be as *bold, precise and compelling* as the trade description itself and must *effectively be brought to the attention* of any person to whom the goods may be supplied, in other words the disclaimer must *equal* the trade description in the extent to which it is likely to get home to anyone interested in receiving the goods.

This 'prominence' requirement has been considered in a substantial number of cases, many of which have understandably been concerned with false mileometer readings. It has been held that general notices on walls and in contractual documents will rarely suffice to effectively prevent the commission of an offence (see *Zawadski* v *Sleigh* [1975] RTR 113, DC; *Waltham Forest London Borough Council* v *T. G. Wheatley (Central Garage) Ltd* (No. 2) [1978] RTR 333, DC). It should be recognised that the necessary degree of prominence to be given to a disclaimer may vary according to the circumstances in particular types of cases. Thus, in *Edward A. Savory and Associates Ltd* v *Dawson* (unreported, Divisional Court 26 Feb 1976), applying the *Norman* v *Bennett* guidelines did not require a disclaimer on every page of the Yellow Pages Directory (see also *R* v *Clarksons Holidays Ltd* (1972) 57 Cr App R 38).

In addition to the prominence requirement, the timing of the disclaimer is of crucial importance if the commission of the offence is to be prevented. The precise moment the disclaimer needs to be employed may vary according to which offence is charged. Thus, in *Norman* v *Bennett* itself, where an offence of 'supplying' was charged, Lord Widgery suggested that the disclaimer would need to be made before the goods were supplied. There is some uncertainty as to the precise moment at which goods are 'supplied' for the purpose of this Act. Whilst in *R* v *Hammertons Cars Ltd* [1976] 1 WLR 1243, Lawton LJ appears to accept a disclaimer may be effective as late as the time of delivery, he warned that a defendant 'may have difficulty in persuading a court that a false trade description has not been applied' (at p. 1248).

Where, however offences of 'applying' or 'offering to supply' are charged, the disclaimer must be contemporaneous with the otherwise false trade description. This is well illustrated by the facts of *Doble* v *David Greig* (above). The offence charged was 'offering to supply' under s. 11(2). The offence was constituted by the display of bottles of Ribena on a supermarket shelf (given the definition of 'offering to supply' under s. 6). A 'disclaimer' at the cash-out desk because it came too late was ineffective, the offence of 'offering to supply' already having been committed. The Court left open the issue as to whether the terms of the disclaimer would have resolved the ambiguity concerning the refund of deposit, had it been placed on the display shelf itself. It follows from this that if the offence of 'applying' is charged the disclaimer must be present at the precise moment at which the alleged offence is committed. Thus, an advertisement of a car for sale stating a false mileometer reading would be unaffected by any disclaimer placed over the reading on the vehicle.

A further point concerning the offence of 'applying' is the controversial issue of whether such an offence can in principle be disclaimed. It has been suggested that a disclaimer is not possible in such circumstances (see *Newman* v *Hackney Borough Council* [1982] RTR 296 per Ormrod LJ at p. 300; *R* v *Southwood, The Times* 1 July 1987). This seems to arise from confusion concerning the nature of liability under s. 1(1)(a). The mistaken view of some members of the judiciary is that all 'applying' offences of necessity involve some dishonesty. If this were the case not only would a disclaimer be of no effect, but the defendant would also be unable to rely on s. 24(1) defences. This is clearly not the case; see, e.g., *Norman* v *Phillips* (1984) 148 JP 741. We accept that where it is shown that there has been dishonesty in 'applying' then in principle no disclaimer should be allowed, although on the guidelines in *Norman* v *Bennett* this would seem theoretically possible.

One final point on disclaimers concerns the burden of proof. As we shall see in the next section below, the burden of proof in respect of s. 24 defences lies squarely with the defendant. On the issue of a disclaimer, however, the burden of proof lies with the prosecution, since the issue raised is in essence whether or not a *prima facie* offence has been committed, i.e., is the disclaimer such as to negate the otherwise false impression?

The development by the courts of the disclaimer is certainly not completely free of difficulty. Our experience tends to show that students do have a problem in grasping the disclaimer concept and, in particular, its relationship to s. 24 defences.

Statutory defences

The first thing you should recognise is the need to be selective in your choice of cases. There is not surprisingly a substantial body of case law in this area. It is true to say however, that only a small number contain points of any significance for examination purposes.

There are several defences contained in s. 24(1) and s. 24(3). The s. 24(3) defences are 'special' in the sense that they only apply to offences of 'supplying' and 'offering to supply' under s. 1(1)(b). The existence of the 'special' defences does not, however, preclude the raising of a defence under s. 24(1) to a charge under s. 1(1)(b). Given the existence of two sets of defences, the examiner might seek to explore your understanding of some important differences between them.

Burden and standard of proof

Section 24 clearly places the onus upon a defendant to establish that he or she is within one or other of the defences. The standard of proof has been held to be on the balance of probabilities (see *McGuire* v *Sittingbourne Co-operative Society Ltd* [1976] Crim LR 268).

Section 24(1) defences

There are two limbs to this defence. In academic terms both are important, but in practice the second limb is more important. Under s. 24(1)(a) the defendant must show that the commission of the offence was due to a mistake, or to reliance on information supplied to him; or to the act or default of another person, or an accident or some other cause beyond his control.

Whilst there has been some suggestion that this first limb of the defence could be abolished, there are several noteworthy points arising from the relevant case law. We shall merely draw attention to these rather than indulge in exhaustive analysis of s. 24(1)(a). The 'mistake' defence is, in the case of limited companies, confined to mistakes committed by those persons who can be said to represent the mind of the company. This would obviously include persons in s. 20 of the Act: 'any director, manager, secretary or other similar officer'. Since the decision in *Tesco Supermarkets Ltd* v *Nattrass* [1972] AC 153, it would seem that this defence may also be raised with regard to persons who, though in the lower orders of management, are still regarded as 'supervisors' rather than 'supervised persons'. It would seem from the decision in *Tesco* that a branch manager of a large retail organisation is not to be regarded as a 'supervisor', though his area or regional manager may well be. Other cases concerning this defence, of which you should be aware, include *Butler* v *Keenway Supermarkets Ltd* [1974] Crim LR 560 and *Birkenhead and District Co-operative Society Ltd* v *Roberts* [1970] 1 WLR 1497.

The most controversial defence is the 'act or default' defence when used by the large company as illustrated by the facts of *Tesco*. It was held in that case that the defendant's *own employee* could be 'another person' within this provision. Despite criticism of this decision it has been applied in a number of cases, including in particular car mileometer cases such as *Lewin* v *Rothersthorpe Ltd* (1984) 148 JP 87. This defence is commonly met in practice and given its controversial nature we suggest you give it close attention.

The 'reliance upon information' defence will rarely be successful. It has been said that the source of the information must be authoritative (see *Taylor* v *Lawrence Fraser (Bristol) Ltd* [1978] Crim LR 43 on the similar defence in other legislation). A failure to check adequately a source may amount to a failure to take 'all reasonable precautions' under s. 24(1)(b) (see below).

The second limb in s. 24(1)(b) requires the person charged to show he 'took *all* reasonable precautions *and* exercised *all* due diligence to avoid the commission of such an offence by himself or any person under his control'. It may be difficult for you to reach any firm conclusions on the facts given in any particular question. We have acknowledged this difficulty in previous chapters in similar circumstances. More important than any conclusion will be your understanding of any relevant cases to which you refer.

Perhaps the first point worth making is that the subsection refers to '*all* reasonable precautions and *all* due diligence'. In *McGuire* v *Sittingbourne Co-operative Society* (above), Lord Widgery CJ drew the attention of magistrates to the danger that the administration of the Act might fall to a 'slipshod level' and emphasised that the onus cast on a defendant is not easily satisfied.

The circumstances which are relevant here may vary according to whether the defendant is pleading 'act or default of another' etc. Most of the cases on the 1968 Act have been concerned with what constitutes reasonable precautions by a company where it is seeking to use the 'act or default' of its own employees. From *Tesco* v *Nattrass* (above) it would seem that it is necessary for the employer to have established an effective system of operation so as to constitute 'all reasonable precautions'. In addition, the 'diligence' requirement would necessitate an efficient system of supervision. You should be aware of what factors satisfied this requirement in the *Tesco* case.

As far as latent defects in goods are concerned, two useful cases are *Sherratt* v *Gerald The American Jeweller* (1970) 114 SJ 147 and *Garrett* v *Boots* (16 July 1980, Divisional Court, unreported). In *Sherratt* the 'obvious precaution' (not taken by the defendant) was to dip one of the allegedly waterproof watches in a bowl of water. In *Garrett* the Divisional Court were of the view that random sampling would suffice. The Court made the point in that case that the precautions required might differ depending on whether the defendant was a large retail organisation or a village shop. This point has been re-affirmed in the recent case of *Denard* v *Abbas* [1987] Crim LR 424 (a case mainly concerned with 'reasonable diligence' under s. 24(3) below), where it was also clearly stated that personal attributes of the defendant, e.g., his command of English and lack of familiarity with the trade, were irrelevant to conviction, though they might be considered on the issue of sentence.

Whilst recognising the difficulties of the small retailer, the courts have treated with some scepticism the argument that the defendant lacked the facilities to carry out the testing of goods (see, e.g., *Hicks* v *Sullam* (1983) 91 Monthly Review 122).

One final point is that the 'precautions' and 'diligence' exercised by the defendant may be regarded as reasonable or sufficient, but may yet fail to provide a defence because they were taken too late 'to prevent the commission' of offences; see, e.g., *Haringey London Borough Council* v *Piro Shoes* [1976] Crim LR 462.

Section 24(3) defences

We wish to make a number of points about these defences in isolation, but in addition we also wish to draw attention to certain points of distinction between these defences and those contained in s. 24(1).

Section 24(3) provides that in any proceedings for an offence of supplying or offering to supply under s. 1(1)(b):

It shall be a defence for the person charged to prove that he *did not know*, and could not with *reasonable diligence* have ascertained, that goods did not *conform to the description* or that the *description had been applied* to the goods.

It is worth noting first of all that there are two separate defences, one relating to the discoverability as to falsity, and the other as to discoverability that the trade description had been applied at all. It is quite clear that in order to establish a *prima facie* offence under s. 1(1)(b), it is *not necessary* for the *prosecution* to show that the defendant knew that a false trade description had been applied. The burden in this respect lies with the defendant, despite the decision in *Cottee* v *Seaton* (above).

The full potential of this defence in wider circumstances has not been explored, as most of the cases have been concerned with motor vehicles. As far as the physical state of vehicles is concerned, the issue has been whether defects were discoverable with 'reasonable diligence'. The case of *Barker* v *Hargreaves* [1981] RTR 197, DC neatly illustrates this issue. That case is important in that Donaldson LJ draws attention to one very clear distinction between s. 24(1) and s. 24(3). Section 24(1) is more general in that it is concerned with prevention whereas s. 24(3) is more specific and relates to the 'particular defects found in the vehicle which form the basis of the charge'. So in *Barker* itself rust which had been concealed by the use of underseal was accepted as not being discoverable by reasonable diligence, whereas corrosion merely hidden by the battery was so discoverable.

Turning to cases concerned with matters other than the physical state of vehicles, e.g., the mileometer reading cases, these illustrate reasonably well the overlap between the s. 24(2) and (3) defences. For example, a person charged under s. 1(1)(b) in respect of a mileometer reading might argue that he had relied upon information supplied to him under s. 24(1) or alternatively that he had no reason to believe the mileometer reading was false (under s. 24(3)). The question then arises as to whether 'all reasonable precautions and all due diligence' amount to the same thing as 'reasonable diligence'. There appears to be no clear judicial statement as to whether there is any difference (see *Barker* v *Hargreaves* (above); *Wandsworth London Borough Council* v *Bentley* [1980] RTR 429, DC; *Crook* v *Howells Garages (Newport) Ltd* [1980] RTR 434, DC).

It should be evident from the above that examiners may seek to explore such points. In our experience students tend to merely recite the provisions in s. 24 without any real attempt to explain the case law and where relevant, the distinctions between the various defences.

Illustrative question

Peter is a freelance photographer who uses his car regularly for travelling in connection with his work. Because of the high mileage involved he adopts the policy of buying a new car every 12 months. In 1987 he trades in his current vehicle for a new one with XYZ Garages Ltd. The mileometer reading on the vehicle traded in is 10,000 miles. XYZ Garages Ltd advertises the same vehicle as follows: 'In excellent condition as new, 10,000 miles guaranteed, £4,000 only'.

The vehicle is bought by Graham and after two weeks he discovers that the vehicle requires £500 of repairs to the engine and gearbox and has some corrosion underneath. On investigation a trading standards officer discovers that the true mileage is in excess of 35,000 miles.

Discuss any possible *criminal* liability of the parties bearing in mind any defences which might be available.

Commentary

Any plan of an answer to this problem should identify the person who may be guilty of one or more offences and also what those offences might be, together with any relevant defences. A possible plan is set out below.

For Peter:

(a)   Possible s. 1(1)(a) in respect of mileometer reading. Problem: 'in the course of trade or business'?
(b)   If not, alternatively, s. 15 Theft Act.
(c)   Section 23: act or default.
(d)   Defences?

For XYZ Garages Ltd:

(a)   Possible offences under s. 1(1)(a): 'excellent condition as new'; '10,000 miles guaranteed'. NB advertisements (s. 5).
(b)   Offences under s. 1(1)(b) 'supplying'.
(c)   Defences: s. 24(1) and 24(3).

Peter

The rubric requires a discussion *only* of *criminal* liability. How often this instruction is overlooked and the examiner is given a discourse on civil liability. Even in some cases where students do recognise this, it is common to find them talking about the consumer 'suing' or prosecuting under the Trade Descriptions Act 1968. It does detract from an answer if you confuse civil and criminal liability or if you are not aware that prosecutions are normally taken by the trading standards/consumer protection department of a local authority.

The prosecuting authority might first consider charging Peter under s.1(1)(a) of the Act, i.e., 'applying' a false trade description, in that it appears implicit in the question that he is responsible for the discrepancy in the mileometer reading. Assuming that to be so, the sole legal difficulty would be whether his transaction with XYZ Garages was conducted by him 'in the course of a trade or business'.

You should be aware that there are two aspects to this issue. The first is whether Peter's activities constitute a business. It was readily accepted in *Davies* v *Summer* (above) that a self-employed individual in similar circumstances satisfied this aspect. The second aspect is that the transaction itself is required to be '*in the course of*' a trade or business. You should make it clear to the examiner that you are aware of the two leading cases which are relevant here, namely *Davies* v *Summer* (above) and *London Borough of Havering* v *Stevenson* (above). The upshot of these cases appears to be that with goods not bought with the primary intention of resale, which are the assets of the business, subsequent disposal would only be '*in the course of*' business if goods of that kind were acquired and disposed of with some degree of frequency and regularity.

Turning to the facts, you should not overlook the deliberate insertion in the question of the sentence 'adopts the policy of buying a new car every 12 months'. This, you might observe, takes this more towards the actual decision in *Stevenson* as opposed to *Davies*. Even if it is not possible to establish that this was in the course of a business Peter may be charged alternatively as mentioned below.

Briefly, you might mention the possibility of a prosecution against Peter under s. 15 of the Theft Act 1968, obtaining property by deception (see *R* v *King (Ian Robert)* [1979] Crim LR 122). In a consumer or commercial law paper a detailed discussion on this point would not be expected.

A more detailed treatment, however, would be expected of the other alternative, namely, a prosecution under s. 23 of the 1968 Act. In dealing with the possibility that Peter has committed such an offence, your answer should spell out the three essential elements.

(a)   Whether on the facts XYZ Garages has committed a *prima facie* offence in regard to the mileometer reading. An important point to be made clear to the examiner is that you understand that it does not matter whether XYZ might have a defence under s. 24. On the facts it would appear that

XYZ have supplied a vehicle to which a false trade description is applied, a *prima facie* offence under s. 1(1)(b).

(b) The interpretation of s. 23 requires that Peter's actions or omissions have to be in some way 'wrongful' (per Wien J. in *Lill Holdings* v *White* (see above)). Furthermore, it was suggested in *Olgeirsson* v *Kitching* (above) that *mens rea* should be established at least where s. 23 is used against a *private* individual. Whilst the evidence seems to suggest that Peter is responsible for the discrepancy, a degree of speculation as to the reason for the discrepancy other than 'clocking' by Peter (e.g., replacement mileometer) would not be out of place.

(c) Finally, it is necessary to establish a sufficient causal link between Peter's wrongful act and the *prima facie* offence of XYZ. Though on the facts there is nothing to suggest the sort of difficulties experienced in *Lill Holdings* v *White*, drawing the examiner's attention to the point can only impress.

In conclusion on Peter's liability, it would seem that he would not be able to take advantage of the statutory defences in s. 24, see *R* v *Southwood, The Times*, 1 July 1987.

XYZ Garages Ltd

We should perhaps begin by recognising that XYZ may be charged either with two offences under s. 1(1)(a), or two offences under s. 1(1)(b). Charges under s. 1(1)(a) are possible because in an advertisement XYZ have 'applied' what is arguably a false trade description 'in excellent condition as new' and they have also repeated a false indication as to mileage. The provision in s. 5 of the Act makes it clear that such an advertisement can be charged as an applying offence.

As we shall see below, which offences are charged may crucially affect the availability of any defences to XYZ Garages Ltd.

One matter common to all these is whether or not there is a false trade description. As regards mileometer readings, it is so well established that the point does not need to be specifically made. However, the other statement by XYZ Garages, namely 'excellent condition, as new' does require some analysis. We shall take these two phrases together rather than to split them. Does it amount to a trade description? We would suggest it does in as much as it is an indication of one of the matters mentioned in s. 2(1), namely, '(d) fitness for purpose, performance, strength . . .' Cases such as *Robertson* v *Dicicco* (above) and *Chidwick* v *Beer* (above) should be cited in support. You might also point out the effect of the provision in s. 3(3) as in *Holloway* v *Cross* that it is sufficient if the statement, though not an indication, is likely to be taken as an indication within s. 2(1).

There is little doubt that in relation to the mileometer reading the trade description (10,000 miles) is clearly false and indeed false *to a material degree* given that the true mileage is in excess of 35,000 miles. We would also consider that a court would decide that the description 'in excellent condition, as new' would be false to a material degree, given the nature and cost of the defects existing in the vehicle and taking into account the relative newness and price paid. Since this is essentially a matter of fact and degree, it may be difficult if not impossible to cite authorities directly in point. However, this should not discourage students from referring to cases by way of illustration (see, e.g., *Robertson* v *Dicicco* (above)).

We need now to consider what defences, if any, might be available to XYZ Garages Ltd. In considering the defences students tend not to relate them to the particulars of the individual offences, but rather regurgitate the provisions, and therefore perhaps fail to convince the examiner that they understand their application.

As outlined above there may be two offences charged under s. 1(1)(a). The *only* defences available in these circumstances are those to be found in s. 24(1). First of all, there is no suggestion on the facts that XYZ Garages Ltd has applied either of the two descriptions *knowing them to be false*. Of course, if that were the case, then the defences would certainly not be available. The default of the company lies rather in the failure to discover facts which render the descriptions false to a material degree. With regard to the mileometer offence, the garage would presumably seek to use the reliance on information or act or default aspects of this defence. In either case, however, the crucial issue is whether the company can satisfy the requirements in s. 24(1)(b), namely 'all reasonable precautions' and 'all due diligence'. The cases (e.g., *Wandsworth LBC* v *Bentley* (above)) suggest that where a second-hand vehicle has been with a number of previous owners, there is a duty to make inquiries into its previous history or use, though the precise extent of the inquiries required may differ according to the facts of any case. However on the facts of our problem, it would seem that Peter has been the only previous owner. If that were the case and Peter had signed the customary assurance warranting the accuracy of the mileage, this might satisfy the 'all reasonable precautions' provision, assuming that there was nothing to put the garage on notice, e.g., the state of the vehicle, so as to require further enquiry. The defects in engine and gearbox would certainly be relevant in this respect, as some indication that the vehicle had done more than the mileage claimed. A student prepared to discuss this is likely to impress the examiner.

With regard to the description, 'excellent condition, as new', the defence which the company is likely to seek to rely upon is the 'act or default' provision. This would involve showing that the advertisement was drafted by an employee who was 'another person' within the meaning of that phrase in *Tesco* v *Nattrass* (above). The facts do not raise this point in particular and we would advise against a lengthy analysis of this issue. Assuming the company could satisfy s. 24(1)(a), it would still have to satisfy s. 24(1)(b). The company would need to show, for example, what system of checks was in operation covering both examination of vehicles and their subsequent description in advertisements. Statements from cases such as *Tesco* (above) or *McGuire* (above) would be relevant in supporting these observations.

If, on the other hand, the charges are brought under s. 1(1)(b) ('supplying'), then the company has another string to its bow, namely, the defences in s. 24(3). The first point which you should make here is that this defence is specific to the particular defect in goods (see Donaldson LJ in *Barker* v *Hargreaves* (above)), compared with s. 24(1) which is more general in its scope. Whether that will make any difference on the facts of our case can only be speculated upon, given the absence of detailed information in the question. Despite this, the point of distinction would be well worth mentioning.

Assuming that XYZ Garages Ltd knew that both descriptions were applied to the goods, the sole issue to be argued here would be that XYZ 'could not with reasonable diligence have ascertained, that the goods did not conform to' the particular descriptions.

As far as the false mileometer reading is concerned, it would seem that 'reasonable diligence' will involve similar factors to those indicated above under 'all reasonable precautions' etc. under s. 24(1)(b).

As far as the actual defects are concerned, *Barker* v *Hargreaves* (above), the leading case, suggests that for this defence to succeed the defects must be latent. If this can be shown to be the case, the company might succeed under s. 24(3), even though it had failed to satisfy s. 24(1)(b) (no proper system of checks, see *Barker* v *Hargreaves* itself). A student conversant with the facts of *Barker* might usefully employ them to show what amounts to *latent* defects and make observations upon the actual defects in the vehicle in this problem question.

As you will have seen the facts of our illustrative question are not particularly lengthy, yet the question raises a significant number of issues. The sheer volume of issues will require you to be extremely careful in the way in which you use the time available. From our attempt to answer the question, you should have realised that there is no necessity to be able to regurgitate verbatim large chunks of sections of the Act. It is sufficient that you know it well enough to be able to precis the substance in a reasonably accurate manner.

TWELVE

TRADE DESCRIPTIONS RELATING TO SERVICES, ACCOMMODATION AND FACILITIES

Introduction

In this second chapter on false or misleading trade descriptions we shall be concentrating on criminal liability for false statements or indications concerning the provision of services, accommodation and facilities. Whilst the law relating to similar indications in respect of the supply of goods, discussed in the previous chapter, has its share of difficulties, it is fair to say that those provisions in the main seem to have worked reasonably well. By way of contrast the law in the area now under discussion is far from satisfactory, as we shall see.

The law relating to the provision of services (s. 14 of the Trade Descriptions Act 1968 apart) was a much neglected area until the Supply of Goods and Services Act 1982 (see chapter 3) attempted to place some of the common law rules upon a statutory footing.

Indeed, the Molony Committee Report (1961, Cmnd. 1781 para. 4.5), in refusing to consider the regulation of services commented:

> In short, we concluded that consideration of consumer needs in respect of services would involve us in such complex and far-ranging investigations, with small prospect of a worthwhile outcome, that our duty lay in focusing upon the more rewarding, but by no means narrow, field within our definition.

The Committee proceeded thereafter to consider the regulation of the supply of goods. No recommendations at all were made in respect of services, despite evidence in those early days of the consumer movement of widespread dissatisfaction which has apparently increased over the years if consideration of the statistics in the Annual Reports of the Office of Fair Trading is anything to go by.

However, for some unexplained reason the Trade Descriptions Act 1968 did in fact, when it made the statute book, contain a section regulating the provision of services. There was little recorded debate upon the section in

Parliament and it might strike you that it was only a half-hearted attempt to deal with the issues.

Certainly, trading standards officers, responsible for the enforcement of the 1968 Act, frequently complain about the deficiencies of s. 14 and there is justification for this view to be found in the reported appeal cases.

As we shall see, in the main, the judiciary appear to have taken a cautious line on the interpretation of s. 14. As a consequence a restrictive approach, perhaps unduly so, has been taken. Reform of s. 14 was canvassed as long ago as 1976 by the Office of Fair Trading (Cmnd. 6628) in its Review of the 1968 Act. Whilst little has so far been done to implement the recommendations in that report, it is useful if you are aware of the reform proposals put forward on s. 14.

You should remember, as pointed out in the previous chapter, that s. 14 creates *criminal* liability. Whilst there may be considerable overlap with the civil law, you must get this distinction clear in your mind. Indeed, as we shall see in the discussion below, the approach of the courts in certain cases has been affected by the issue of whether the facts give rise or not to concurrent civil liability (see Lord Widgery in *Beckett* v *Cohen* [1973] 1 All ER 120 at pp. 121-2). This of itself, causes difficulties for students in attempting to obtain a perspective on the s. 14 provisions.

Substantive difficulties

We shall assume you are familiar with the provisions of s. 14. There seem to us to be a few major areas of difficulty with regard to the section as it stands. These are the *mens rea* requirements, the issue of future statements, the issue of prices and the meaning of 'services, accommodation or facilities'. In addition, there is as yet some unsettled controversy about whether s. 14 controls misleading as opposed to false indications.

Before going on to discuss these issues, it is worth observing that, compared with ss. 1-6, s. 14 is much briefer. For example, there is no attempt to list, as in s. 2(1) the various types of indication which constitute trade descriptions. This brevity may be a consequence of Parliament's unease at the thought of creating a criminal offence arising from the provision of services (see the comments in the Report of the OFT, cited above, para. 9 onwards). It has also contributed to the uncertainty surrounding s. 14 as a whole.

Mens rea requirement

As we saw in the previous chapter, offences under s. 1 are strict liability in nature. Section 14 expressly includes a *mens rea* requirement in subsection

(1)(a) and (b). You should note the precise wording of these subparagraphs, as it appears something may turn upon the position of the words (see *Wings Ltd* v *Ellis* [1984] 3 All ER 577).

Somewhat ironically the *mens rea* requirement had not proved much of a stumbling block to successful prosecutions until *Wings Ltd* v *Ellis* (above) if the reported appeal cases are anything to go by. Whilst proof of *knowledge* of falsity might be difficult normally involving proof of dishonesty, the 'recklessness' requirement appears to have been considerably relaxed in favour of the prosecution. It seems that there is no need to establish dishonesty under s. 14(1)(b), if regard is paid to s. 14(2)(b) (which seems clear on its wording) and the cases of *M.F.I. Warehouses Ltd* v *Nattrass* [1973] 1 All ER 762 and *Cowburn* v *Focus Television Rentals Ltd* [1983] Crim LR 563. An examiner would certainly expect you to have a good knowledge of the *M.F.I.* case at least and the test to be applied. The Divisional Court in that case rejected the defence argument that 'recklessness' was to be given its normal common law meaning according to *Derry* v *Peek* [1889] 14 AC 337 (see also *Sunair Holidays Ltd* v *Dodd* [1970] 2 All ER 410, per Lord Parker CJ at p. 411). In *M.F.I.* v *Nattrass* (at p. 768) Lord Widgery CJ stated:

I have accordingly come to the conclusion that 'recklessly' in the context of the 1968 Act does not involve dishonesty. Accordingly it is not necessary to prove that the statement was made with that degree of irresponsibility which is implied in the phrase 'careless whether it be true or false'. I think it suffices for present purposes if the prosecution can show that the advertiser did not have regard to the truth or falsity of his advertisement even though it cannot be shown that he was deliberately closing his eyes to the truth, or that he had any kind of dishonest mind.

In that case the evidence showed that the company's chairman studied the offending advertisement 'for five or ten minutes thereabouts . . . but did not think through sufficiently the implications thereof . . .'.

The Divisional Court took the view that this was 'recklessness'. Some would argue that on this interpretation the standard to justify conviction is one of carelessness only.

Turning back to the *mens rea* requirement under s. 14(1)(a), namely, making a statement knowing it to be false, you ought to be fully aware of the important implications of *Wings Ltd* v *Ellis* (above). There seems little doubt that there is no small amount of confusion about this decision by the House of Lords. What the case appears to be saying is that the offence under s. 14(1)(a) is a 'half-*mens rea*' offence, namely, that there must be knowledge as to the falsity of a statement, but there need be no *mens rea* as to the actual *making* of the statement itself. This appears to mean that when the customer was reading the Wings brochure in January 1982, whilst the company did not know they were making any statement in that brochure, liability on that point was strict. Therefore, as long as they knew at some stage that the relevant part of the brochure was incorrect, a conviction, subject to the availability of the s. 24 defences, would be upheld. The Divisional Court [1984] All ER 1046 had got itself in a tangle by resorting to the concept of the 'result' crime (see *R* v *Miller* [1983] 2 AC 161, which you should be familiar with from your criminal law studies). The House of Lords rejected this approach, but in doing so opened the way for perhaps even more confusion (see Taylor and Stephenson (1985) 48 MLR 340). A good knowledge of this case and the differing approaches taken by their Lordships would certainly impress an examiner.

With regard to the *mens rea* requirement, there is one further important point which relates to our earlier discussion in chapter 11 on the significance of *Tesco Supermarkets Ltd* v *Nattrass* [1972] AC 153. For there to be corporate liability under s. 14 of the 1968 Act, the prosecution must establish that one of the 'high-ranking' officials in the corporate body has the necessary *mens rea*. As we have seen before, the line appears to be drawn at quite a high level in the company hierarchy. Two good illustrations of the way this principle works are *M.F.I.* v *Nattrass* (above) and *Wings Ltd* v *Ellis* (above). In the former case it was the chairman of the company who had the necessary 'reckless' state of mind. In *Wings* an alternative charge under s. 14(1)(b) (recklessness) was laid against the company in respect of a photograph in the same brochure. The photograph gave a false impression of one of the facilities at the hotel in question; indeed it was a picture of another hotel altogether. The evidence showed that photograph was approved by a person described as a 'contracts manager'. The Divisional Court [1984] 1 All ER 1046 held (and this point was not appealed) that such a person was not within the class described as 'the ruling officers' of the company. The Court also took the view that nobody within the 'ruling officers' was guilty of any 'recklessness' in setting up the system to prevent errors of this kind arising.

Finally, the Review by the Office of Fair Trading suggested the removal of the *mens rea* requirement, subject to limited exceptions, to bring s. 14 into line with s. 1, but the chances of this taking place are remote.

Future intention

You will no doubt recall from your study of the civil law relating to misrepresentation (see Taylor, SWOT *Law of Contract*, 2nd ed pp. 121-42) that there is a problem concerning statements about the future. Such statements are not capable of being true or false at the time they are made. A similar problem has bedevilled the application of s. 14 of the 1968 Act. This was clearly highlighted in the cases of *Beckett* v *Cohen* [1973] 1 All ER 120 and *R* v *Sunair Holidays Ltd* [1973] 2 All ER 1233. In *Beckett* v *Cohen* the promises by the builder were considered to be about the future: they might give rise to a contractual action, i.e., for breach of warranty, but could not be the basis for a criminal prosecution (see also *Sunair Holidays Ltd* v *Dodd* [1970] 2 All ER 410). However, the balance has to some extent been redressed in favour of the consumer by the House of Lords in the leading case of *British Airways Board* v *Taylor* [1976] 1 All ER 65. Again, this is a case with which you should make yourself very familiar, particularly the statement by Lord Wilberforce (at p. 68):

> There may be inherent in a promise an implied statement as to a fact, and where this is really the case, the court can attach appropriate consequences to any falsity in, or recklessness in the making of, that statement. Everyone is familiar with the proposition that a statement of intention may itself be a statement of fact, and so capable of being true or false.

His Lordship did go on, however, to give a similar warning as given in *Beckett* v *Cohen* (above) that s. 14 was not designed to create criminal liability out of something which can only be regarded as a breach of warranty.

Searching for the implied statement of fact may involve fine distinctions (see *British Airways Board* v *Taylor* itself and also *Banbury* v *Hounslow London Borough Council* [1971] RTR 1). In a sense one can always find some implicit fact in a statement about the future. However, trading standards officers are often, it seems, reluctant to take up prosecutions where a statement is in any way concerned with statements about the future. Of course, there is a close connection here with the *mens rea* requirement (see *Sunair Holidays Ltd* v *Dodd* (above)), in that where circumstances are regarded as being beyond the control of the maker of the offending statement, it may well be difficult to satisfy the *mens rea* requirement in any event.

Prices

Whether or not a false statement as to the price of services and so on falls within s. 14 is controversial. The Divisional Court came to the view in the series of cases (see *Newell* v *Hicks* (1984) 148 JP 307, *Dixon Ltd* v *Roberts* (1984) 148 JP 513 and *Kinchin* v *Ashton Park Scooters* (1984) 148 JP 540) that s. 14, on its wording did not apply to prices. However, some of the heat may have gone out of this controversy (though we feel that it is likely to generate enough heat of itself) by virtue of the passing of the Consumer Protection Act Part III which eventually should control statements as to prices regarding services, accommodation and facilities. Part III is dependent upon the drawing up of an appropriate Code of Practice and it may be some time before it comes into force. It is as well, therefore, to be aware of the problems under s. 14 as it stands.

Services, accommodation, facilities

Much of the difficulty surrounding these words has been concentrated upon the distinction between 'services' or 'facilities' on the one hand and something which whilst similar, is thought to be more closely analogous to the provision of goods. There is understandably perhaps no attempt in the Act at a definition of any of these matters.

The word 'accommodation' has, however, established itself as meaning 'short-term' accommodation only. Therefore, any false statements about holiday or hotel accommodation have been treated as being caught by s. 14. Indeed many of the reported cases on this section have revolved around problems concerning holiday accommodation. There may, of course, be an overlap here with 'facilities', in that false statements about the provisions of accommodation may include false statements about facilities available, for example, in a hotel (see *Wings Ltd* v *Ellis*, above).

On the face of it 'services' and 'facilities' are both capable of an extremely wide meaning, although a rather restrictive interpretation has been placed upon one or the other in a few cases. 'Services' have been defined as 'doing something for somebody' (per Goff LJ in *Newell* v *Hicks* at p. 313), whereas a facility is considered to be 'providing somebody with the "wherewithall" to do something for himself' (also per Goff LJ in *Newell* v *Hicks*). In *Newell* the failure to supply a video recorder free with every car purchased during a particular period was regarded as a promise concerning the supply of goods rather than a 'facility'. In *Kinchin* v *Ashton Park Scooters* (1984) 148 JP 540 the failure to obtain insurance as promised for a customer did fall within s. 14 as a facility (see also *Dixons* v *Roberts* (1984) 1 JP 513 and *Westminster City Council* v *Ray Alan (Manshops) Ltd* [1982] 1 All ER 771 as other examples of the restrictive approach).

The main reason given in these cases for a restrictive interpretation seems to be the fact that the statute creates criminal liability and consequently any doubt about the meaning of words should be resolved in favour of the defendant. This allied with the judicial fear of superimposing criminal consequences for what is often considered to be nothing more than a minor civil breach results in a watered down section with immense enforcement difficulties as far as trading standards officers are concerned.

The areas of difficulty discussed above certainly provide an examiner with plenty of scope for testing examination questions. Such a question might be of the essay type inviting a critical assessment of the provisions of s. 14. On the other hand it is a relatively straightforward task for an examiner to construct a problem question which covers the major issues on the section. We have chosen a problem as our specimen question. As you will see it is something of a 'kitchen-sink' problem, as it attempts to deal with a whole host of issues on s. 14.

Illustrative question

In January 1987 John decided to book a holiday in Cornwall with Sunshine Holidays Ltd, after glancing through their 1987 brochure. In the brochure the hotel chosen by John was described as being 'right on the beach' and 'the ideal spot for a quiet holiday'. The brochure boasted of heated indoor and outdoor swimming pools and an evening baby-sitting service 'which will enable you to enjoy the facilities of this luxury hotel'. The brochure also promised free holiday insurance for every holiday booked before the end of January 1987. On return from his holiday with his young family, John complained to his local trading standards department that the hotel was at the top of a three hundred foot cliff with the beach below. He also complained that the cliff top was a gathering place for the local youths on their motorbikes and that the noise went on late into the night. Additionally, the outdoor pool seemed a lot smaller than indicated in the photograph in the brochure, it was not heated, and in fact it was still in the process of construction. It also appeared that the babysitting service was wrongly indicated as being available at the hotel, and that the company knew of the error by November 1986. John's invoice indicated that he had been charged for the holiday insurance premium.

Discuss any possible *criminal* liability of Sunshine Holidays Ltd.

Commentary

Introduction

Where to start is the obvious question.

It is one we have just faced when starting this commentary. We perhaps all share that same feeling of panic when presented with a large number of facts and potential issues in a question of this kind. There seems to be so much to say about the facts and not enough time in which to do the saying. However, one can assume that when setting this question the examiner had in mind some, if not all, of the problems raised by s. 14 of the 1968 Act and the reported case law thereon. It is likely that in a question of this kind that there will be some need to explore the difficulties surrounding the *mens rea* requirement, corporate liability and the difficulty concerning statements about the future. Equally, the distinction between the provision of services and facilities on the one hand and the supply of goods may be one which the examiner exploits to the full.

Perhaps the first point to note with this problem is the rubric. You are asked to discuss *criminal* liability only. Time spent discussing actionable misrepresentation or breach of contract is wasted, although brief comparison, where appropriate, may impress the examiner. In addition, you are asked to consider the position of *Sunshine Holidays Ltd*, not that of any individual within the company. This should, of course, ring bells: issues of corporate liability, *mens rea, Tesco* v *Nattrass, Wings* v *Ellis*, etc.

There are several 'statements' in the problem about which John may complain to the trading standards officer. One way of dealing with the question might be to begin by looking at them individually and seeing whether any offence has been committed.

'Right on the beach'

This statement is obviously one of existing fact. We are told that the hotel is on a 300 foot high cliff. Is there any offence in respect of the statement that it is 'right on the beach?' Under s. 14 it is an offence in the course of trade or business, subject to the *mens rea* requirement, to make a false statement as to, amongst other matters, the location of any accommodation. It is clearly established that the type of accommodation includes holiday accommodation and the exact position of the hotel, i.e., whether 'right on the beach' or not, is an issue of location. Section 14(4) requires that for a statement to be 'false', it must be 'false to a material degree'. Is the fact that the hotel is at the top of a 300 foot cliff something which makes the statement materially false? There does not seem to be much doubt on this issue. In *Thomson Travel Ltd* v *Roberts* (1984) 148 JP 666 the Divisional Court refused to disturb the justices, finding that there was an offence where a similar description had been applied and the breach was man-made and access to the sea was by means of ladders down the side of a concrete wall. The issue was what effect the statement would have on the mind of ordinary readers of the brochure.

Given that there appears to be a false trade description here, the only real issue which might be raised is that of the requirement that for there to be a conviction under s. 14(1)(a) or (b), *mens rea* is an essential ingredient. We have little evidence here that the company, through one of its high-ranking officials (see *Tesco* v *Nattrass* (above)) knew that the hotel was perched on a high cliff top. On the other hand, the cases of *M.F.I.* v *Nattrass* and *Cowburn* v *Focus* (above) both illustrate the comparative ease with which the Divisional Court was satisfied that there was 'recklessness' on the part of the respective companies. The 'recklessness' may be the failure to have in operation a system of checks on statements going into a company's literature. Presumably, Sunshine Holidays Ltd would have to show that the responsibility for placing material in brochures was given to a trusted, but low-ranking employee, whose *mens rea* could not be therefore attributed to the company itself. It seems clear, however, that this particular aspect of 'delegated' responsibility has not been thought through properly by the courts and there is no direct authority on it. Subject to that point, it would seem there is a good chance of a successful conviction under s. 14(1)(b).

'The ideal spot for a quiet holiday'

This again appears to be a factual statement relating to the provision of accommodation, in particular its location or amenities. Similarly, it would surely be accepted by a court that the statement appears to be false to a material degree in the circumstances depicted. The difficulty facing the prosecution in this instance may relate to the problem that the statement might be regarded as a statement about the future, as we have seen in the cases of *Beckett* v *Cohen* (above) and also *Sunair Holidays Ltd* v *Dodd* [1970] 2 All ER 410. In the latter case a holiday brochure stated 'all twin-bedded rooms with . . . terrace'. A particular client was provided with a room without a terrace. It was held that no offence was committed by the holiday company, as the statement was true at the time made, the company having contracted with the owner of the hotel for such rooms. The situation in our problem is slightly different, but a court might take a similar view, unless it could be shown that the holiday company was aware of the disturbance created by the local youngsters. In addition, the prosecution might well fail on the *mens rea* requirement. The events may be considered to be outside the company's control in these circumstances, although, again, if it could be shown that it had been put on notice about the noise problem, it might be possible for the prosecutor to establish 'recklessness' on its part. The prosecutor's ability to do this may well depend upon considerations expressed in the previous discussion on the statement about the hotel's location 'right on the beach'.

'Heated indoor and outdoor swimming pools'

The prosecutor may no doubt face similar problems with regard to this particular statement. The complaints about this statement refer to the outdoor pool. The first issue is whether pictorial representations fall within s. 14. The answer from the cases seems to be that they can. In *Wings* v *Ellis* (above) it was accepted at both Divisional Court and House of Lords level that the photograph of the wrong hotel could constitute an indication for the purposes of s. 14 (although the conviction on that count was not upheld by the Divisional Court and this point was not taken before the House). In *R* v *Clarksons Holidays Ltd* (1972) 57 Cr App R 38 an artist's impression of a hotel was regarded as such an indication. Given that this point is established, the prosecution would have to show that the indication was 'false to a material degree' as required by s. 14(4). On the facts we are told the outdoor pool 'seemed a lot smaller than indicated in the brochure'. Thus, if this was sufficient to mislead the ordinary average person, then it would be false to a material degree.

Turning to the fact that the pool was not heated as claimed, the solution might well depend on whether the pool was ever heated or not. The usual difficulty faces the prosecutor here. The statement could be regarded as one about the future — a mere contractual warranty, breach of which might give an individual consumer a remedy but would not provide a basis for a successful prosecution.

However, as was pointed out by Lord Wilberforce in *British Airways Board* v *Taylor* (above): 'a promise or forecast may contain by implication a statement of present fact. The person who makes the promise may be implying that his present intention is to keep it or that he has at present the power to perform it' (per McKenna J in *R* v *Sunair Holidays Ltd* [1973] 2 All ER 1233 at p. 1236). If the pool had never been heated, and it could be inferred from the brochure that the statement related to an existing state of affairs, then the prosecution might succeed (see *R* v *Sunair Holidays Ltd* (above) and *R* v *Clarksons Holidays Ltd* (above)). Of course, if the pool had been heated at the time of the issue of the brochure, but for some reason, for example, necessary repairs, was not heated at the time of John's visit, the prosecutor would have considerable difficulty in satisfying the court that there had been a breach of s. 14. The question leaves you to speculate a little on this point.

One additional factor might point more favourably in the direction of the prosecution. The question states that the pool was still in the course of construction. Again, it might be inferred from the photograph that the pool existed at the time of issue of the brochure. If so, the case of *R* v *Clarksons Holidays Ltd* indicates that a prosecution on that basis would succeed. In that case an artist's impression of a hotel was seen as an indication that a hotel existed, complete and ready for visitors, namely, a statement of existing fact, and not one about the future.

'Babysitting service available'

This is clearly a breach of contract or an actionable misrepresentation. What the examiner is interested in here, however, is the issue of *mens rea* with particular reference to *Wings* v *Ellis* (above). You may recall that in that case an error was made in a brochure about the availability of air-conditioning at a particular hotel. At the time of issue of the brochure the holiday company was unaware of the error. This came to light subsequently but before the brochure was read by the aggrieved consumer. At that stage the company made attempts to correct the false statement. The House of Lords held that an offence was committed in these circumstances, but left the door open for defendants in similar circumstances to plead the statutory defence in s. 24 of the 1968 Act. It would seem that an offence was committed by the company in January 1987, it having the necessary *mens rea* by November 1986, unless the company can show it took 'all reasonable precautions' and exercised 'all due diligence' to avoid the commission of the offence (s. 24(1)(b)). Presumably, if the company could show that they had taken steps to inform staff and outside travel agents of the error, as had been done in *Wings*, then this might satisfy the statutory defence requirements. It should be remembered that *Wings* were unable to rely on the defences, however, because they had not been pleaded. The case is therefore not a direct authority on this issue, and regard should be had to some of the cases discussed in the previous chapter in relation to s. 24(1)(b).

It seems therefore that there is a reasonable chance, subject to the availability of the s. 24 defence, that Sunshine Holidays Ltd will be convicted under s. 14(1)(a) in respect of this matter. We have assumed, of course, the necessary *mens rea* was attributable to some high-ranking officer of the company, unlike the position on the second charge in *Wings* v *Ellis* (above) in relation to the photograph, where the state of mind in question was that of a junior employee only.

'Free holiday insurance'

Again, there seems little doubt that the failure to meet this particular promise would be actionable under civil law principles. However, as will have been gathered from a discussion earlier in this chapter, this issue has caused considerable difficulty for prosecutors seeking to use s. 14 of the 1968 Act.

It could be argued that this is a statement about the future, a mere contractual warranty; however, that point has never been forcefully argued in the reported cases. What has been discussed is whether s. 14 applies to prices. In *Newell* v *Hicks* (above) it was said that s. 14 did not cover statements or indications about the price of services, accommodation or facilities. In any event, in that case the free supply was one of goods, i.e., a video recorder, and was for that reason outside the scope of s. 14. However, in *Kinchin* v *Ashton Park Scooters* (above) there was a similar promise, as here, with regard to insurance. This was regarded as the provision of a 'facility', and the prosecutor's appeal against the justices' decision on this point was upheld by the Divisional Court. However, the Divisional Court still maintained that s. 14 did not apply to prices, but appears to apply to situations where a service or facility is stated to be 'free' but is not provided at all. Mann J (at p. 544) states quite specifically that if the insurance had been provided at a price, then the difficulty in *Newell* v *Hicks* would have arisen. It would seem on the facts that s. 14 would not apply, as the insurance facility has been provided at a price thus distinguishing *Kinchin* v *Ashton Park Scooters*.

We have seen that what appeared to be a complex set of facts, when broken down in this way, can be dealt with comfortably even in an examination context. This is achieved by being aware of the major points of difficulty which your examiner might wish to explore before you enter the examination room.

INDEX

TITLES IN THE SERIES

SWOT Constitutional and Administrative Law
SWOT Law of Evidence
SWOT Company Law
SWOT Law of Contract
SWOT Revenue Law
SWOT Family Law
SWOT Land Law
SWOT Criminal Law
SWOT Equity and Trusts
SWOT Commercial and Consumer Law
SWOT A-Level Law
SWOT Law of Torts
SWOT Jurisprudence
SWOT Employment Law
SWOT English Legal System